Lecture Notes in Artificial I

Edited by J. G. Carbonell and J. Siekma

Subseries of Lecture Notes in Computer Science

Lecture Notes in Artificial Intelligence   4211

Edited by J. G. Carbonell and J. Siekmann

Subseries of Lecture Notes in Computer Science

Paul Vogt   Yuuya Sugita   Elio Tuci
Chrystopher Nehaniv (Eds.)

Symbol Grounding and Beyond

Third International Workshop on the Emergence
and Evolution of Linguistic Communication, EELC 2006
Rome, Italy, September 30 – October 1, 2006
Proceedings

Springer

Series Editors

Jaime G. Carbonell, Carnegie Mellon University, Pittsburgh, PA, USA
Jörg Siekmann, University of Saarland, Saarbrücken, Germany

Volume Editors

Paul Vogt
Tilburg University, ILK/Language and Information Science
P.O. Box 90153, 5000 LE Tilburg, The Netherlands
E-mail: p.a.vogt@uvt.nl

Yuuya Sugita
RIKEN Brain Science Institute, Behavior and Dynamic Cognition Lab.
2-1 Hirosawa, Wako-shi, Saitama 351-0198, Japan
E-mail: sugita@bdc.brain.riken.go.jp

Elio Tuci
Université Libre de Bruxelles, IRIDIA
Avenue F. Roosevelt 50, CP 194/6, 1050 Brussels, Belgium
E-mail: etuci@ulb.ac.be

Chrystopher Nehaniv
University of Hertfordshire, School of Computer Science
Adaptive Systems & Algorithms Research Groups
College Lane, Hatfield, Hertfordshire, AL10 9AB, UK
E-mail: C.L.Nehaniv@herts.ac.uk

Library of Congress Control Number: 2006932800

CR Subject Classification (1998): I.2.11, I.2.6-7, I.6, F.1.1-2, H.3.1, K.4, H.5, J.4

LNCS Sublibrary: SL 7 – Artificial Intelligence

ISSN   0302-9743
ISBN-10   3-540-45769-0 Springer Berlin Heidelberg New York
ISBN-13   978-3-540-45769-5 Springer Berlin Heidelberg New York

Springer is a part of Springer Science+Business Media

springer.com

© Springer-Verlag Berlin Heidelberg 2006
Printed in Germany

Typesetting: Camera-ready by author, data conversion by Scientific Publishing Services, Chennai, India
Printed on acid-free paper   SPIN: 11880172   06/3142   5 4 3 2 1 0

Preface

This volume is the collection of papers and abstracts of the Third Annual International Workshop on the Emergence and Evolution of Linguistic Communication (EELCiii), held in Rome from September 30 to October 1, 2006. This workshop was the third in line after previous editions held in Kanazawa (Japan) in 2004 and in Hatfield (UK) in 2005. Although the previous events were published as post-proceedings, this event was the first to have its proceedings published at the workshop. Three types of papers were elicited: full papers, invited full papers and invited abstracts. All full papers were peer-reviewed by the International Programme Committee.

The workshop's focus was on the evolution and emergence of language. This is a fast-growing interdisciplinary research area with researchers coming from disciplines such as anthropology, linguistics, psychology, primatology, neuroscience, cognitive science and computer science. Although most papers focus on evolution, a number of papers focus more on language acquisition. This was highly welcomed, since research on language acquisition (both from psychology and artificial intelligence) is extremely important in gaining insights regarding language evolution and, not least, regarding the theme of this workshop 'Symbol Grounding and Beyond.'

Despite the interdisciplinarity of the field and – in principle – of the EELC series, most contributions stem from computer science (mainly artificial intelligence and artificial life). This is not surprising, because this was also the case in previous workshops and because this workshop was part of the 'Simulation of Adaptive Behavior' conference (SAB 2006), a.k.a. 'From Animals to Animats.'

We would like to thank those involved in the organisation of SAB 2006, especially Stefano Nolfi, for their assistance in organising the workshop, the members of the Programme Committee for their assistance in reviewing the papers, the invited speakers (Peter Gärdenfors, Naoto Iwahashi, Elena Lieven, Deb Roy and Luc Steels) and, of course, all authors of the contributions in this collection.

June 2006

Paul Vogt
Yuuya Sugita
Elio Tuci
Chrystopher Nehaniv

Organisation

EELCIII was organised by the Organising Committee as part of the Simulation of Adaptive Behavior conference.

Organising Committee

Paul Vogt (Tilburg University, The Netherlands)   Chair
Yuuya Sugita (RIKEN BSI, Japan)   Co-chair
Elio Tuci (Université Libre de Bruxelles, Belgium)   Co-chair
Chrystopher Nehaniv (University of Hertfordshire, UK)   Co-chair

Programme Committee

Takaya Arita (University of Nagoya, Japan)
Tony Belpaeme (University of Plymouth, UK)
Bart de Boer (University of Groningen, The Netherlands)
Angelo Cangelosi (University of Plymouth, UK)
Tecumseh Fitch (University of St. Andrews, UK)
Takashi Hashimoto (JAIST, Japan)
Jim Hurford (University of Edinburgh, UK)
Takashi Ikegami (University of Tokyo, Japan)
Simon Kirby (University of Edinburgh, UK)
Caroline Lyon (University of Hertfordshire, UK)
Davide Marocco (ISTC, National Research Council, Italy)
Chrystopher Nehaniv (University of Hertfordshire, UK)
Stefano Nolfi (ISTC, National Research Council, Italy)
Kazuo Okanoya (RIKEN BSI, Japan)
Tetsuo Ono (Future University Hakodate, Japan)
Domenico Parisi (ISTC, National Research Council, Italy)
Akito Sakurai (Keio University, Japan)
Andrew Smith (University of Edinburgh, UK)
Kenny Smith (University of Edinburgh, UK)
Luc Steels (Vrije Universiteit Brussel, Belgium)
Yuuya Sugita (RIKEN BSI, Japan)
Jun Tani (RIKEN BSI, Japan)
Satoshi Tojo (JAIST, Japan)
Elio Tuci (Université Libre de Bruxelles, Belgium)
Paul Vogt (Tilburg University, The Netherlands)

Table of Contents

A Hybrid Model for Learning Word-Meaning Mappings⋆

Federico Divina[1] and Paul Vogt[1,2]

[1] Induction of Linguistic Knowledge / Language and Information Science
Tilburg University, P.O. Box 90153, 5000 LE Tilburg, The Netherlands
[2] Language Evolution and Computation Research Unit, School of Philosophy,
Psychology and Language Sciences, University of Edinburgh, UK
{f.divina@uvt.nl, paulv}@ling.ed.ac.uk

Abstract. In this paper we introduce a model for the simulation of language evolution, which is incorporated in the New Ties project. The New Ties project aims at evolving a cultural society by integrating evolutionary, individual and social learning in large scale multi-agent simulations. The model presented here introduces a novel implementation of language games, which allows agents to communicate in a more natural way than with most other existing implementations of language games. In particular, we propose a hybrid mechanism that combines cross-situational learning techniques with more informed feedback mechanisms. In our study we focus our attention on dealing with referential indeterminacy after joint attention has been established and on whether the current model can deal with larger populations than previous studies involving cross-situational learning. Simulations show that the proposed model can indeed lead to coherent languages in a quasi realistic world environment with larger populations.

1 Introduction

For language to evolve, the language has to be transmitted reliably among the population, which is only possible if the individual agents can learn the language. In human societies, children have to learn for instance the sounds, words and grammar of the target language. In the current paper, we focus solely on the evolution and acquisition of word-meaning mappings. The way children acquire the meanings of words still remains an open question. Associating the correct meaning to a word is extremely complicated, as a word may potentially have an infinite number of meanings [1].

Different mechanisms that children may adopt when acquiring the meanings of words have been suggested, see, e.g., [2] for an overview. For example, Tomasello has proposed that *joint attention* is a primary mechanism [3]. According to this

⋆ This research and the New Ties project is supported by an EC FET grant under contract 003752. We thank all members the New Ties project for their invaluable contributions. Opinions and errors in this manuscript are the authors' responsibility, they do not necessarily reflect those of the EC or other New Ties members.

P. Vogt et al. (Eds.): EELC 2006, LNAI 4211, pp. 1–15, 2006.

mechanism, children are able to share their attention with adults on objects, e.g., through gaze following or pointing. Moreover, children can learn that adults have control over their perceptions and that they can choose to attend to particular objects or aspects of a given situation. This allows children to focus their attention on the same situation experienced by adults, thus reducing the number of possible meanings of a word.

This mechanism, however, is not sufficient, because it is still uncertain whether a word relates to the whole situation, to parts of the situation or even to a completely different situation. This is known as the *referential indeterminacy* problem illustrated by Quine [1] with the following example: Imagine an anthropologist studying a native speaker of an unfamiliar language. As a rabbit crosses their visual field, the native speaker says "gavagai" and the anthropologist infers that "gavagai" means *rabbit*. However, the anthropologist cannot be completely sure of his inference. In fact, the word "gavagai" can have an infinite number of possible meanings, including *undetached rabbit parts*, *large ears*, *it's running*, *good food* or even *it's going to rain*.

To overcome this problem, additional mechanisms have been proposed to reduce the referential indeterminacy. Among these is a representational bias known as the *whole object bias* [4], according to which children tend to map novel words to whole objects, rather then to parts of objects. Another mechanism that children appear to use is the *principle of contrast* [5], which is based on the assumption that if a meaning is already associated with a word, it is unlikely that it can be associated with another word.

There is also evidence that children can acquire the meanings of words more directly by reducing the number of potential meanings of words across different situations [6,7]. This *cross-situational learning* can work statistically by maintaining the co-occurrence frequencies of words with their possible meanings [8,9] or simply by maintaining the intersection of all situations in which a word is used [10,11]. Crucially, cross-situational learning depends on observing a sufficient degree of one-to-one mappings between words and meanings. Although theoretically, the level of uncertainty (i.e. the number of confounding – or background – meanings) in situations may be quite large, this may have a large impact on the time required to learn a language [11].

Cross-situational learning yields poor results when the input language is less consistent regarding the one-to-one mapping. This has been found in simulation studies of language evolution with increased population sizes [9]. In such simulations, different agents create many different words expressing the same meaning when they have not yet communicated with each other. So, the more agents there are, the more words can enter a language community during the early stages of evolution. In models that use explicit meaning transfer, there are positive feedback loops that reduce the number of words sufficiently over time, allowing the language to converge properly [12]. However, when there is no positive feedback loop, as is the case with cross-situational learning, there appears to be no efficient mechanism for reducing the number of words in the language. A possible solution to this problem could be to include an additional mechanism that imposes a bias toward one-to-one mappings between words and meanings [13].

In this paper we propose a hybrid model for the evolution of language that combines joint attention, cross-situational learning and the principle of contrast as mechanisms for reducing the referential indeterminacy. In addition, a feedback mechanism and related adaptations are used as a synonymy damping mechanism. This model is used to investigate the effect that context size has on the development of language, but more importantly it is used to investigate how this model can deal with large populations. The model is embedded in the New Ties project[1], which aims at developing a benchmark platform for studying the evolution and development of cultural societies in very large multi-agent systems [14].

The paper is organised as follows: in the next section, we provide a brief description of the proposed model (for details, consult [14,15]). In Section 3 we present some experiments, whose aims are to show that the proposed hybrid model can lead to the evolution of a coherent lexicon in large population sizes and with varying context sizes. The results are discussed in Section 4. Finally, Section 5 concludes.

2   The Model

2.1   New Ties Agent Architecture

The New Ties project aims at developing a platform for studying the evolution and development of cultural societies in a very large multi-agent system. In this system, agents are inserted in an environment consisting of a grid world in which each point is a location. The world, which is inspired by Epstein & Axtell's [16] sugar scape world, is set up with tokens, edible plants, building bricks, agents, different terrains of varying roughness, etc. The aim for the agents is to evolve and learn behavioural skills in order for the society to survive over extended periods of time. As part of these skills, language and culture are to develop.

At each time step each agent receives as input a set of perceptual features and messages, which constitute the context of an agent, and outputs an action (see Fig. 1 for the basic agent architecture). These actions are collected by the environment manager, and when all agents have been processed, the collected actions are executed and the environment is updated.

The perceptual features an agent receives represent both objects and actions that occur in its visual field. These features are processed with a categorisation mechanism based on the discrimination game [17] (a detailed description of this mechanism is given in [14,18]). Basically, each object is mapped onto a set of categories, where each category corresponds to a feature. So, if an object is described by n features, it will be categorised into n categories. Messages are processed with a language interpretation module, described in Section 2.2, and also yield a set of categories. All these categories are stored in the short-term memory (STM), which can be accessed by the control module, as well as all other modules.

---

[1] New Ties stands for New Emerging World models Through Individual, Evolutionary and Social learning. See http://www.new-ties.org

Perceptual
input   Messages

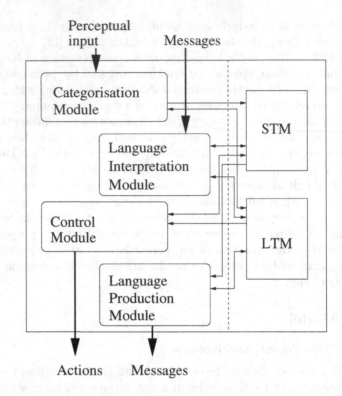

Actions   Messages

Fig. 1. The basic architecture of a New Ties agent. Perceptual features of objects and actions are processed by the categorisation module, while messages are interpreted with the language interpretation module. The control module outputs actions and the language production module produces outgoing messages. Various sources of knowledge are stored in the short- and long-term memories.

Once the perceptual features and messages have been processed, the controller is used to determine the action to perform. This controller is represented by a *decision Q-tree* (DQT), which is a decision tree that can change during an agent's lifetime using reinforcement learning [14]. The possible actions include, among others, *move, turn left, turn right, mate, talk, shout,* ... In case the output of the DQT is either the *talk* or *shout* action, the agent must produce a message, which is done by the language production module, described below. Each action performed costs a certain amount of energy, and when an agent's energy level decreases to zero or below, it dies. Energy levels can be increased by eating plants. Agents also die when they reach a predefined age.

Agents start their life with a small initial DQT, which, as mentioned above, can be changed by reinforcement learning. This initial DQT is the result of evolution. When two agents reproduce, they produce an offspring who inherits its genome from its parents, subject to cross-over and mutations. This genome carries the code for producing the initial DQT and other biases, which regulate, for instance, the 'socialness' of the agent. This socialness gene is a bias for

	m_1	$\ldots$	m_N
w_1	σ_{11}	$\ldots$	σ_{1N}
$\vdots$	$\vdots$	$\vdots$	$\vdots$
w_M	σ_{M1}	$\ldots$	σ_{MN}

	m_1	$\ldots$	m_N
w_1	P_{11}	$\ldots$	P_{1N}
$\vdots$	$\vdots$	$\vdots$	$\vdots$
w_M	P_{M1}	$\ldots$	P_{MN}

Fig. 2. A simplified illustration of the lexicon. The lexicon consists of two matrices that associate meanings m_j with words w_i. The left matrix stores association scores σ_{ij} and the right matrix stores co-occurrence probabilities P_{ij}.

an agent to be social; the more social an agent is, the more frequently it will communicate and the more likely it is to provide more information regarding the meaning of a message. Unlike standard evolutionary algorithms, reproduction is not processed cyclical, but acyclical, i.e., two agents can reproduce when they decide to, but only if they are of different sex and in nearby locations.

2.2 Communication and Learning Word-Meaning Mappings

The language evolves in the society by agents' interacting through language games. While doing so, each individual constructs its own lexicon, which is represented in the long-term memory (LTM) by two association matrices (Fig. 2). Each matrix associates words w_i with meanings m_j. The first matrix stores association scores σ_{ij}, while the second stores co-occurrence probabilities P_{ij}. The former is updated based on feedback the agents may receive regarding the effectiveness (or success) of their interaction. However, as this feedback is not always available, the agents also maintain the co-occurrence frequencies of words and the potential meanings as they co-occur in a given situation (or context). The two matrices are coupled via the *association strength, $strL_{ij}$*, which is calculated as:

$$strL_{ij} = \sigma_{ij} + (1 - \sigma_{ij})P_{ij}. \tag{1}$$

This coupling allows the agents to infer the right word-meaning mappings across different situations using the co-occurrence probabilities when there has been little feedback. However, when there has been sufficient feedback on the language use of the agents, the association score σ_{ij} may become high enough to overrule the co-occurrence probabilities.

Both matrices are updated after each language game. If a language game is considered successful based on the feedback mechanism, the association score σ_{ij} of the used association is increased by

$$\sigma_{ij} = \eta \cdot \sigma_{ij} + 1 - \eta, \tag{2}$$

where $\eta = 0.9$ is a constant learning parameter. In addition, the scores of competing associations are laterally inhibited by

$$\sigma_{ij} = \eta \cdot \sigma_{ij}. \tag{3}$$

An association α_{nm} is competing if either the word is the same ($n = i$) or the meaning ($m = j$), but not both. If the game has failed according to the feedback mechanism, σ_{ij} is also decreased this way. The association score is unchanged if no feedback is processed.

In each game, irrespective of its outcome, the co-occurrence frequencies f_{ij} of words with potential meanings in that situation are increased, thus affecting the co-occurrence probabilities:

$$P_{ij} = \frac{f_{ij}}{\sum_i f_{ij}}. \tag{4}$$

The reason for adopting this dual representation is that earlier studies have indicated that using the mechanism for updating the association scores (Eqs. 2 and 3) work much better than for updating the co-occurrence probabilities (Eq. 4) if there is feedback, while the opposite is true for cross-situational learning [19].

Unlike standard implementations, such as [17,18], a language game is initiated by an agent when its controller decides to talk or shout[2], or otherwise with a certain probability proportional to socialness gene. This agent (the speaker) then selects an arbitrary object from its context as a *target object*[3] and decides on how many words it will use to describe the object. This number, expressed in the *task complexity* T_c, is determined by generating a random number between 1 and 5 following a Gaussian distribution with the average age of the target audience in tens of 'New Ties years' (NTYrs)[4] as its mean and a standard deviation of 0.75. This way, the agent will tend to produce shorter messages when addressing a young audience and longer messages when addressing an older audience.

Depending on this task complexity, the agent selects arbitrarily T_c different categories that represent the object. Recall that each category relates to one perceptual feature of an object, such as the object's colour, shape, distance or weight. For each category, the speaker then searches its lexicon for associations that have the highest strength $strL_{ij}$. If no such association is found, a new word is invented as an arbitrary string and added to the lexicon. Each word thus found is then appended to the message which is distributed to the agent(s) in the speaker's vicinity.

On certain occasions, for instance, when the hearer had signalled that it did not understand the speaker, the speaker may accompany the message with a pointing gesture to draw the attention to the target (such a gesture is only produced with a probability proportional to the socialness gene mentioned earlier). This way, the agents establish joint attention, but still the hearer does not necessarily know exactly what feature of the object is signalled (cf. Quine's problem).

---

[2] The 'talk' action is directed to only one visible agent, while 'shout' is directed to all agents in the audible vicinity of the initiator.

[3] In later studies we intend to make this selection depending on the decision making mechanism determined by the DQT, so the communication will be more functional with respect to the agent's behaviour.

[4] In the current paper, a year in 'New Ties time' equals to an unrealistic 365 time steps.

When an agent receives a message, its language interpretation module tries to interpret each word in the message by searching its lexicon for associations with the highest strength $strL_{ij}$. If the association score σ_{ij} of this element exceeds a certain threshold (i.e., $\sigma_{ij} > \Theta$, where $\Theta = 0.8$), then the hearer assumes the interpretation to be correct. If not, the hearer may – with a certain probability proportional to the socialness gene – consider the interpretation to be incorrect and signal a 'did not understand' message, thus soliciting a pointing gesture; otherwise, the hearer will assume the interpretation was correct.

In case the interpretation was correct, the hearer may – again with a probability proportional to its socialness gene – signal the speaker that it understood the message, thus providing feedback so that both agents increase the association score of used lexical entries and inhibit competing elements as explained above. In all cases, the co-occurrence probability P_{ij} is increased for all categories in the context that have an association with the expressed words. In case the speaker had pointed to the object, this context is reduced to the perceptual features of this object. Otherwise, the context contains all categories of all visible objects, which may differ from those the speaker sees – including the target object. All interpretations are added to the STM, which the controller uses to decide on the agent's next action.

When no interpretation could be found in the lexicon, the agent adds the novel word to its lexicon in association with all categories valid in the current context (i.e., either all objects and events perceived or the object that was pointed to). The frequency counters of these associations are set to 1 and the association scores σ_{Nj} are initialised with:

$$\sigma_{Nj} = (1 - \max_i(\sigma_{ij}))\sigma_0, \tag{5}$$

where $\max_i(\sigma_{ij})$ is the maximum association score that meaning m_j has with other words w_i, $\sigma_0 = 0.1$ is a constant, and $i \neq N$. This way, if the agent has already associated the meaning (or category) m_j with another word w_i, the agent is biased to prefer another meaning with this novel word. Hence, this implements a notion of the principle of contrast [5]. Note again that the hearer may not have seen the target object and thus may fail to acquire the proper meaning.

3 Experiments

In the experiments we test the effectiveness of the model described in the previous section. In particular, we are interested to see whether reasonable levels of communicative accuracy can be reached with relatively large populations. In addition, we investigate the influence of considering a different number of perceptual features that agents have at their disposal for inferring word-meaning mappings. In order to focus on these questions, the evolutionary and reinforcement learning mechanisms were switched off. So, although agents could reproduce, each agent has exactly the same hand-crafted controller that did not change during their lifetimes. As a result, in the simulations reported here, agents only

move, eat, reproduce (with no evolutionary computation involved) and communicate with each other. When an agent's energy level decreased below zero, they
died. The same happens when agents reach a certain age (set at 80 'New Ties
years', i.e. 29,200 time steps).

We performed a set of experiments in which we varied the number of features
considered for each object, from a minimum of 2 to a maximum of 10 features.
Varying the number of features has an influence on the number of possible meanings in the language. The following table indicates how many meanings there are
for the different number of features available:

No. of features	2	3	4	5	6	7	8	9	10
No. of meanings	10	16	19	23	26	35	40	45	48

Remember that a category relates to one feature, so the more features are
used to describe an object, the more possible meanings can be associated to a
word. Effectively, increasing the number of features increases the context sizes. A
recent mathematical model describing cross-situational learning [11] shows that
learning word-meaning mappings is harder when the context size is larger. So,
we expect that considering a higher number of features will lead to the evolution
of a lower level in communicative accuracy, or to a slower learning rate.

In addition to reducing the number of features, referential indeterminacy can
be reduced by means of pointing. As mentioned, the probability with which
agents point is proportional to the socialness gene. As the evolutionary mechanisms are switched off in these experiments, the socialness gene is now initialised
individually with a random value.

The initial population size is set to 100 agents. When the agents reach the age
of 10 NTYrs (3,650 time steps), they start to reproduce. So, from then onward
the population size can grow, though this may not happen if the agents tend to
die faster than they reproduce.

Recall that all agents are evaluated once during each time step. So, during one
time step, multiple language games can be played by different agents. Moreover,
different agents can speak to one another simultaneously, as they do not wait
for their turn. Playing one language game takes 2-3 time steps: (1) sending a
message, (2) receiving a message, occasionally, (3) signalling feedback and (4)
receiving feedback.

The simulations are evaluated based on *communicative accuracy*. Communicative accuracy is calculated each 30 time steps by dividing the total number
of successful language games by the total number of language games played
during this period. A language game is considered successful if the hearer interpreted the message from the speaker such that the interpreted category exactly
matched the intended category (so not the object). Simulations were repeated
5 times with different random seeds for each condition and the results reported
are averages over these 5 trials.

Figure 3 (top) shows communicative accuracy for the cases with 2, 6 and 10
features. In all cases, accuracy increased to a level between 0.50 (10 features) and
0.68 (2 features) during the first 30 time steps. After this, accuracy first increased

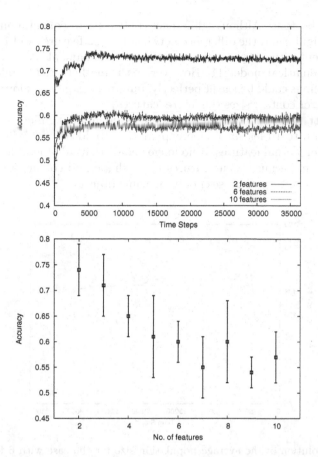

Fig. 3. (Top) The evolution of communicative accuracy (y-axis) over time (x-axis) for the conditions with 2, 6 and 10 features. Notice the odd scale on the y-axis. (Bottom) Communicative accuracy measured at the end of each simulation, averaged over the 5 trials with their standard deviation. The results relate to the number of perceptual features varied from 2 to 10 with incremental steps (x-axis).

quite rapidly and then stagnated more or less around 0.57 (10 features), 0.60 (6 features) and 0.73 (2 features). Although the language is not learnt perfectly in any condition, accuracy is reasonable and much better than chance. For instance, in the case where there are 6 features, chance is between 1/26 (if all possible meanings are in the context – cf. above mentioned table) and 1/6 (if the target object was pointed to).

For comparison, we tested the model in a simulation where pointing was used to *explicitly* transfer the intended *meaning* (i.e. categories) – at least in those interactions where pointing was used. Under this condition, communicative accuracy yielded on average 0.97 ± 0.02 at the end of the simulations.

It is clear that the levels of communicative accuracy decreased when the number of features increased up to 6 or 7 features, after which there is no more significant change (Fig. 3 bottom). Although differences between subsequent numbers of features are not significant, the difference between using 2 features and 7 features is. This is consistent with our prediction mentioned earlier and also with the findings from the mathematical model [11]. However, in the mathematical model all word-meaning mappings could be learnt perfectly, but at the expense of longer learning periods for larger context sizes (i.e. more features).

It is not yet fully understood why there is no more significant change for variation from 6 to 10 features. One explanation could be that when there are more than 6 perceptual features, it no longer holds that all objects are described by every feature, because some features (e.g., shape and colour) are shared by all objects, while others (e.g., sex) only by some objects.

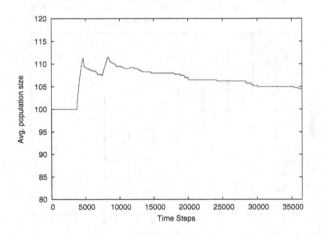

Fig. 4. The evolution of the average population size for the case with 6 features. All other simulations revealed a similar evolution.

Figure 4 shows the evolution of the average population size in the simulations with 6 features. We see that the first 3,650 time steps (10 NTYrs), the population size remains constant at 100 agents. This is because during this period, agents only start reproducing when they reached an age of 10 NTYrs. We then see a rapid increase of the population size to 110 agent, after which the population size somewhat fluctuates until it eventually slowly decreases, though the total number remains larger than 100. The decrease is due to the fact that giving birth costs a large amount of energy, which is passed on to the offspring. So agents who are less fit will have a large chance of dying after giving birth. The issue here is that these changes in the population do not seem to alter the evolution of accuracy a lot, though around the points where there is a large inflow or outflow of agents, this does seem to have some effect. This is consistent with findings from earlier simulations on language evolution, e.g., [20].

It is important to stress that these experiments are different from those focusing only on cross-situational learning as in [8,9,11]. In those experiments, cross-situational learning was the only learning mechanism. In these experiments, feedback regarding a game's success is provided in approximately 12% of the language games, while messages were accompanied with a pointing gesture in about 42% of all games. Note that one game can have both a pointing gesture and feedback, so none were used in an estimated 50%. Per time step, approximately 27% of all agents initiated a language game, so assuming that the population size was on average 105 over the entire period of the experiment, a total of approximately 1 million language games were played at the end of the experiments.

4   Discussion

In this paper we investigate some aspects of learning word-meaning mappings regarding Quine's problem of referential indeterminacy. In particular, we are interested in how agents can evolve a shared lexicon regarding various characteristics of objects without using explicit meaning transfer. Although agents do not always point to target objects, but when it happens, hearers still cannot determine exactly what characteristics (or features) of objects are intended by the speaker. Our proposed solution is to use cross-situational learning for such instances. However, as this learning mechanism has proved to be relatively slow and difficult to scale up in terms of population size [9], we combined this method with learning techniques based on positive feedback and the principle of contrast.

The results achieved with this model are reasonable. The population can develop a communication system with an accuracy of about 50-70% quite rapidly, while further improvement on accuracy is somewhat slower yielding levels of accuracy between 60-75% at the end of the simulations. The initial speed of learning seems very fast, but one has to realise that the agents do not communicate with all other agents. Instead, the only communicate with agents within their vicinity. In the current setting, there were groups of around 3-4 agents quite near to each other. So, although the population is larger than in any previous study using cross-situational learning, it will take a long time before all agents would have communicated with many different agents. It is unclear in the current simulations what the reach of an agent was (i.e. the number of different agents it communicated with).

The stagnation of communicative accuracy is thought to be caused by − at least − three aspects: 1) the influx of new agents, 2) the increase of task complexity and 3) mismatches in perceived contexts by different agents participating in a language game. The first two aspects start to have an influence at time step 3,650 − the time that the first agents reach an age of 10 NTYrs. This is around the same period where the stagnation starts to occur. The third aspect is caused by the 'situatedness' of the agents in their environment, because two agents cannot be at the same location simultaneously, and also because their orientation can be quite different (see [21] for a discussion). Furthermore, if an object is obscured by another one for a particular agent, this need not be the case for another agent. If the other agent already learnt the meaning of this word reliably, there is no problem, but otherwise the hearer will assume the word means something that he sees. This can be problematic for cross-situational learning, which heavily depends on consistent and reliable input [9]. Despite all this, the agents perform well beyond chance. In the future, we will assess in more detail what the exact effects of these aspects are.

The latter aspect can partly be solved using pointing, though – as mentioned – this only occurred on average in about 42% of all interactions. Pointing gestures can be initiated spontaneously by the speaker with a certain probability, but can also be solicited by the hearers when they send a negative feedback signal. In such cases, the context is reduced to the number of perceptual features of one object, which equals 2 in the simplest case investigated and 10 in the most difficult case. Since the language games will fail frequently early on, many negative feedback signals are sent, in which case the speaker is likely to repeat the message, but now accompanied by a pointing gesture. This way, agents can engage in a sort of 'dialogue', where the speaker repeats himself to make himself understood if requested by the hearer.

It must be stressed that the success is probably only partly due to the cross-situational learning. It is, to some extent, also due to the positive feedback that is provided when the hearer considers the language game to be successful. Recall that feedback is provided when the association score σ_{ij} exceeds a certain threshold Θ or – if this is not the case – with a probability that is inversely proportional to the value of socialness gene (which was assigned randomly in the current simulations). During the early stages of word learning, we can only expect the latter case to hold, so when through cross-situational learning a hearer has selected one possible interpretation, the association score σ_{ij} is reinforced occasionally. This association needs to be reinforced 16 times before the association score exceeds the threshold, which is set to $\Theta = 0.8$. Until then, the agents rely on cross-situational learning, accompanied by occasional 'blind' adaptations of the association scores σ_{ij}. This is, then, similar to the synonymy damping mechanism proposed in [13], which has a positive effect on disambiguating the language during cross-situational learning.

In [22], we investigated the role of feedback in a related model simulating the Talking Heads experiment. There it was found that only when feedback was used frequently enough, the results were better than when feedback was not used at all (i.e. when the learners could only rely on a variant of cross-situational learning). However, in those simulations feedback forced the speaker to point at the object and, since in those simulations objects were represented by only one category, pointing identified the target meaning more precisely. We are currently investigating more thoroughly what the role of feedback is in this model.

It is also important to realise that the language is relatively small. In case there are 2 features, an agent has only 10 categories, but in case of 10 features an agent has a total of 48 categories. Although learning individual words can take longer when there are less meanings (because it can take longer before distracting meanings no longer compete), this does not hold for the entire language, provided the context size is substantially smaller than the total number of meanings [11]. So, the smaller the language, the easier it should be learnt.

It is yet unclear what the influence of the principle of contrast is in this model, because we did not compare these results with a simulation where the principle of contrast was switched off. This will be carried out in future experiments. It is interesting to note, however, that we implemented the principle of contrast as a loose bias, rather than as a strong principle that would rule out competing word-meaning mappings entirely.

One may wonder why this particular study is carried out in a complex environment as the current one, while a similar study could have been carried out in a much more simpler simulation setting. We agree this is true, but it is important to realise that this is the first in a series of experiments being set up in the New Ties project. There are many more planned; some of which may indeed be done using a simpler set up (e.g., for investigating the effect of the principle of contrast), but most will relate to the evolution of more complex behaviours that would allow the population to remain viable over extended periods of time. Such experiments will involve various combinations of learning mechanisms to allow the population to evolve and learn how to behave properly in their complex environment. These learning mechanisms include evolutionary learning, individual (reinforcement) learning and social learning. Especially the latter is of interest, because we intend to set up experiments in which the language that evolves will be used to share information concerning the way the controller is structured, thus allowing agents to copy such structures in order to acquire more similar controllers.

5   Conclusions

In this paper we have presented a new hybrid model for the simulation of language evolution, and in particular the evolution of shared lexicons. This model is incorporated in the New Ties project, whose aim is to set up large scale simulations to study the evolution of cultural societies by combining evolutionary, individual and social learning techniques.

Using the model we show how a combination of different learning mechanisms, which include pointing as a means of establishing joint attention, the principle of contrast, a positive feedback mechanism and cross-situation learning allow agents to infer the meaning of words. In particular, we show that this model can – in contrast to previous studies [9] – deal well with relatively large populations. One reason for this ability is that the feedback mechanism acts as a synonymy damping mechanism, similar to a recent study by De Beule et al. [13].

The study further shows that the model is quite robust (but definitely not perfect) when agents need to infer the meaning when there is more referential indeterminacy, though learning is somewhat hampered in terms of communicative accuracy. Indirectly, this confirms another recent study by Smith et al. [11], who mathematically proved that cross-situational learning can work well with different levels of referential indeterminacy, though the learning speed is affected such that higher levels of indeterminacy require longer learning periods. The difference with the current study is that in the mathematical study language can be learnt with 100% accuracy, but under the assumption that an ideal language exists which needs to be learnt by one individual who receives consistent input. In the current simulation, such assumptions do not hold.

As one of the objectives of the New Ties project is to set up a benchmark platform for studying the evolution of cultural societies, which includes the evolution of language, we believe this study is a first promising step showing what sort of studies can be carried out with this platform.

References

1. Quine, W.V.O.: Word and object. Cambridge University Press (1960)
2. Bloom, P.: How Children Learn the Meanings of Words. The MIT Press, Cambridge, MA. and London, UK. (2000)
3. Tomasello, M.: The cultural origins of human cognition. Harvard University Press (1999)
4. Macnamara, J.: Names for things: a study of human learning. MIT Press, Cambridge, MA (1982)
5. Clark, E.: The principle of contrast: A constraint on language acquisition. In MacWhinney, B., ed.: Mechanisms of language acquisition. Lawrence Erlbaum Assoc., Hillsdale, NJ (1987) 1–33
6. Akhtar, N., Montague, L.: Early lexical acquisition: the role of cross-situational learning. First Language (1999) 347–358
7. Houston-Price, C., Plunkett, K., Harris, P.: 'word-learning wizardry' at 1;6. Journal of Child Language **32** (2005) 175–190
8. Smith, A.D.M.: Intelligent meaning creation in a clumpy world helps communication. Artificial Life **9(2)** (2003) 559–574
9. Vogt, P., Coumans, H.: Investigating social interaction strategies for bootstrapping lexicon development. Journal of Artificial Societies and Social Simulation **6** (2003)
10. Siskind, J.M.: A computational study of cross-situational techniques for learning word-to-meaning mappings. Cognition **61** (1996) 39–91
11. Smith, K., Smith, A., Blythe, R., Vogt, P.: Cross-situational learning: a mathematical approach. In Vogt, P., Sugita, Y., Tuci, E., Nehaniv, C., eds.: Proceedings of the Emergence and Evolution of Linguistic Communication (EELCIII), Springer (2006)
12. Baronchelli, A., Loreto, V., Dall'Asta, L., Barrat, A.: Bootstrapping communication in language games: Strategy, topology and all that. In Cangelosi, A., Smith, A., Smith, K., eds.: The evolution of language; Proceedings of Evolang 6, World Scientific Publishing (2006)
13. De Beule, J., De Vylder, B., Belpaeme, T.: A cross-situational learning algorithm for damping homonymy in the guessing game. In: ALIFE X. Tenth International Conference on the Simulation and Synthesis of Living Systems. (2006) to appear.
14. Gilbert, N., den Besten, M., Bontovics, A., Craenen, B.G., Divina, F., Eiben, A., et. al.: Emerging artificial societies through learning. Journal of Artificial Societies and Social Simulation **9** (2006)
15. Divina, F., Vogt, P.: Modelling language evolution in a complex ecological environment. ILK Research Group Technical Report Series no. 06-01 (2006)
16. Epstein, J.M., Axtell, R.: Growing artificial societies: social science from the bottom up. MIT Press, Cambridge, MA. (1996)

17. Steels, L.: The synthetic modeling of language origins. Evolution of Communication **1(1)** (1997) 1–34
18. Vogt, P.: The emergence of compositional structures in perceptually grounded language games. Artificial Intelligence **167** (2005) 206–242
19. Vogt, P.: Lexicon Grounding on Mobile Robots. PhD thesis, Vrije Universiteit Brussel (2000)
20. Steels, L., Kaplan, F.: Situated grounded word semantics. In: Proceedings of IJCAI 99, Morgan Kaufmann (1999)
21. Vogt, P., Divina, F.: Language evolution in large populations of autonomous agents: issues in scaling. In: Proceedings of AISB 2005: Socially inspired computing joint symposium. (2005) 80–87
22. Divina, F., Vogt, P.: Perceptually grounded lexicon formation using inconsistent knowledge. In: Proceedings of the VIIIth European Conference on Artificial Life (ECAL2005), Springer-Verlag (2005) 644–654

Cooperation, Conceptual Spaces
and the Evolution of Semantics

Peter Gärdenfors[1]and Massimo Warglien[2]

[1] Lund University Cognitive Science, Kungshuset, S-22222 Lund, Sweden
Peter.Gardenfors@lucs.lu.se
[2] Department of Business Economics, Ca' Foscari Università, Venezia, Italy
warglien@unive.it

Abstract. We start by providing an evolutionary scenario for the emergence of semantics. It is argued that the evolution of anticipatory cognition and theory of mind in the hominids opened up for cooperation about future goals. This cooperation requires symbolic communication. The meanings of the symbols are established via a "meeting of minds." The concepts in the minds of communicating individuals are modelled as convex regions in conceptual spaces. We then outline a mathematical framework based on fixpoints in continuous mappings between conceptual spaces that can be used to model such a semantics.

1 Communication and Meaning: An Evolutionary Perspective

When communication first appears, it is the communicative *act* in itself and the context it occurs in that is most important, not the expressive form of the act [1]. As a consequence, the *pragmatic* aspects of language are the most fundamental from an evolutionary point of view. When communicative acts (later speech acts) in due time become more varied and eventually conventionalized and their contents become detached from the immediate context, one can start analyzing the different *meanings* of the acts. Then *semantic* considerations become salient. Finally, when linguistic communication becomes even more conventionalized and combinatorially richer, certain markers, a.k.a. *syntax*, are used to disambiguate the communicative contents when the context is not sufficient to do so. Thus syntax is required only for the subtlest aspects of communication – pragmatic and semantic features are more fundamental.

This view on the evolutionary order of different linguistic functions stands in sharp contrast to mainstream contemporary linguistics. For followers of the Chomskian school, syntax is the primary study object of linguistics; semantic features are added when grammar is not enough; and pragmatics is a wastebasket for what is left over (context, deixis, etc). However, we believe that when the goal is to develop a theory of the evolution of communication, the converse order – pragmatics before semantics before syntax – is more appropriate. In other words, there is much to find out about the evolution of communication, before we can understand the evolution of semantics, let alone syntax.

In support of the position that pragmatics is evolutionarily primary, we want to point out that most human cognitive functions had been chiselled out by evolution

P. Vogt et al. (Eds.): EELC 2006, LNAI 4211, pp. 16–30, 2006.

before the advent of language. We submit that language would not be possible without all these cognitive capacities, in particular having a theory of mind and being able to represent future goals (see [2]). This position is not uncontested. Some researchers argue that human thinking cannot exist in its full sense without language (e.g. [3]). According to this view, the emergence of language is a cause of certain forms of thinking, e.g. concept formation.

However, seeing language as a cause of human thinking is like seeing money as a cause of human economics [4, p. 94]. Humans have been trading goods as long as they have existed. But when a monetary system does emerge, it makes economic transactions more efficient and far reaching. The same applies to language: hominids have been communicating long before they had a language, but language makes the exchange of meaning more effective. The analogy carries further. When money is introduced in a society, a relatively stable system of *prices* emerges. Similarly, when linguistic communication develops, individuals will come to share a relatively stable system of *meanings*, i.e. components in their mental spaces, which communicators can exchange between each other. In this way, language fosters a *common structure* of the mental spaces of the individuals in a society.

Within traditional philosophy of language, a semantics is seen as a mapping between a language and the world. From an evolutionary perspective, this view has severe problems. For one thing, it does not involve the users of the language. In particular, it does not tell us anything about how individual user can "grasp" the meanings determined by such a mapping [5]. In this article, we want to propose a radically different view of the evolution of semantics based on a "meeting of minds." According to this view, the meanings of expressions do not reside in the world or solely in the mental schemes of individual users, but they emerge from the communicative interactions between the language users.

The first part of this paper (sections 2 and 3) presents an evolutionary scenario for the emergence of a "socio-cognitive" semantics. We shall argue that the evolution of anticipatory cognition and theory of mind in the hominids opened up for cooperation about future goals. This cooperation requires symbolic communication. The meanings of the symbols are established via a "meeting of minds." In the second part of the paper (sections 4-6), we outline a mathematical framework based on fixpoints in continuous mappings between conceptual spaces that can be used to model such a semantics.

This view on how meanings are established gains additional support from a different direction. In a variety of computer simulations and robotic experiments (e.g. [6], [7], [8], [9], [10], [11], [12]), it has been shown that a stable communicative system can emerge as a result of iterated interactions between artificial agents, even though there is nobody who determines any "rules" for the communication. A general finding of the experiments is that the greater number of "signallers" and "recipients" involved in communication about the same outer world, the stronger is the convergence of the reference of the messages that are used and the faster the convergence is attained. Still, different "dialects" in the simulated community often emerge. However, the "mental spaces" that have been used for robots in these simulations have, in general, been very simplistic and assumed to be identical in structure for all individuals.

2 Cooperation for Future Goals

Language is the solution to certain problems concerning communication. But animals communicate without language. So what are the communicative reasons for developing a more complicated system like human symbolic language? Our answer is that humans have a capacity to communicate about their future goals.

To elaborate this position, we must analyze some of the cognitive prerequisites for symbolic language. Bischof [13] and Bischof-Köhler [14] argue that animals other than humans cannot anticipate future needs or drive states. Their cognition is therefore bound to their present motivational state (see also [15]). This hypothesis, which is called the Bischof-Köhler hypothesis [16], is supported by the current evidence concerning planning in non-human animals.

Gulz [15] calls planning for present needs *immediate planning* while planning for the future is called *anticipatory planning*. Humans can predict that they will be hungry tomorrow and save some food, and we can imagine that the winter will be cold, so we start building a shelter already in the summer. There is nothing in the available evidence concerning animal planning, notwithstanding all its methodological problems, which suggests that any other genus than *Homo* can represent their *future* desires (the recent results by Mulcahy and Call [17] are not really counterevidence to the thesis). The cognition of other animals concerns here and now, while humans are mentally both here and in the future.

Anticipatory planning is a component in a more general anticipatory cognition that is a hallmark of *Homo sapiens* [18]. It also includes episodic memory [19] and other aspects of "mental time travel" [16], [20]. A central question is what factors along the hominid line have created selective evolutionary forces that have resulted in anticipatory cognition in general (including episodic memory) and anticipatory planning in particular (also cf. [21]).

One answer is provided by Osvath and Gärdenfors [18], who argue that the Oldowan culture led to the co-evolution of transport and anticipatory planning. The hominid life on the savannah during the Oldowan era opened up for many new forms of cooperation for future goals. For example, Plummer [22, p. 139] writes: "Given that body size often predicts rank in the carnivore guild, an individual *Homo habilis* would likely not have fared well in a contest with many of its contemporary carnivores. Competition with large carnivores may have favoured cohesive groups and coordinated group movements in *Homo habilis*, cooperative behaviour including group defence, diurnal foraging (as many large predators preferentially hunt at night) with both hunting and scavenging being practiced as the opportunities arose, and the ability (using stone tools) to rapidly dismember large carcasses so as to minimize time spent at death sites."

For most forms of cooperation among animals, it seems that mental representations are not needed. If the common goal is *present* in the actual environment, for example food to be eaten or an antagonist to be fought, the collaborators need not focus on a joint representation of it before acting. If, on the other hand, the goal is distant in time or space, then a *mutual* representation of it must be produced before cooperative action can be taken. For example, building a common dwelling requires coordinated planning of how to obtain the building material and advanced collaboration in the construction. In general terms, cooperation about future goals requires that *the mental spaces of the individuals be coordinated* (or, in some cases, negotiated).

3 The Need for Symbols in Communication About Future Goals

Symbolic language is the primary tool by which humans can make their inner worlds known to each other. In previous work [2], [18], [23], [24], it has been proposed that there is a strong connection between the evolution of anticipatory cognition and the evolution of symbolic communication. In brief, the argument is that symbolic language makes it possible to *cooperate about future goals* in an effective way.

Language is based on the use of representations as stand-ins for entities, actual or just imagined. Use of such representations replaces the use of environmental cues in communication. If somebody has an idea about a goal she wishes to reach, she can use language to communicate her thoughts. In this way, language makes it possible for us to coordinate our visions about the future – our minds can meet. The question that has to be answered is why symbolic communication is necessary for this kind of communication.

Tomasello [25, p. 95] defines symbolic communication as the process by which "one individual attempts to manipulate the attention of, or to share attention with, another individual. In specifically linguistic communication [...] this attempt quite often involves both (a) reference, or inviting the other to share attention to some outside entity (broadly construed), and (b) predication, or directing the other's attention to some currently *unshared* features or aspects of that entity [...]." We cannot fully accept this definition. One aspect that is missing in his characterization is that depending on the character of the "outside entity," different cognitive demands on the individual whose attention is manipulated will be relevant. To understand the differences, one must distinguish between (1) entities that are present in the shared environment, (2) entities that are not present in time or space but about which there is some common knowledge, and (3) entities that are unknown to the other individual. Communication about future goals often involves entities of the third kind.

Depending on which type of entity is communicated about, different minimal forms of communication are required. It becomes very natural to map the three kinds of entities to be communicated about to Peirce's [26] triad of index, icon and symbol:

(1) If the entity is present, then *indexical* communication, for example pointing, is sufficient. Animal communication consists almost exclusively of signals, referring to what is present at the moment in the environment, be it food, danger or a mate. This form of communication does not presume that the signaller ascribes any mental representation of the communicated object in the mind of the receiver. It is important to note that this kind of communication does not require any form of symbolic communication. (This is another reason we do not fully accept Tomasello's definition presented above.) Consequently, as long as all communication concerns present entities, there will be no evolutionary pressures for the use of symbols.

(2) If the communicated entity is not present, direct signalling will not work. If I want to refer to a deer that I saw down by the riverside yesterday, merely pointing will not help, nor will a call signal. This form of communication clearly requires representations that are detached from the present [2]. *Iconic miming* may establish the reference, but only if the signaller and receiver have sufficient *common knowledge* about the indicated entity and there are sufficient cues from previous communication or the environment to make it possible for the receiver to identify the object. (This would be a case of what is called triadic miming in [27]. When the relevant entity is

an action, this form of communication works particularly well. By using icons, one agent can show another how to act in order for the two of them to reach a common goal. Icons can work as imperatives, urging the agents to "Do like this!" [23].

(3) The most difficult type of communication concerns *novel* entities that do not yet exist. Collaboration about future, non-existent goals falls within this category. Here the signaller can neither rely on common knowledge about the entity, nor on cues from the environment. Iconic communication might work in exceptional cases, but we submit that it is for this kind of communication that *symbols* prove their mettle. For example, if I have come up with an idea about how to build a new kind of defence wall around our camp, it is very difficult to see how this can be communicated by miming alone. In particular, if the communication involves the *predication* of Tomasello's definition above, that is, directing the other's attention to some currently unshared features or aspects of that entity, symbols seem to be crucial. Such a predication process will also require the productivity and compositionality of a symbolic system.

In this characterization we use "symbolic communication" in a basically Peircian way, meaning that the act is conventional and breaks up compositionally into meaningful sub-acts that relate systematically to each other and to other similar acts [27], [28]. This form of communication is, as far as we know, uniquely human. In this context it should be noted that Tomasello's [25, p. 95] definition of symbolic communication that was presented above also covers what we call indexical and iconic cases.

An important feature of the use of symbols in cooperation is that they can set the cooperators free from the goals that are available in the present environment. The future goals and the means to reach them are picked out and *shared* through the symbolic communication. This kind of sharing gives humans an enormous advantage concerning cooperation in comparison to other species. We view this advantage as a strong evolutionary force behind the emergence of symbols. More precisely, we submit that there has been a co-evolution of cooperation about future goals and symbolic communication (cf. the "ratchet effect" discussed in [4], pp. 37-40 and [18]. However, without the presence of anticipatory cognition, the selective pressures that resulted in symbolic communication would not have emerged. However, once symbolic communication about future goals has been established, it can be used for other purposes, for example, sharing myths and rituals.

We want to show that this kind of sharing mental representations leads to the emergence of a semantics, that is, a set of shared meanings. In our opinion, semantics can be seen as conventionalized pragmatics [29]. One important question then concerns how the cognitive structure of the semantic conventions looks like. Here, so called cognitive semantics offers a cue to one part of the answer (e.g. [29], [30], [31]). According to cognitive semantics, the meanings of words can be represented as "image schemas" in the heads of the communicators. These schemas are abstract mental pictures having an inherent spatial structure constructed from elementary topological and geometrical structures like "container," "link" and "source-path-goal." A common assumption is that such schemas constitute the representational form that is common to perception, memory, and semantic meaning.

However, a general problem for such a semantic theory is: if everybody has their own mental space, how can we then talk about a representation being *the* meaning of an expression? In other words, how can individual mental representations become conventions? Therefore, the question in focus will be: how can language help us *share* our mental spaces?

In the computer simulations and robotic experiments performed by Steels and others, the typical communicative situation is a "guessing game" [8] where the signaller, by uttering an expression, tries to make the recipient identify a particular object in the environment. It should be noted that in such guessing games (as in Wittgenstein's language games), the participants are only concerned with finding the appropriate referent among those that are present on the scene. In contrast, communication about *non-present* referents, which are in focus here, demands that the communicators have more advanced representational capacities.

4 Semantics as a Meeting of Minds

Our view on the evolution of symbolic communication puts novel, non-present and even fictitious referents in focus. Therefore, a semantic theory that starts from reference to the world seems unnatural from our perspective. Our task is to develop a semantic theory that fits with the evolutionary account presented above. In our view, the semantics does not consist of a mapping from linguistic expressions to an external world, but is rather constituted of the individuals' mental spaces and mappings between them. In brief, we see semantics as a meeting of the minds and hence we advocate a form of socio-cognitive semantics.

As a comparison, consider the "cognitive semantics" where image schemas have been core carriers of meaning. An image schema is a conceptual structure that belongs to a particular individual. However, when the authors within cognitive linguistics write about image schemas, they are often presented as structures that are *common* to all speakers of a language. However, in the socio-cognitive type of semantics we model in the next section, we do not assume that everybody has the same meaning space, but only that there exist well-behaved mappings between the meaning spaces of different individual – "well-behaved" in the sense that the mappings have certain mathematical properties (to be specified in the following section). As we shall argue, semantic equilibria can exist without assuming shared spaces. The semantics will be represented by a *fixpoint* in the mapping between individual mental spaces.

The fundamental role of communication is to affect the states of mind of others. A meeting of the minds means that the representations in the minds of the communicators will become sufficiently compatible so that successful joint action can arise. Thus we conceive of semantics as a *product of communication* – meanings arise as a result of communicative interactions. The mental space that generates the meanings for a particular individual is partly determined from the individual's interaction with the world, partly from her interaction with others and partly from her interaction with herself (e.g. in the form of self-reflection). This view does not entail that different individuals mean the same thing by using an expression, only that their communication is sufficiently successful.

As a preparation for our analysis of communication about novel and non-present objects as a basis for semantics, let us consider a theoretical scenario proposed by Freyd [32]. The main theme of her paper is that knowledge, by the fact that it is *shared* in a language community, imposes *constraints* on individual cognitive representations. She argues that the structural properties of individuals' mental spaces have evolved because "they provide for the most efficient sharing of concepts," and proposes that a dimensional structure with a small number of values on each dimension will be especially "shareable." This process of creating shared meanings is continually ongoing: the interplay between individual and social structures is in eternal co-evolution. The effects are magnified when communication takes place between many individuals (cf. the simulations by Steels and others).

The constraints of sharing concepts can be discussed in relation to the image schemas of cognitive semantics. Even if different individuals do not have identical schemas, there are good reasons to assume that they have developed a high degree of similarity. One is that since basic image schemas are supposed to represent perceptual and other bodily experiences, the very fact that humans have similar constitutions makes it likely that our representations are very similar. Another reason is that if the image schema corresponding to a particular expression is markedly different for two individuals, it is likely that this will lead to problems of communication. A desire for successful communication will therefore lead to a gradual alignment among the members of a linguistic community of the image schemas.

Image schemas provide a bridge between a focus on shared meanings and a focus on the common shape of underlying conceptual structures that facilitate mutual understanding and the successful interaction between possibly different but similarly structured mental spaces. After all, we can communicate effectively even if we do not share the same mental representation. For example, in communication between children and adults, children often represent their concepts using fewer dimensions, and dimensions that are different from those of the adults.

Our aim is to model how a common structure in individual mental spaces will ensure the existence of a "meeting of minds," and how semantics may be grounded in the formal properties of such interaction.

5   Meeting of Minds as Fixpoints in Communication Games

In this section we outline, in rather broad terms, a mathematical framework for semantics as "meeting of the minds".

As long as communication is conceived as a process through which the mental state of an individual affect the mental state of another one, a "meeting of the minds" is a condition in which both individuals find themselves in compatible states of mind that do not require further processing. Just like covenants shake hands after reaching an agreement on the terms of a contract, speakers may reach a point in which both believe they have understood what they are talking about. Of course, they may actually mean different things, just like the terms of a contract might prove to be interpreted differently by the covenants. But it is enough that, in a given moment and a given context, speakers may reach a point in which they feel there is a mutual understanding – no matter whether mutual agreement implies or not that they mean the same thing.

A very common mathematical way to define such kind of state would be to identify it as a fixpoint. A fixpoint x^* of a function $f(x)$ is a point in which the function maps x^* on itself ($f(x^*) = x^*$). But what kind of object is a function that reaches a fixpoint when minds agree? The most natural candidate for such a semantics is a function that maps language expressions on mental states, and vice-versa – a kind of interpretation function and its inverse. So, in our framework minds meet when the interpretation function mapping states of mind on states of mind via language finds a resting point – a fixpoint.

Using fixpoints is, of course, not new to semantics. The semantics of programming languages often resort to fixpoints to define the "meaning" of a program. Its meaning is where the program will stop (for a remarkable review, see [33]). In a different vein, Kripke's [34] theory of truth is grounded on the notion of a fixpoint – in his case the fixpoints of a semantic evaluation function are at the focus of his interest. Fixpoints are also crucial in other fields, such as the study of semantic memory: content-addressable memories usually store information as a fixpoint of a memory update process (the canonical example being [35]).

However, here we make a fairly different use of the fixpoint notion to define our "meeting of minds" semantics, since we consider the fixpoints of an interactive, social process of meaning construction and evaluation. From this point of view, our use of fixpoints resembles more the one made by game theorists to define states of mutual compatibility of individual strategies. To some extent, we are following the tradition of communication games ([36], [37], etc), but to this tradition we are adding some assumptions about the *topological* and *geometric* structure of the individual mental spaces that will allow us to specify more substantially how the semantic emerges and what properties it has.

Our argument is that some types of topological and geometric properties of mental representations are more likely to engender meetings of minds, because they lend more naturally fixpoints to communication activities. Thus, we shift from the conventional emphasis on the way we share the same concepts to an emphasis on the way the "shape" of our conceptual structures makes it possible for us to find a point of convergence. A parallel with the pragmatics of conversation in the Gricean tradition comes to the mind: just like maxims of conversation ensure that talk exchanges find a mutually accepted direction, we explore the complementary notion that the way we shape our concepts deeply affects the effectiveness of communication.

On this ground, we make an implicit selection argument: just like wheels are round because they make transportation efficient, we expect to identify the shapes of concepts that are selected to make communication smooth.

It turns out that structural properties of conceptual representations that grant the existence of meetings of minds are to a large extent already familiar to cognitive semantics and in particular to the theory of conceptual spaces. These basic properties are the metric structure induced by similarity, the closed/bounded nature of concepts, convexity of conceptual representation, and the assumption that natural language, with all its resources, can "translate" (spatial) mental representations with reasonable approximation. In what follows, we will make more precise these notions and the role they play in a "meeting of minds" semantics theory.

Our first step is to assume, following [38], that conceptual spaces are made out of primitive *quality dimensions* (often rooted in sensorial experience) and that similarity provides the basic metric structure to such spaces. The dimensions represent various "qualities" (colour, shape, weight, size, position …) of objects in different domains.

While the nature of psychologically sound similarity measures is still highly contro-versial (and presumably differs between domains), numerous studies suggest that it is a continuous function of Euclidean distance in the conceptual spaces. Consequently, we will assume, as a first approximation, that conceptual spaces can be modelled as *Euclidean spaces*.

It is not only in humans that one finds these kinds of representations. For example, Gallistel [39] devotes an entire chapter to "Vector spaces in the nervous system." in his book on learning mechanisms in biological systems. He writes [39, p. 477]: "The purpose of this chapter is to review neurophysiological data supporting the hypothesis that the nervous system does in fact quite generally employ vectors to represent prop-erties of both proximal and distal stimuli. The values of these representational vectors are physically expressed by the locations of neural activity in anatomical spaces of whose dimensions correspond to descriptive dimensions of the stimulus." Further-more, it is well known that even fairly simple neural processing mechanisms can approximate arbitrary continuous functions [40].

In [38], it is proposed that *concepts* can be modelled as *convex regions* of a con-ceptual space. While convexity may seem a strong assumption, it is a remarkably regular property of many conceptual representations grounded in perception (e.g., colour, taste, pitch). Furthermore, we will soon argue that convexity is crucial for assuring the effectiveness of communication.

There are interesting connections between analyzing concepts as convex regions and the *prototype theory* developed by Rosch and her collaborators (see, for example, [30], [41], [42], [43]). When concepts are defined as convex regions of a conceptual space, prototype effects are indeed to be expected. In a convex region one can de-scribe positions as being more or less central. In particular, in a Euclidean space one can calculate the centre of gravity of a region.

It is possible to argue in the converse direction too and show that if prototype the-ory is adopted, then the representation of concepts as convex regions is to be ex-pected. Assume that some quality dimensions of a conceptual space are given, for example the dimensions of colour space, and that we want to decompose it into a number of categories, for example colour concepts. If we start from a set of proto-types $p_1, ..., p_n$ of the concepts, for example the focal colours, then these should be the central points in the concepts they represent. The information about prototypes can be used to generate concepts by stipulating that p belongs to the same concept as the *closest* prototype p_i. It can be shown that this rule will generate a decomposition of the space – the so-called *Voronoi tessellation*. An illustration of the Voronoi tessella-tion is given in figure 1.

A crucial property of the Voronoi tessellation of a conceptual space is that it al-ways results in a decomposition of the space into *convex* regions (see [44]). In this way, the Voronoi tessellation provides a constructive geometric answer to how a similarity measure together with a set of prototypes determine a set of categories.

As long as concepts are closed and bounded regions of conceptual spaces, they ac-quire one more crucial topological property: *compactness*. Euclidean metrics, com-pactness and convexity set the stage for our fixpoint argument. But before getting there, a last point must be made briefly. A basic tenet of cognitive semantics is that language can preserve the spatial structure of concepts. One way to say it is that

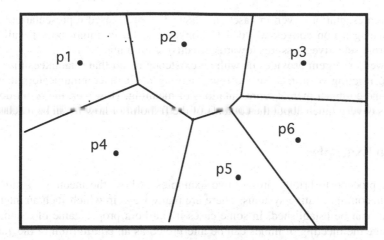

Fig. 1. Voronoi tessellation of the plane into convex sets

language can preserve the neighbourhood relations among points of conceptual spaces. In topology, a neighbourhood preserving function is nothing but a continuous function. In other words, assuming that language can preserve neighbourhood relations of conceptual spaces implies assuming that language can establish a continuous mapping between mental spaces of different individuals – and a continuous mapping of the product space of individual mental spaces on itself. While this continuity assumption may seem extreme, it basically says that natural language must have enough plasticity to map neighbourhoods of points in a conceptual space on neighbourhoods of points in another conceptual space – or in the space itself. Furthermore, as we shall see, this assumption can be relaxed to assume that such continuous mappings can be suitably approximated.

Now all ingredients are there, and we can simply remind you of one of the most fundamental results of analysis, Brouwer's [45] theorem: each continuous map of a convex, compact set on itself has at least one fixpoint. In the present context, this result basically tells us that, no matter what is the content of individual mental representations, provided that such representations are "well shaped" and that language is plastic enough to preserve the spatial structure of concepts, there will always be at least one point representing a "meeting of minds." Furthermore, given a continuous function and convex compact spaces, whenever such spaces can be decomposed in smaller convex closed subsets (they can be "triangulated"), there will always be a function mapping such decomposition on itself (called a "simplicial approximation") that will approximate the continuous function, and preserve its fixpoint property. In other words, such fixpoints may be still approximated by a coarser mapping.

After this short and very informal mathematical detour, our central claim should become apparent: whenever the facility to reach a meeting of minds matters, convex mental representations provide a background over which language can deploy most of its power. We see this as an indirect explanation of why concepts are in general convex. Please note that we are not claiming that convex representations are "faithful" representations of the world – we just claim that since they are effective, one should find them quite widespread. In fact, our claim implies that one should expect to find convex representations even in cases in which they are biased representations of the world: seeing a non convex world with convex spectacles might be a peculiar bias arising from selective pressures towards effective communication.

Brouwer's theorem provides us with an existence result that guarantees that an appropriate meeting of minds can be found among a set of communicators that have convex and compact mental representations of meaning. However, the result does not in itself say very much about the contents of the fixpoint or how it can be reached.

6 Two Examples

We now proceed to briefly present two examples of how the meeting of minds can emerge in communicative systems. There are many ways in which such an interactive semantics can be established. In some cases it can be a proper game of communication, where the meeting of minds can be interpreted as an equilibrium of the game. In other cases, it can result from simpler adaptive processes that do not require strategic reasoning.

Jäger and van Rooij [46] provide an example of the first kind. Their domain is the colour space and the problem they approach is how a common meaning for colour terms can develop in a communication game. In their example, there are only two players: s (signaller) and r (receiver). It is assumed that the two players have a common conceptual space C for colour. Jäger and van Rooij define the space as a "continuous space" but from their following claims, it clearly must be a compact and convex space, such as a colour circle or a colour spindle. There is also a fixed and finite set M of n messages that the signaller can convey to the receiver. The colour space C can also be interpreted as a state space from which Nature draws points according to some continuous distribution p. The signaller can choose a *decomposition* S of the space C in n subsets assigning to each colour a unique message. The receiver can choose where to locate n points, corresponding to the meaning assigned to each of the n messages by the signaller.

The goal of the communication game is to maximize the average similarity between the intention of the signaller and the interpretation of the receiver. The communication game unfolds as follows. Nature chooses some point in the colour space, according to some fixed probability distribution. The signaller s knows the choice of nature, but the receiver r does not. Then s is allowed to send one of the messages to r. The receiver r in turn picks a point in the colour space. In the game, s and r maximize utility if they maximize the similarity between nature's choice and r's "interpretation". Here is it only assumed that the similarity is a monotonically decreasing function of the Euclidean distance in the colour space between nature's choice and r's choice.

A Nash equilibrium of the game is a pair (R*, S*), where R* is an n-tuple of points of C and S* is a decomposition (in n subsets) of C, such that both are a best response to each other. Jäger and van Rooij [46] show how to compute the best response functions for each player. The central result of their paper can be restated by saying that if the colour space is convex and compact and the probability and similarity functions are continuous, then there exists a Nash equilibrium, and it corresponds to a Voronoi tessellation of the colour space (which results in convex subsets).

They also show how, in a simplified evolutionary version of the game, convex colour regions can emerge as the evolutionary stable solutions of the game. Jäger and van Rooij's model is also interesting because it provides an illustration of how a discrete system of signs (there are only n signs in their communication game) can give rise to continuous functions mapping agents' mental representations on themselves. In their example, signs define an array of locations in the colour space, and the "best response function" of s and r continuously maps configurations of such array of points as responses to decompositions of C, and vice versa. In this language game, "language" has to be plastic enough to grant the continuity of the "best response" function, and the meaning space C must have enough topological structure to afford the existence of fixpoints. Language plasticity is given here by the possibility to continuously deform the decomposition S and the location of the points of R.

As a second example, Hutchins [47] provides a case that is more loosely related to a game structure, but where fixpoints with a semantic valence result form simple adaptive dynamics shaped by communication. He models how individuals may reach an agreement over an interpretation of potentially incomplete and noisy signals from the environment. Each individual is represented as a constraint satisfaction network, in which nodes represent features (corresponding to quality dimensions in a conceptual space) of the world and connections between nodes impose some coherence between configurations of features.

Communication between agents is modelled through connections between nodes of different agents. Through such connections the state of mind of an agent affects the states of mind of the other agents by transmitting the activation values of its nodes. In other words, communication continuously maps the state of minds of each agent on the states of mind of other agents in a feature space: Imagine a "feature-based" language through which agents can express their beliefs about the state of the world.

Hutchins shows by simulations how agents starting form different beliefs can converge towards fixpoints that represent consensual interpretations of the state of the world. Consensus needs not to correspond to "reality": In many cases it is a form of groupthink, convergence to beliefs dominated more by peer pressure than truth. Revisiting more formally Hutchins' model, Marchiori and Warglien [48] prove that communication can give rise to new fixpoints that were not contained in individual initial memories – i.e. there may be genuine new meanings arising as meetings of minds among communicating agents.

7 Conclusion

In this article, we have first told a story about the evolution of communication based on the unique human capacity for planning for future goals. A consequence of our story is that in order for communication about non-present objects to succeed, the minds of the interlocutors must meet. In the second part of the paper, we have then presented a framework for how this process can be modelled as a fixpoint semantics. To some extent, we have followed the tradition of communication games, but the most innovative part of our model is the assumptions about the *topological* and *geometric* structure of the mental spaces of the communicators. We have focused on the compactness and convexity of these spaces and, following Gärdenfors' [38] work on conceptual spaces, argued that these assumptions are very natural. These assumptions make it possible for us to apply Brouwer's fixpoint theorem, which in this context, is interpreted as saying that for communicators with "well-behaved" mental spaces, there will always exist a meeting of their minds that represents the meaning of the expressions they use. We have also outlined two examples of how such a meeting can be achieved.

The fixpoint semantics that we have presented provide us with rather new perspectives on the functioning of semantics for natural languages. We hope to develop the model to show that this perspective is fruitful and that it can solve many of the problems for classical forms of semantics, for example problems concerning the reference of expressions for non-existing objects and that it can shed new light on the meaning of metaphors.

References

1. Winter, S.: Expectations and Linguistic Meaning. Lund University Cognitive Studies 71, Lund (1998)
2. Gärdenfors, P.: How Homo Became Sapiens: On the Evolution of Thinking. Oxford University Press, Oxford (2003)
3. Dennett, D.: Consciousness Explained. Little, Brown and Company, Boston (1991)
4. Tomasello, M.: The Cultural Origins of Human Cognition. Harvard Unversity Press, Cambridge, MA (1999)
5. Harnad, S.: The Symbol Grounding Problem. Physica D. 42 (1990) 335-46
6. Hurford, J.: The Evolution of Language and Languages. In: Dunbar, R., Knight, C., Power, C. (eds): The Evolution of Culture. Edinburgh University Press, Edinburgh (1999) 173-193
7. Kirby, S.: Function, Selection and Innateness: The Emergence of Language Univerals. Oxford University Press, Oxford (1999)
8. Steels, L.: The Talking Heads Experiment. Laboratorium, Antwerp (1999)
9. Steels, L.: Social and Cultural Learning in the Evolution of Human Communication. In: Oller, K., Griebel, U. (eds.): The Evolution of Communication Systems. MIT Press, Cambridge, MA (2004) 69-90
10. Kaplan, F.: L'émergence d'un lexique dans une population d'agents autonomes. Ph. D. Thesis. Laboratoire d'Informatique de Paris 6, Paris (2000)
11. Vogt, P.: Bootstrapping Grounded Symbols by Minimal Autonomous Robots. Evol. of Comm. 4 (2000) 89-118
12. Vogt, P.: The Emergence of Compositional Structures in Perceptually Grounded Language Games. Artif. Intell. 167 (2005) 206-242
13. Bischof, N.: On the Phylogeny of Human Morality. In: Stent, G. (ed.): Morality as a Biological Phenomenon. Abako, Berlin (1978) 53-74
14. Bischof-Köhler, D.: Zur Phylogenese menschlicher Motivation. In: Eckensberger, L.H., Lantermann, E.D. (eds.): Emotion und Reflexivität. Urban & Schwarzenberg, Vienna (1985) 3-47
15. Gulz, A.: The Planning of Action as a Cognitive and Biological Phenomenon. Lund University Cognitive Studies 2, Lund (1991)
16. Suddendorf, T., Corballis M.C.: Mental Time Travel and the Evolution of Human Mind. Genetic, Social and General Psychology Monographs 123 (1997) 133-167
17. Mulcahy, N.J., Call, J.: Apes Save Tools for Future Use. Science 312 (2006) 1038-1040.

18. Osvath, M., Gärdenfors, P.: Oldowan Culture and the Evolution of Anticipatory Cognition, Lund University Cognitive Studies 121, Lund (2005)
19. Tulving, E.: How Many Memory Systems are There? Am. Psychologist 40 (1985) 385-398
20. Suddendorf, T., Busby J.: Mental Time Travel in Animals? Trends in Cog. Sci. 7 (2003) 391-396
21. Savage-Rumbaugh, E.S.: Hominin Evolution: Looking to Modern Apes for Clues. In: Quiatt, D., Itani, J. (eds.): Hominin Culture in Primate Perspective. University Press of Colorado, Niwot (1994) 7-49
22. Plummer T.: Flaked Stones and Old Bones: Biological and Cultural Evolution at the Dawn of Technology. Yearbook of Phys. Anthrop. 47 (2004) 118-164
23. Brinck, I., Gärdenfors, P.: Co-operation and Communication in Apes and Humans. Mind and Lang. 18 (2003) 484-501
24. Gärdenfors, P.: Cooperation and the Evolution of Symbolic Communication. In Oller, K., Griebel, U. (eds.): The Evolution of Communication Systems. MIT Press, Cambridge, MA (2004) 237-256
25. Tomasello, M.: On the Different Origins of Symbols and Grammar. In: Christansen, M.H., Kirby, S. (eds.): Language Evolution. Oxford University Press, Oxford (2003) 94-110
26. Peirce, C.S.: The Collected Papers of Charles Saunders Peirce. Vols. 1-4. Harvard University Press, Cambridge, MA (1931-35)
27. Zlatev, J., Persson, T., Gärdenfors, P.: Bodily Mimesis as the "Missing Link" in Human Cognitive Evolution. Lund University Cognitive Studies 121, Lund (2005)
28. Deacon, T.W.: The Symbolic Species. Penguin Books, London (1997)
29. Langacker, R.W.: Foundations of Cognitive Grammar, Vol. 1. Stanford University Press, Stanford, CA (1987)
30. Lakoff, G .: Women, Fire, and Dangerous Things. The University of Chicago Press, Chicago, IL (1987)
31. Talmy, L.: Force Dynamics in Language and Cognition. Cognitive Science 12 (1988) 49-100
32. Freyd, J.: Shareability: The Social Psychology of Epistemology. Cognitive Science 7 (1983) 191-210
33. Fitting, M.: Fixpoint Semantics for Logic Programming: A Survey. Theor. Comput. Sci. 278 (2002), 25-51
34. Kripke, S.: Outline of a Theory of Truth. J. of Phil. 72 (1975) 690-716
35. Hopfield, J.J.: Neural Networks and Physical Systems with Emergent Collective Computational Abilities. Proc. Nat. Acad. of Sci. 79 (1982), 2554–2558
36. Lewis, D.: Convention. Harvard University Press, Cambridge, MA (1969)
37. Stalnaker, R.: Assertion. Syntax and Semantics 9 (1979) 315-332
38. Gärdenfors, P.: Conceptual Spaces: The Geometry of Thought. MIT Press, Cambridge, MA (2000)
39. Gallistel, C. R.: The Organization of Learning. MIT Press, Cambridge, MA (1990)
40. Hornik, K., Stinchombe, H., White, H.: Multilayer Feedforward Networks are Universal Approximators. Neural Networks 2 (1989) 359-366
41. Rosch, E.: Cognitive Representations of Semantic Categories. J. of Exp. Psych.: General 104 (1975) 192–233
42. Rosch, E.: Prototype Classification and Logical Classification: The Two Systems. In: Scholnik, E. (ed.): New Trends in Cognitive Representation: Challenges to Piaget's Theory. Lawrence Erlbaum Associates, Hillsdale, NJ (1978) 73–86
43. Mervis, C., Rosch, E.: Categorization of Natural Objects. Ann. Rev. of Psychol. 32 (1981) 89–115

44. Okabe, A., Boots, B., Sugihara, K.: Spatial Tessellations: Concepts and Applications of Voronoi Diagrams. John Wiley & Sons, New York (1992)
45. Brouwer, L.E.J.: Über ein eindeutige, stetige Transformation von Flächen in sich. Mathematische Annalen 69, blz. (1910) 176-180
46. Jäger, G., van Rooij, R.: Language Structure: Psychological and Social constraints, Synthese (to appear)
47. Hutchins, E.: Cognition in the Wild. MIT Press, Cambridge, MA (1995)
48. Marchiori, D., Warglien, M.: Constructing Shared Interpretations in a Team of Intelligent Agents: The Effects of Communication Intensity and Structure. In: Terano, T., Kita, H., Kaneda, T., Arai, K., Deguchi, H. (eds.): Agent-Based Simulation: From Modeling Methodologies to Real-World Applications. Springer Verlag, Berlin (2005)

Cross-Situational Learning: A Mathematical Approach

Kenny Smith[1], Andrew D.M. Smith[1], Richard A. Blythe[2], and Paul Vogt[1,3]

[1] Language Evolution and Computation Research Unit, University of Edinburgh
[2] School of Physics, University of Edinburgh
[3] ILK/Language and Information Science, Tilburg University, The Netherlands
{kenny, andrew, paulv}@ling.ed.ac.uk, R.A.Blythe@ed.ac.uk

Abstract. We present a mathematical model of cross-situational learning, in which we quantify the learnability of words and vocabularies. We find that high levels of uncertainty are not an impediment to learning single words or whole vocabulary systems, as long as the level of uncertainty is somewhat lower than the total number of meanings in the system. We further note that even large vocabularies are learnable through cross-situational learning.

1 Introduction

One of the design features of human language is the *arbitrary* relationship between words and their meanings [1] — they are not related iconically, through perceptual similarity, but merely by convention. Learning word-meaning mappings is therefore far from trivial, yet when children acquire language, they learn the meanings of a large number of words very quickly. This phenomenon is known as *fast mapping* [2]. Precisely how children achieve this remains to be established.

The problem of *referential indeterminacy* in acquiring word–meaning mappings was famously illustrated by Quine [3]. He imagined an anthropologist interacting with a native speaker of an unfamiliar language. As a rabbit runs by, the speaker exclaims "gavagai", and the anthropologist notes that "gavagai" means RABBIT. Quine showed, however, that the anthropologist cannot be sure that "gavagai" means RABBIT; in fact, it could have an infinite number of possible meanings, such as UNDETACHED RABBIT PARTS, DINNER or even IT WILL RAIN.

Developmental linguists have proposed many mechanisms which children may use to overcome referential indeterminacy in word learning (see [4,5] for overviews). Tomasello, for instance, proposes that the core mechanism is *joint attention* [6,7]; children understand that adults use utterances to refer to things, and upon hearing an utterance they attempt to attend to the same situation as their caregivers. Establishing joint attention in this way reduces the number of potential meanings a word might have, although Quine shows that this cannot be sufficient. Researchers have proposed a number of representational biases (e.g. the *whole object bias* [8] and the *shape bias* [9]) and interpretational constraints (e.g. *mutual exclusivity* [10] and the *principle of contrast* [11]) which might act to further reduce the indeterminacy problem.

P. Vogt et al. (Eds.): EELC 2006, LNAI 4211, pp. 31–44, 2006.

Further evidence suggests that children may learn the meaning of many words more straightforwardly, by simply disambiguating potential meanings across different occasions of use [12,13]. There is evidence that this process, known as *cross-situational learning*, takes place from a very early age [14]. Cross-situational learning is unlikely to provide a complete account of word learning, but does allow us to consider word learning in the absence of sophisticated cognitive mechanisms.

Understanding how children learn the meaning of words is not only a key question in developmental linguistics, but is also fundamentally an evolutionary issue. Firstly, accounting for the design feature of arbitrariness requires us to understand how the apparent problems introduced by arbitrary meaning-word mappings might be resolved. Secondly, an account of the evolution of the capacity for language must begin with a clear specification of the explanandum — for example, must the capacity for language include domain-specific word learning strategies? Finally, the indeterminacy of meaning is itself a important issue in the literature on the computational modelling of linguistic evolution [15,16]

In this paper, we present a mathematical model of cross-situational language learning and use it to quantify some basic properties of the learnability of words and vocabularies. In the following section, we describe cross-situational learning in more detail. Our formalisation is introduced in section 3, where we quantify the learnability of individual utterances. In section 4, we extend the model to quantify the learnability of a whole language. Finally, in section 5 we discuss the study's implications, and explore extensions of the model to address more realistic treatments of language structure, use and learning.

2   Cross-Situational Learning

Cross-situational learning is a technique for working out the reference of an utterance, based on multiple exposures to the utterance's use in context. When an utterance is produced, the context of its use will provide a number of candidate meanings for that utterance. From a hearer's point of view, each of these is in principle equally plausible, and there is no obvious motivation for choosing between them. If the same utterance is produced in a different situation, however, a different set of possible meanings may be suggested by that situation. The hearer can make use of this, by taking the intersection of the two sets of possible meanings, in order to (potentially) reduce the ambiguity of the utterance.

Cross-situational learning has been modelled computationally by Siskind [17], who showed that it could indeed be used to learn word-meaning mappings. In his model, a learner is exposed to a corpus of artificial sentences, each of which is paired with a set of possible meanings. Initially, the learner associates each word with all possible meanings. When hearing a word in a new situation, however, the learner eliminates any existing meanings for that word which are not consistent with the new situation.

Variants of the cross-situational model have been used to simulate the evolution of lexicons in multi-agent systems [16,18], in which meanings are built up through interaction with the world and other individuals. In these experiments, Smith [18] and Vogt [16] have separately shown that conventionalised vocabularies can emerge and persist through cross-situational learning. Our focus in this paper is similar to Siskind's — we are interested in the learnability of an existing vocabulary system, rather than the negotiation of shared vocabularies in a population. However, our approach is different — rather than modelling cross-situational learning computationally, we seek as far as possible an exact mathematical characterisation of the properties of the system. This paper represents a preliminary stage in this process.

3   The Mathematical Model of Cross-Situational Learning

In this section, we describe a mathematical model which we can use to specify the probability of a learner learning the meaning of a word cross-situationally. In every episode of exposure to an utterance, the hearer observes a situation which provides both the intended meaning of the utterance (the *target* meaning) and a set of other meanings incidentally provided by the situation (the *context*).

Assume that the context has the same number of members C in each episode, but the members are chosen at random and without duplication from the larger set of M possible meanings.[1] There are therefore $\binom{M}{C}$ different possible contexts.

Let the context in episode E_e be C_e. If, after e episodes, a non-target meaning has occurred in every episode $E_1 \ldots E_e$, then that meaning is called a *confounder* — this recurring meaning is an equally plausible meaning for the utterance as the target meaning, given that it too is present in all e situations where the utterance is used. Let the number of confounders after e episodes be K_e, and let us assume that the meaning of a word is successfully learned after e episodes if there are no confounders left ($K_e = 0$) — when $K_e = 0$, the target meaning is the only one which has occurred in every one of the e episodes.

3.1   An Illustration

Let us take a simple example, with $C = 3$ and $M = 5$. The 10 possible contexts are enumerated in Fig. 1, and we assume for this exposition that they are equiprobable, and that each therefore occurs with a probability of $\binom{M}{C}^{-1}$. In the graphical notation in Fig. 1, each context is represented as a row of M boxes, with each box representing a meaning. A cross in a box denotes that that meaning is present in the given context.

Note that there are necessarily C confounders ($K_1 = C$) after E_1 — each of the meanings in context C_1 has occurred as often as the target meaning, namely once. Let us now investigate what happens in episode E_2, taking context $E_1 = \{m_1, m_2, m_3\}$ as an example, and combining it with each possible context which

---

[1] Note that M is *exclusive* of the target meaning. In other words, there are $M + 1$ possible meanings, and any situation provides $C + 1$ unique meanings: the target and C unique additional meanings.

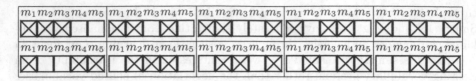

Fig. 1. Enumeration of $\binom{M}{C} = 10$ possible contexts, with $C = 3$ and $M = 5$

could occur in episode E_2. Fig. 2 below shows the 10 resultant combinations, the number of confounders K_2, and the confounder meanings highlighted in grey.

$K_2 = 3$	$K_2 = 2$	$K_2 = 2$	$K_2 = 2$	$K_2 = 2$
$K_2 = 1$	$K_2 = 2$	$K_2 = 2$	$K_2 = 1$	$K_2 = 1$

Fig. 2. Combinations of contexts after E_2, with the number of confounders K_2, and the confounder meanings highlighted in grey

We can see in Fig. 2 that the set of confounders remaining after episode E_2 is dependent on the set of confounders from E_1, and the meanings in C_2. We can ignore all meanings which did not occur in C_1, as they can never be confounders — a single non-occurrence in one episode is enough to rule out a particular meaning as a confounder. More generally, the set of confounders K_e after episode E_e depends on the set of confounders after the previous episode E_{e-1} , namely K_{e-1}, and the set of meanings chosen in context C_e.

Let the probability of having n confounders after e episodes $P(K_e = n)$ be $P_n(e)$. The probability that a word is successfully learned after e episodes is therefore $P_0(e)$. After E_2, and assuming $C_1 = \{m_1, m_2, m_3\}$, we can see in Fig. 2 that $P_3(2) = \frac{1}{10}$; $P_2(2) = \frac{6}{10}$; $P_1(2) = \frac{3}{10}$ and $P_0(2) = \frac{0}{10}$. Note in this case that it is impossible to have learned a word after two episodes $(P_0(2) = 0)$, because the context is larger than half of the number of possible meanings $(C > \frac{M}{2})$, and so it is impossible to select disjoint sets for C_1 and C_2. It should be clear that the choice of $C_1 = \{m_1, m_2, m_3\}$ in this example is unimportant: the same probabilities for each value of K_2 are obtained for every possible choice for C_1.

What happens, however, when there are fewer than C confounders at the previous timestep $(K_{e-1} < C)$? To examine this situation we have to look at a further episode, E_3. Let's take $C_1 = \{m_1, m_2, m_3\}$, $C_2 = \{m_1, m_2, m_4\}$ as an example, giving $K_2 = 2$, and combine it with all possibilities for C_3, as depicted in Fig. 3.

We can see that for $K_2 = 2$, given $C_1 = \{m_1, m_2, m_3\}$ and $C_2 = \{m_1, m_2, m_4\}$, the probabilities are $P_2(3) = \frac{3}{10}$, $P_1(3) = \frac{6}{10}$, $P_0(3) = \frac{1}{10}$. The choice of C_1 and C_2

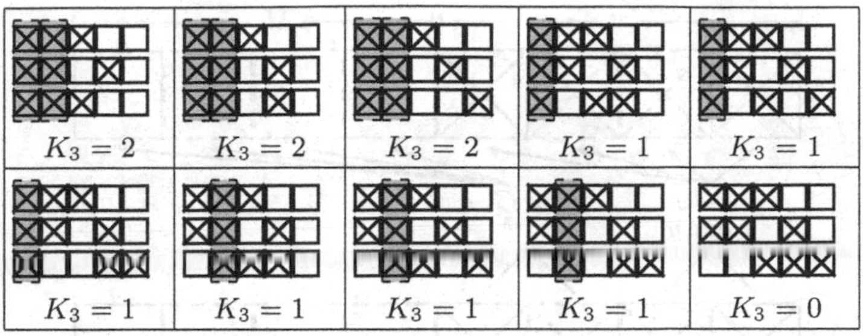

Fig. 3. Combinations of contexts after E_3, with the number of confounders (K_3), and the confounder meanings highlighted in grey

is again unimportant, as the same probabilities for each value of K_3 are obtained for each combination where $K_2 = 2$. Similar calculations can be carried out for $K_2 = 1$, by choosing (for instance) $C_1 = \{m_1, m_2, m_3\}$ and $C_2 = \{m_1, m_4, m_5\}$.

3.2 Calculating Semantic Inferrability

In general, the transition probability $Q(x|y)$, i.e. that there will be x confounders after episode e, given that there were y confounders after episode $e-1$, is:

$$Q(x|y) = \binom{y}{x} \times \binom{M-y}{C-x} \times \binom{M}{C}^{-1} \qquad (1)$$

The first term $\binom{y}{x}$ is the number of ways of correctly selecting *confounders*: y is the number of confounders at time $e-1$ (call this the confounding set), and x is the number of confounders we want to have at time e. There are therefore $\binom{y}{x}$ ways in which the desired number of confounders x can be chosen from the confounding set y. The second term $\binom{M-y}{C-x}$ is likewise the number of ways of correctly selecting non-confounders: $M - y$ gives the number of meanings which are *not* confounders at time $e-1$ (call this the non-confounding set). Recall that every context has C members, so if there are x confounders in a valid context, then we must also select $C - x$ non-confounders from the non-confounding set. There are clearly $\binom{M-y}{C-x}$ ways of choosing the desired number of non-confounders $C - x$ from the non-confounding set $M - y$, as shown in Fig. 4. The number of valid contexts which satisfy the desired condition is the product of these two expressions, divided by the total number of possible contexts, to produce the overall transition probability Q.

Therefore, the probability $P_n(e)$, that there will be n confounders after e episodes is:

$$P_n(e) = \sum_{i=n}^{C} P_i(e - 1) \times Q(n|i) . \qquad (2)$$

We have already seen, however, that if $e = 1$, then the number of confounders is necessarily C, so for completeness (2) should be extended to cover the case

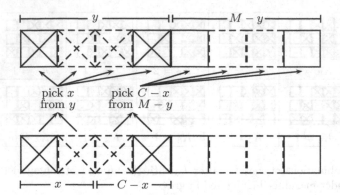

Fig. 4. Building a context of size C, made up of x confounders chosen from the y members of the confounding set, and $C - x$ non-confounders chosen from the $M - y$ members of the non-confounding set.

where $e = 1$:

$$P_n(e) = \begin{cases} 1 & \text{if } e = 1, n = C, \\ 0 & \text{if } e = 1, n \neq C, \\ \displaystyle\sum_{i=n}^{C} P_i(e-1) \times Q(n|i) & \text{otherwise.} \end{cases} \quad (3)$$

In Appendix A, we solve (3) to give the following explicit formula for $P_n(e)$:

$$P_n(e) = \binom{C}{n} \sum_{i=n}^{C} (-1)^{i-n} \binom{C-n}{i-n} (p_i)^{e-1} \quad (4)$$

where

$$p_i = \frac{\binom{M-i}{C-i}}{\binom{M}{C}} = \begin{cases} 1 & \text{for } i = 0 \\ \frac{C(C-1)...(C-i+1)}{M(M-1)...(M-i+1)} & \text{for } i > 0 \end{cases} \quad (5)$$

is the probability that a particular subset of i members of the C confounders in the first episode E_1 appear in any subsequent episode.

3.3 Word Learnability Results

Using either (3) or (4), therefore, we can quantify the learnability of an *individual* word — the probability that an individual word will be learned, $P_0(e)$ — which depends on M, C, and e. Fig. 5 shows word learnability for $M = 50$, for various values of C. Two basic results are apparent: (i) A word cannot be learned when $C = M$, as confounders can never be eliminated; (ii) For all other cases, learnability increases over time, although it may be the case (for example, when C is high) that learnability remains at zero for a number of exposures, before becoming non-zero.

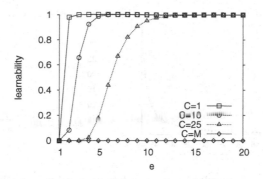

Fig. 5. Word learnability given $M = 50$, for various C

We can also quantify the number of episodes e^* required to learn a word with probability $1 - \epsilon$. Fig. 6 (a) shows e^* given $M = 50$, with $\epsilon = 0.01$, for various context sizes. Expected values are derived from Eqn. (3), exact values by Monte Carlo simulation[2]. It is clear that the results from the Monte Carlo simulation closely match the results from the mathematical model. In addition, we see that (iii) the smaller the context size, the quicker a word can be learned; (iv) as C approaches M, it takes a long time to learn a word, as confounders are only rarely eliminated. Fig. 6 (b) shows e^* given $C = 5$, with $\epsilon = 0.01$, for various M. We can see that (v) words can be learned more rapidly as the number of meanings increases; as M increases, it becomes less likely that any one meaning will recur in every context with the target meaning.

4   Quantifying the Learnability of a Whole Language

The model described in the previous section only considers the learnability of a *single word*. One conclusion is that, given a fixed context size, the meaning of a particular word is easier to learn if that word is part of a large system for conveying a large number of distinct meanings (M is large). This suggests that we need to consider the learnability of a whole vocabulary system consisting of a number of words, each of which conveys a particular meaning, rather than considering word learnability in isolation.

In order to do this, we must first introduce a minor change to our notation. When considering the learnability of a single word, we were concerned with the number of meanings *other than the target meaning*, and the number of meanings in the context *other than the target meaning*. We denoted these as M and C respectively. When quantifying the learnability of a whole set of words, we are necessarily interested in cases where the target meaning for a particular word may also occur as a non-target meaning for some usage of some other word. Let

---

[2] In the simulation, a learner works through a series of exposures, eliminating candidate meanings. e^* is the number of episodes required to achieve learnability of $1 - \epsilon$ averaged over 1000 such simulations.

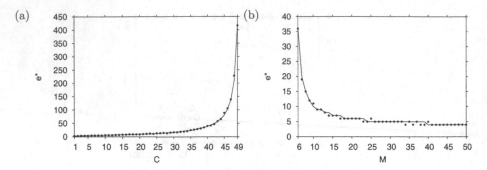

Fig. 6. The number of episodes required to learn a word with probability 0.99 varies with the number of meanings and the context size; (a) shows e^* given $M = 50$, for various C, (b) shows e^* given $C = 5$, for various M. Lines are expected values, points are actual (Monte Carlo simulation) values.

us therefore call the total number of lexicalised meanings in a vocabulary system $\bar{M}$. In every episode of exposure to an utterance conveying one of these meanings, the hearer observes a situation which provides both the target meaning and a context of other meanings. The number of meanings involved in the context, *inclusive of the target meaning*, is given by $\bar{C}$. The $C = \bar{C}-1$ non-target meanings in the context are chosen at random and without duplication from the larger set of $M = \bar{M} - 1$ possible meanings. In other words, $\bar{M}$ and $\bar{C}$ are inclusive, rather than exclusive, of the target meaning.

It is convenient, at least initially, to consider the situation where only W of the total number of possible meanings $\bar{M}$ are ever chosen as the target. We seek now $R_W(e)$, the probability that all W of these words have been learned after e episodes; the probability that the whole language has been learned is then given by the special case $W = \bar{M}$. To obtain this, we must average over all W^e sequences of utterances. Some particular sequences may, or may not, be equivalent to one another depending on what inferences are made by the learner. If, for example, the learner assumes that different words do not have the same meaning, then the order with which the words are presented matters. Under this assumption, if the word for a meaning is learned then that meaning can no longer act as a confounder for the remaining meanings. This induces non-trivial interactions between episodes in which different words are uttered. On the other hand, if the learner entertains the possibility that two words may have the same meaning, then they must wait until all meanings other than the target have been ruled out. In this latter case, the probability that a meaning has been learned is independent of the order in which the words are presented, and thus depends only on the number of times a particular meaning has been chosen as the target. In this much simpler case, which we will focus on here, only the number of times a word is uttered is important: order of presentation does not matter.

In this case, the probability of learning all W words is given by

$$R_W(e) = \langle P_0(e_1)P_0(e_2)\cdots P_0(e_W)\rangle \qquad (6)$$

where the angle brackets denote an average over the probability distribution of sequences of e episodes in which the first word of interest is the target e_1 times, the second e_2 and so on. This distribution is the multinomial distribution

$$\frac{1}{W^e} \binom{e}{e_1 e_2 \cdots e_W} = \frac{1}{W^e} \frac{e!}{e_1! e_2! \cdots e_W!}$$

constrained such that $\sum_i e_i = e$. The functions $\Pi_0(e_i)$ appearing in Eqn. (6) are as given by Eqn. (4). It is possible to calculate this average exactly; unfortunately, the expression that results is rather unwieldy and extremely difficult to interpret. We thus derive instead an approximation to $R_W(e)$ that admits a clearer insight into the learnability of an entire language.

This approximation is obtained by focusing on the regime where the language is learnt to a high probability, i.e., where $R_W(e) = 1 - \epsilon_W$ and the parameter ϵ_W is small. For example $\epsilon_W = 0.01$ corresponds to having learned the words with 99% certainty. In Appendix B, we present the details of this approximate approach which results in the following expression for the probability of learning W of $\bar{M}$ words after e episodes:

$$R_W(e) \approx \sum_{k=0}^{W} \binom{W}{k} (1 - \bar{M})^k \left[1 - \frac{k}{W} \left(\frac{\bar{M} - \bar{C}}{\bar{M} - 1} \right) \right]^e . \tag{7}$$

Since each term in the series is progressively smaller, and the relative size of each term is roughly equal to the absolute size of the previous term, the series can be truncated at $k = 1$ as long as ϵ_W is sufficiently small. Inverting this truncated expression gives an indication of the time taken to learn the whole language with probability $1 - \epsilon_W$. It reads

$$e^* \approx \frac{\ln[\epsilon_W] - \ln[W(\bar{M} - 1)]}{\ln \left[1 - \frac{1}{W} \left(\frac{\bar{M} - \bar{C}}{\bar{M} - 1} \right) \right]} . \tag{8}$$

Since various approximations have been made to arrive at this formula, it is worth testing its validity by comparing with data from Monte Carlo simulations. Fig. 7 shows the match between expected and actual (obtained from simulation) values given various values of ϵ, $\bar{C}$ and $\bar{M} = W$. As can be seen from the figures, there is close agreement between the actual and expected values as long as ϵ_W is not large (Fig. 7 (a)) and $\bar{C}$ is not small (Fig. 7 (b)). The former condition is easily understood, since ϵ_W was assumed to be small throughout the derivation of (7) and (8). Meanwhile, a closer analysis of the approximations used in Appendix B to derive these expressions shows that strong fluctuations in the number of episodes required to learn a single word lead to the breakdown of the approximation when $\bar{C}$ is small.

Fig. 7 (b) shows e^* given $M = 50$, $\epsilon_W = 0.01$, for various context sizes. It is apparent that (i) the smaller the context size, the quicker a whole vocabulary can be learned; (ii) as $\bar{C}$ approaches $\bar{M}$, it takes a long time to learn a word, as confounders are only rarely eliminated. In other words, $\bar{C}$ does not have to

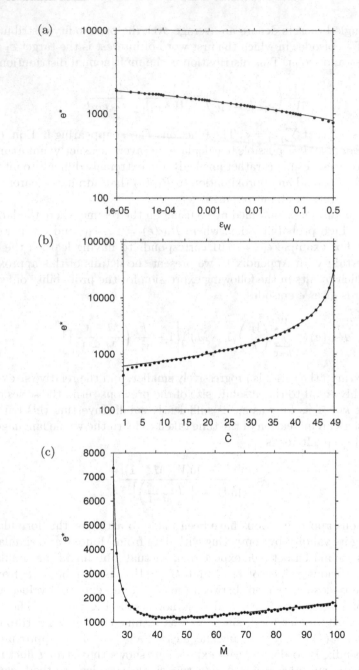

Fig. 7. The number of episodes needed to learn a whole vocabulary with probability $1 - \epsilon_W$. (a) shows e^* given $\bar{M} = 50, \bar{C} = 25$, for various ϵ_W. (b) shows e^* given $\bar{M} = 50, \epsilon_W = 0.01$, for various $\bar{C}$. (c) shows e^* given $\bar{C} = 25, \epsilon_W = 0.01$, for various $\bar{M}$. Lines are expected values, points are actual (Monte Carlo) values. Note log scales on (a) and (b).

be very small for a vocabulary to be learned in a reasonable time, as long as it is fairly small *relative to* $\bar{M}$. Fig. 7 (c) shows e^* given $\bar{C} = 25, \epsilon_W = 0.01$, for various $\bar{M}$. Here we see that (iii) it is easiest to learn a whole language when $\bar{C}$ is less than $\bar{M}$ and both are relatively small.

Fig. 7 (c) further suggests that, once $\bar{M}$ is significantly greater than $\bar{C}$, e^* increases linearly with $\bar{M}$. In fact, putting $W = \bar{M}$ in Eqn. (8) suggests that the rate of increase is slightly greater than linear. Specifically, one finds that once $\bar{M}$ has greatly exceeded the larger of $\bar{C}$ and $\ln \epsilon_W$,

$$e^* \sim 2\bar{M} \ln \bar{M} . \tag{9}$$

In other words, (iv) while the time taken to learn a vocabulary of a particular size increases superlinearly with respect to the size of that vocabulary, there is no critical value of $\bar{M}$ beyond which e^* increases dramatically — large vocabularies are learnable through cross-situational learning.

5 Discussion

We have outlined a mathematical formulation of cross-situational learning, and presented some basic results linking word and vocabulary learnability to the size of the vocabulary system, the number of candidate meanings provided by a context of use, and the amount of time for learning. Based on these results, it is tempting to speculate on the human case, particularly from an evolutionary perspective — for example, we might claim that humans have a long period of developmental flexibility to allow them time to learn a large vocabulary system, or that humans have evolved a number of biases for word-learning to reduce the effective context size during word learning and make large vocabularies learnable in a fairly short period of time.

However, several shortcomings in the model as it stands need to be addressed before such speculations can be entertained (if at all). Firstly, and most importantly, we have considered both words and meanings to be unstructured atomic entities. The model as it stands is therefore better interpreted as quantifying the learnability of a *holistic* system. In *compositional* systems, such as language, meanings are structured objects and utterances are structured sequences of words. We are currently extending this model to explore such a situation, in order to contrast the learnability of words in systems of different structural kinds.

Secondly, we assume that all meanings occur with uniform probability. This is unlikely to be exactly true, and it may be that the frequency of communicatively-relevant situations is highly non-uniform, possibly Zipfian [19]. How does this affect word learnability? Again, we are extending our model to allow us to investigate such questions.

Finally, as discussed in section 4, we have assumed that the meaning of each word is learned independently — learning something about the meaning of one word tells you nothing about the meaning of another word. We know, however, that this assumption is not true for humans, who instead appear to assume that if one word has a particular meaning, then no other word will have that same meaning — this is mutual exclusivity [10]. How much, if at all, does mutual exclusivity simplify the learning of words in holistic or structured systems? We are also investigating this question using a Monte Carlo version of our model.

The model outlined here is, we feel, an important first step on the path to a more thorough and formal understanding of the developmental and evolutionary problem of word learning.

References

1. Hockett, C.F.: The origin of speech. Scientific American **203** (1960) 88–96
2. Carey, S., Bartlett, E.: Acquiring a single new word. Papers and Reports on Child Language Development **15** (1978) 17–29
3. Quine, W.v.O.: Word and Object. MIT Press, Cambridge, MA (1960)
4. Bloom, P.: How Children Learn the Meanings of Words. MIT Press, Cambridge, MA (2000)
5. Hall, D.G., Waxman, S.R., eds.: Weaving a Lexicon. MIT Press, Cambridge, MA (2004)
6. Tomasello, M.: The cultural origins of human cognition. Harvard University Press, Harvard (1999)
7. Tomasello, M.: Constructing a language: a usage-based theory of language acquisition. Harvard University Press (2003)
8. Macnamara, J.: Names for things: a study of human learning. MIT Press, Cambridge, MA (1982)
9. Landau, B., Smith, L.B., Jones, S.S.: The importance of shape in early lexical learning. Cognitive Development **3** (1988) 299–321
10. Markman, E.M.: Categorization and naming in children: problems of induction. Learning, Development and Conceptual Change. MIT Press, Cambridge. MA (1989)
11. Clark, E.V.: The lexicon in acquisition. Cambridge Studies in Linguistics. Cambridge University Press, Cambridge (1993)
12. Akhtar, N., Montague, L.: Early lexical acquisition: the role of cross-situational learning. First Language (1999) 347–358
13. Klibanoff, R.S., Waxman, S.R.: Basic level object categories support the acquisition of novel adjectives: evidence from pre-school aged children. Child Development **71** **(3)** (2000) 649–659
14. Houston-Price, C., Plunkett, K., Harris, P.: 'Word-Learning Wizardry' at 1;6. Journal of Child Language **32(1)** (2005) 175–189
15. Smith, A.D.M.: Establishing communication systems without explicit meaning transmission. In Kelemen, J., Sosík, P., eds.: Advances in Artificial Life. Springer-Verlag, Heidelberg (2001) 381–390
16. Vogt, P., Coumans, H.: Investigating social interaction strategies for bootstrapping lexicon development. Journal of Artificial Societies and Social Simulation **6**(1) (2003) http://jasss.soc.surrey.ac.uk/6/1/4.html.
17. Siskind, J.M.: A computational study of cross-situational techniques for learning word-to-meaning mappings. Cognition **61** (1996) 39–91
18. Smith, A.D.M.: Intelligent meaning creation in a clumpy world helps communication. Artificial Life **9**(2) (2003) 175–190
19. Zipf, G.K.: The Psycho-Biology of Language. Routledge, London (1936)
20. Wilf, H.S.: Generatingfunctionology. Academic Press (1994)

A   Exact Solution for the Single Word Case

The exact solution given in Eqn. (4) can be obtained in two ways: (i) by diago-
nalisation of the matrix of transition probabilities $Q(x|y)$; or (ii) by applying the
"inclusion-exclusion" principle (or sieve method) from combinatorics. In this Appendix, we outline the latter approach which, as explained by Wilf [20, p.110], is
useful when "it is relatively easy to see how many objects have at least a certain
number of properties and maybe more". The sieve method, he goes on to explain,
converts this "at least" information into the desired "exactly" information.

In our application, we seek $P_n(e)$, the probability that n of the initial C confounders are present in each of a number e of episodes. The "at least" information
here is the probability p_n that a specific subset of n confounders appears in each
of e episodes, along with maybe some other confounders. This probability is
given by p_n^{e-1} Eqn. (5), since the desired subset is always present in the first
episode (by definition), and then with probability p_n in subsequent episodes.

The sieve method then states that the probability of having a subset of N
confounders present in every episode is given by the sum

$$P_n(e) = \sum_{i=n}^{C} (-1)^{i-n} \binom{i}{n} \sum_{i\text{-subsets of } C \text{ confounders}} p_i^{e-1} \tag{10}$$

$$= \sum_{i=n}^{C} (-1)^{i-n} \binom{i}{n}\binom{C}{i} p_i^{e-i} \tag{11}$$

where we have used the fact that there are $\binom{C}{i}$ distinct subsets of size i contained
within a set of C objects. The result (4) then follows from the fact that $\binom{i}{n}\binom{C}{i} = \binom{C}{n}\binom{C-i}{i-n}$, as can be verified by writing the binomial coefficients explicitly in
terms of factorials.

B   Approximate Solution for the Multiple Word Case

We are interested in determining the probability $R_W(e)$ that W of $\bar{M}$ meanings
have been learnt after a total number of e episodes in the regime where $R_W(e) \approx 1$. Our approach rests on the following observation: if all W words are to be learnt
with certainty $1 - \epsilon_W$ (ϵ_W being a small parameter), each of the factors $P_0(e_i)$ in
Eqn. (6) should contribute an amount approximately equal to $1 - \frac{\epsilon_W}{W}$. That is,
every word has to be learnt (on average) to a *higher* level of certainty; the value
of ϵ for a single word (ϵ_1) is approximately equal to $\frac{\epsilon_W}{W}$. Looking at Fig. 5, we
see that to achieve this high level of single-word learnability, many utterances of
each individual word are required in order to eliminate all confounding meanings.
The upshot of this is that, since e_i is expected to be large, the expression for
$P_0(e_i)$, Eqn. (4), is well approximated by the first two terms in the series. We
henceforth assume that we can write

$$P_0(e_i) \approx 1 - (M-1)\left(\frac{\bar{C}-1}{\bar{M}-1}\right)^{e_i}. \tag{12}$$

Using this approximation in Eqn. (6) we find

$$R_W(e) \approx \left\langle \prod_{i=1}^{W} \left[1 - (\bar{M} - 1) \left(\frac{\bar{C} - 1}{\bar{M} - 1} \right)^{e_i} \right] \right\rangle \tag{13}$$

$$= \sum_{k=0}^{W} \binom{W}{k} (1 - \bar{M})^k \left\langle \left(\frac{\bar{C} - 1}{\bar{M} - 1} \right)^{e_1 + e_2 + \cdots + e_k} \right\rangle. \tag{14}$$

The average over the multinomial distribution can then be computed by noting the identity

$$\sum_{e_1} \sum_{e_2} \cdots \sum_{e_W} \binom{e}{e_1 e_2 \cdots e_W} u_1^{e_1} u_2^{e_2} \cdots u_W^{e_W} = (u_1 + u_2 + \cdots + u_W)^e \tag{15}$$

which yields Eqn. (7). As we note in the text, the approximation (12) holds as long as fluctuations in the number of episodes in which a particular meaning is the target are small relative to the mean.

Dialog Strategy Acquisition and Its Evaluation for Efficient Learning of Word Meanings by Agents

Ryo Taguchi, Kouichi Katsurada, and Tsuneo Nitta

Graduate School of Engineering, Toyohashi University of Technology
1-1 Hibariga-oka, Tempaku-cho, Toyohashi-city, 441-8580 Japan
{taguchi, katurada, nitta}@vox.tutkie.tut.ac.jp
http://www.vox.tutkie.tut.ac.jp/

Abstract. In word meaning acquisition through interactions among humans and agents, the efficiency of the learning depends largely on the dialog strategies the agents have. This paper describes automatic acquisition of dialog strategies through interaction between two agents. In the experiments, two agents infer each other's comprehension level from its facial expressions and utterances to acquire efficient strategies. Q-learning is applied to a strategy acquisition mechanism. Firstly, experiments are carried out through the interaction between a mother agent, who knows all the word meanings, and a child agent with no initial word meaning. The experimental results showed that the mother agent acquires a teaching strategy, while the child agent acquires an asking strategy. Next, the experiments of interaction between a human and an agent are investigated to evaluate the acquired strategies. The results showed the effectiveness of both strategies of teaching and asking.

1 Introduction

As demand grows for more natural communication with human-like agents such as anthropomorphic agents, avatars, animated agents, talking heads, etc., research and development have begun on allowing people to communicate with such agents using the advanced interface of multi-modal interaction (MMI).

When receiving input modalities such as speech and gesture, the agents with MMI integrate the multiple modalities and interpret them, then they hold a conversation sometimes according to the context. However, because the current MMI technologies enable us only to interact with the agents along dialog scenarios described by system designers, the applications are quite limited. MMI without dialog scenarios requires autonomous agents who acquire the knowledge of multimedia objects in the real world and interact with humans under this commonly grounded knowledge. Namely, the agents need to acquire the meanings of words through interactions with end-users in the real world. Moreover, automatic acquisition of dialog strategies used for word meaning acquisition is another important function when making the learning effective.

Roy et al. [1] and Iwahashi et al. [2] respectively proposed mechanisms to acquire word meanings that represent relations among visual features of objects and acoustic features of human speeches using machine learning methods. With the help of these

P. Vogt et al. (Eds.): EELC 2006, LNAI 4211, pp. 45–56, 2006.
© Springer-Verlag Berlin Heidelberg 2006

mechanisms, robots learn to understand word meanings in the real world. On the other hand, Levin et al. [3] and Singh et al. [4] investigated how to adapt dialog strategies to the environment by applying reinforcement learning to a human-machine interaction corpus. In the two approaches, interpretation of unknown utterances and adaptation of dialog strategies are separately investigated, however, we should apply both of them to the interaction at the same time because interpretation and dialog control depend on each other. In the case of children's language acquisition, a parent teaches his/her child through cooperative interaction and the child acquires not only word meanings but also dialog strategies.

We are developing Infant Agents (IAs) that are modeled after the word meaning acquisition and the dialog strategy acquisition process of human infants [5]. IAs automatically acquire dialog strategies through interactions among IAs. In this paper, we propose a method for dialog strategy acquisition that uses each other's comprehension level which is inferred from an agent's or a human's facial expressions and utterances. The experiments on dialog strategy acquisition are carried out through interaction between two IAs. Then, we confirm the effectiveness of the acquired strategies through the interaction between a human and an IA.

In section 2 we explain IAs and a dialog strategy acquisition method. In section 3 we conduct the experiments on automatic acquisition of dialog strategies. In section 4 we evaluate the acquired strategies. Lastly, in section 5, we describe the conclusions of this paper.

2   Infant Agent

We are developing IAs modeled after human infants [5]. IAs learn word meanings through human–IA interaction, then share the word meanings acquired by each other via a network. This knowledge-sharing is achieved through interaction in the same manner that humans learn from one another. Furthermore, IAs, through interaction between themselves, automatically acquire dialogue strategies which are needed to efficiently learn each other's knowledge.

2.1   Learning of Word Meanings

The experiments are executed in a virtual space on a computer. There are nine objects in this space. Each object has visual features such as shape and color. Such object features are categorized into six types (globe, triangle, cube, red, blue, and white). In the first step of the learning, an IA chooses an object and asks a question to a counterpart, which is a human or another IA. This question is performed by pointing at the object, not by speaking. We call this asked object a topic object. Then, the counterpart teaches one or two words representing the object features by his/her/its utterance. For simplicity, we assume that IAs have a mechanism for converting the utterance into a phoneme sequence, and IAs directly receive a phoneme sequence as the utterance (see Fig. 1). However, each phoneme contained in the sequence is incorrectly received with probability 0.1. When receiving a pair of a phoneme sequence and object features, the IA divides the phoneme sequence into words by referring to its Word Memory that stores frequencies of words and object features. If the phoneme sequence contains an unknown word, the IA newly registers the pair of the word and the object features in its Word Memory. If known words appear in the phoneme sequence, the IA increments their frequencies. Then, the IA calculates the conditional probability $P(x \mid w)$, where w is a word and x is an object feature. If the probability meets the following three conditions, the IA acquires a relation between the word w and the feature x as the meaning of w.

(1) A word w has been learned more than 3 times.
(2) $P(x \mid w) > 0.9$
(3) Only one feature x meets the condition (2).

Object Feature	Phoneme Sequence	Object Feature	Phoneme Sequence
Globe	/maru/	Red	/aka/
Triangle	/saNkaku/	Blue	/ao/
Cube	/sikaku/	White	/siro/

Fig. 1. Object features and phoneme sequences. Each phoneme sequence represents the object feature written on the left.

2.2 IA's Actions and Facial Expressions

In the above section, we explained the algorithm for the learning of word meanings that is applied to IAs. In the IA–IA interaction or the human–IA interaction, IAs carry out in turn the actions such as asking a question and teaching words. The actions are chosen according to the IA's dialog strategy. The dialog strategies should be controlled according to the comprehension level of each other. For example, when there are few words that are known by a counterpart, it is more efficient to teach one word because it is difficult for IAs to divide an utterance containing two words into correct words. And IAs have to choose according to each other's comprehension level either by teaching or asking. However, the counterpart's comprehension level must be inferred by IAs because it cannot be referred to directly. Therefore, in this paper, we assume that IAs and humans change their own facial expression as a representation of their comprehension of the counterpart's last utterance. We also give IAs a mechanism that infers the comprehension level from the counterpart's facial expressions and utterances. In the following sections, we explain the actions, facial expressions, and inference mechanism of IAs.

2.2.1 Actions
IAs can carry out the following six actions.

(1) "NO ACT": Nothing is done.
(2) "CHANGE A TOPIC": An IA changes a topic by choosing an object randomly.
(3) "ASK": An IA asks a question by pointing at a topic object.
(4) "IMITATE": An IA imitates a counterpart's utterance.
(5) "ADD A WORD": An IA randomly chooses a word from its Word Memory and adds it to its Speech Register.
(6) "SPEAK": An IA utters the contents of its Speech Register.

A dialog starts when one of the IAs carries out "ASK" after "CHANGE A TOPIC". Then, IAs perform in turn one of the six actions according to their strategies which are under learning. After an IA carries out the above (1), (3), (4) or (6), the counterpart's turn comes, or the IA takes its turn again after carrying out "CHANGE A TOPIC" or "ADD A WORD".

"CHANGE A TOPIC" can be carried out repeatedly up to 9 times. This means that an IA can strategically choose one from nine objects. For example, according to a strategy it can perform "CHANGE A TOPIC" until it finds an unknown object.

"ADD A WORD" can be carried out repeatedly up to 2 times and "SPEAK" can be carried out after it. "ADD A WORD" is an action to randomly choose a word from the IA's Word Memory and add it to its Speech Register that stores words to be uttered. However, we assume that the added words represent features of a topic object. IAs construct a teaching utterance by iterating this action. "SPEAK" is an action to speak the content stored in the Speech Register.

"IMITATE" is an action to imitate a counterpart's utterance. By performing this action, IAs can check whether taught utterances were conveyed correctly.

2.2.2 Inference of Comprehension Level

When the counterpart's facial expression becomes comfortable or neutral after an IA teaches words, the IA considers that the counterpart already knows the correct meanings of the words, and so adds the words to its own Shared Word Memory. The Shared Word Memory stores those words that have been shared with a counterpart. And, when a counterpart's utterance does not conflict with the knowledge held by an IA, the IA adds the uttered words to its own Shared Word Memory. For their own dialog strategies, IAs use the information of the Shared Word Memory as a reflection of the counterpart's comprehension level.

2.2.3 Facial Expressions

IAs have three types of facial expression: neutral, comfortable, and uncomfortable. When new word meanings are acquired or new words are shared, an IA's facial expression becomes comfortable. If an unknown word is contained in a counterpart's utterance, the IA's facial expression becomes uncomfortable. In other cases, the IA's facial expression remains neutral.

2.3 Dialog Strategy Acquisition

We use Q-learning as a strategy acquisition mechanism. Q-learning [6] is one of the online Reinforcement Learning algorithms and is widely used to optimize an agent's behavior. The following sections explain the states and rewards which are used in Q-learning.

2.3.1 States of Q-Learning

In order to acquire dialog strategies based on a past dialog history and the comprehension level of a counterpart, IAs recognize states by using not only the information for expressing current dialog situations (such as a counterpart's facial expressions and actions) but the contents of each IA's Word Memory and Shared Word Memory. Specifically, a state is recognized for the following 8-dimensional information.

(1) Counterpart's action
(2) Counterpart's facial expression
(3) Own last action
(4) Own facial expression
(5) The number of words that represent features of a topic object
(6) The number of shared words in (5)
(7) The number of words in the Speech Register
(8) The number of shared words in the Speech Register

2.3.2 Rewards of Q-Learning

In order to realize cooperative learning of word meanings, rewards should be given according to not only an IA's own learning situation but also the counterpart's learning situation. Therefore, we calculate rewards r as follows.

$$r = \frac{r_1 + r_2}{2}, \tag{1}$$

where r_1 is a reward according to the IA's own learning situation and r_2 is a reward according to the counterpart's facial expression.

Table 1 shows actual values of rewards.

Table 1. Rewards of Q-learning

	r_1
New word meanings were acquired, where n is the number of the acquired words at once.	20n
New words were added into IA's Shared Words Memory.	5
"CHANGE A TOPIC" or "ADD A WOED" was paformed.	0
The other cases.	-1

	r_2
The counterpart's facial expression became comfortable.	5
The counterpart's facial expression became neutral or uncomfortable.	-1

3 Experiments of Dialog Strategy Acquisition

3.1 Experimental Setup

We investigate the acquisition of dialog strategies through the interaction between two IAs designed in the previous section. Six words are used in our experiments, where all of them are given as initial knowledge to the IA that is called IA1. The other IA is called IA2 and does not have the initial knowledge.

We define a dialog as a sequence of interaction until IA2 acquires all word meanings or until 100 turns have passed. At the beginning of each dialog, the word meanings learned by IA2 are reset, however, the strategy of each IA is preserved and is continuously learned across the dialogs. In the experiment, 100,000 dialogs are iterated and both IAs acquire dialog strategies according to their own initial knowledge. Each IA decides its action based on the ε-greedy policy in the learning step, where ε is set to 0.1. The learning rate of Q-learning is decreased from 0.1 to 0.001, according to the frequency of learning, and the discount rate of Q-learning is set to 0.9.

After the dialog strategy acquisition, we execute 1,000 dialogs between IA1 and IA2 following the acquired strategies in order to evaluate their efficiency. In the dialogs to be evaluated, the IAs do not learn dialog strategies. Each IA chooses its action on the basis of the greedy policy that is following the highest Q-value at any time. Then, we compare its efficiency with the efficiency of the interaction between two agents whose strategies have been designed by us; one of the agents is an IA that has been given the role of teacher and is called TA, and the other is an IA that has been given the role of learner and is called LA. The TA has the initial knowledge while the LA has none. Their strategies are as follows: The TA randomly chooses between "ADD A WORD" and "SPEAK". The LA randomly chooses an object and asks about it.

3.2 Experimental Results

First, we show how the actions of IA1 and IA2 change by the strategy acquisition. Figure 2 shows that the IAs before the strategy acquisition choose each action with a constant proportion regardless of dialog situations. On the other hand, Figure 3 shows that the IAs after the strategy acquisition choose actions according to the progress of the dialogs. And, after the strategy acquisition, IA1 has a tendency to choose teaching actions such as "ADD A WORD" and "SPEAK", and IA2 has a tendency to choose learning actions such as "CHANGE A TOPIC", "ASK" and "IMITATE". These results show that each IA acquired a teaching strategy or an asking strategy according to its own initial knowledge.

Next, we show an example of interaction between the IAs that follow the acquired strategies in Fig. 4. In the first turn, IA1 taught the word "maru". Then IA2 tried to imitate IA1's utterance but heard it wrongly and said, "matu." In the second turn, IA1 made IA2 correctly learn the word by teaching "maru" again. When IA2 could correctly speak the word, IA1 considered that the word had been shared with IA2. Then IA1 began to teach two words as shown in the third turn. In each of the first, second and fifth turns, IA1 taught one word, because "maru" or "sikaku" had not been shared. IA1's strategy can efficiently teach words according to the counterpart's comprehension level. IA2 could learn correct words by imitating IA1's utterance as shown in the second turn. Moreover, when IA2's facial expression was neutral or IA2 acquired new word meanings, IA2 changed the topic object, as shown in the fifth, eighth and ninth turns. IA2's strategy is efficient because it can appropriately change a topic object according to IA2's own comprehension level.

Finally, we show the efficiency of the IA1–IA2 interaction and the TA–LA interaction in Fig. 5. Figure 5 shows that the IA1–IA2 interaction is more efficient than the TA–LA interaction.

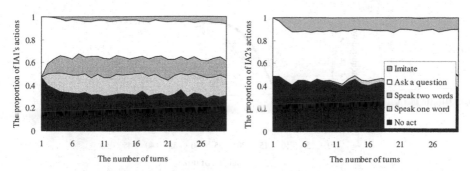

Fig. 2. Actions of IA1 (left) and IA2 (right) before strategy acquisition

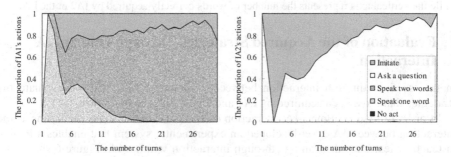

Fig. 3. Actions of IA1 (left) and IA2 (right) after strategy acquisition

0	start of dialog
1	IA2:(- -) IA2 indicated a bule globe.
	IA1:(- -) IA1 said, "maru."
2	IA2:(x x) IA2 imitated IA1's utterance and said, "matu."
	IA1:(x x) IA1 said, "maru."
3	IA2:(x x) IA2 imitated IA1's utterance and said, "maru."
	IA1:(^_^) IA1 considered "maru" as a shared word and said, "maruao."
4	IA2:(x x) IA2 imitated IA1's utterance and said, "maruao."
	IA1:(^_^) IA1 considered "ao" as a shared word and said, "aomaru."
5	IA2:(-) IA2 indicated a red cube.
	IA1:(- -) IA1 said, "sikaku."
6	IA2:(x x) IA2 imitated IA1's utterance and said, "sikaku."
	IA1:(^_^) IA1 considered "sikaku" as a shared word and said, "sikakuaka."
7	IA2:(x x) IA2 imitated IA1's utterance and said, "sikakuaka."
	IA1:(^_^) IA1 considered "aka" as a shared word and said, "akasikaku."
8	IA2:(- -) IA2 indicated a red triangle.
	IA1:(- -) IA1 said, "sankakuaka."
9	IA2:(x x) IA2 acquired the meaning of "aka" and indicated a blue cube.
	IA1:(- -) IA1 said, "sikakuao."
10	IA2:(^_^) IA2 acquired the meanings of "sikaku" and "ao".

Fig. 4. Interaction example between IA1 and IA2

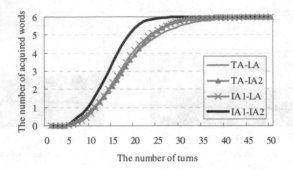

Fig. 5. Performance of acquired strategies. The horizontal axis represents the number of turns while the vertical axis represents the number of words correctly acquired by IA2 or the LA.

4   Evaluation of the Acquired Strategies Through Human–IA Interaction

In this section, through interaction between a human and an IA, we evaluate the strategies that have been acquired by IA1 and IA2 in the above section.

In order to realize human–IA interaction on the basis of the same conditions as the interaction between IAs, we developed an experimental system that enables a human to teach or learn word meanings through interaction with an IA. Figure 6 shows the execution screen of the experimental system. In the virtual space of the experiment, there are an IA and nine objects. A human, or an experimental subject, can choose the face icon that represents his/her facial expression every time an IA speaks. When it is the human's turn, he/she can point at an object or input his/her utterance from a keyboard. The IA's utterance is displayed on a computer screen for three seconds.

We prepare the following two types of experiment.

Experiment (1): Evaluation of acquired teaching strategies: an experimental subject plays the role of a learner and learns word meanings from utterances of IAs.

Experiment (2): Evaluation of acquired learning strategies: an experimental subject plays the role of a teacher and teaches word meanings to IAs.

Fig. 6. Human–IA Interaction System

We evaluate the performance of each acquired strategy. In both experiments, the subjects are seven undergraduates. In experiment (1), they interact with IA1 and the TA given only the role of a teacher. In experiment (2), they interact with IA2 and the LA. In the experiments, subjects are requested to understand IAs' strategies (roughly) in preliminary interaction with the IAs.

4.1 Evaluation of the Acquired Teaching Strategies

In this experiment, experimental subjects learn word meanings from utterances of IAs.

4.1.1 Experimental Setup

The IAs teach the same six words as the above experiments of Section 3. Each word represents the shape or color of objects such as "cube" or "red". However, the experiments will fail if the experimental subjects already know these words. Therefore, in order to prepare words that are not known by any subject, IAs automatically generate the phoneme sequences of the words at the beginning of each dialog. Specifically, IAs randomly choose 2 to 4 syllables from 45 types of syllable, which are prepared beforehand by us, and combine them to create words such as "HEKE" and "EUREKA". The experimental subjects know that a word spoken by IAs represent either the shape or color of objects. Namely, in this task, the experimental subjects translate IAs' language into our language. The IA's utterance is displayed on a computer screen for three seconds. Every time IAs speak, the experimental subjects write down the meanings of the words on specified paper.

We compare IA1 that acquired the teaching strategy through the above experiment with the TA that decides randomly on the number of teaching words and speaks them.

4.1.2 Experimental Results and Discussion

In the TA–human interaction, the experimental subjects took about 12 turns to acquire the above six words on average. On the other hand, in the case of the IA1–human interaction, it was about 8 turns (see Fig. 7).

By using the paired t-test, we assessed the significance of the difference between TA and IA1. The result showed a significant difference between them (level of significance of the test $P = 0.02 < 0.05$) and demonstrated the effectiveness of IA1's strategy on the interaction with humans.

Compared with the above IA–IA interaction (see Fig. 5), the experimental subjects were able to acquire the words about two times as quickly as IAs. One of the reasons for the result is the fact that humans use relationships between words to acquire word meanings. For example, when a red cube is called "KOKE" and then a red triangle is called "KOKEMOMO", IAs acquire the meanings of "KOKE" as a word representing the color red. Also, the experimental subjects too are able to acquire the meanings. Furthermore, by using the knowledge "word meanings do not overlap each other", they can acquire the meaning of "MOMO" as a word representing the shape of a triangle.

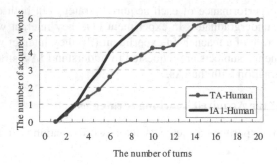

Fig. 7. The number of words correctly acquired by humans when IAs are teachers

4.2 Evaluation of the Acquired Learning Strategies

In this experiment, experimental subjects teach word meanings to IAs.

4.2.1 Experimental Setup

The experimental subjects teach the same six words as in the above experiment.

We compare IA2 that acquired the learning strategy through the experiment of Section 3 with the LA that invariably asks about a different object. In the above IA–IA interaction, IAs can teach multiple words at a time, but in this interaction, the experimental subjects invariably teach only one word in order to simplify their task. We assume that there is no recognition error.

4.2.2 Experimental Results and Discussion

In the human–LA interaction, the LA took about 30 turns to acquire the above six words on average. On the other hand, in the case of the human–IA2 interaction, it was about 24 turns (see Fig. 8).

By using the paired t-test, we assessed the significance of the difference between LA and IA2. The result showed a significant difference between them (level of significance of the test $P = 0.03 < 0.05$) and demonstrated the effectiveness of IA2's strategy on the interaction with humans.

IA2 becomes more efficient as it acquires more words, because, as discussed, IA2 asks preferentially about objects for which it has not yet acquired many words.

Next, in order to compare the teaching strategies of the experimental subjects with IA's strategy under the same conditions, we show the results of the interaction between the TA' that invariably teaches only one word and the LA or IA2 in Fig. 8. In this interaction, we assume that there is no recognition error. Figure 8 shows that the experimental subjects can teach more efficiently words to both LA and IA2 than the TA'. One of the reasons for the result is the fact that humans can memorize teaching history including IAs' response and can intentionally teach those words that have not yet been acquired by IAs. Moreover, the experimental subjects were using not only their memories but also high reasoning ability. For example, when an IA2 sequentially indicated cubes of different colors, an experimental subject inferred that "IA2 does not know the word representing cube" from the behavior of IA2. However, there were some ineffectual teachings, such as an experimental subject taught words that

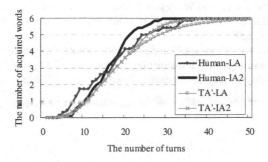

Fig. 8. The number of words correctly acquired by IA2 or the LA,when humans are teachers

had already been acquired by an IA, so the difference between human's teachings and IA's teachings is smaller than that of Section 4.1.2.

5 Conclusion

In this paper, we proposed a novel method for dialog strategy acquisition that uses the counterpart's comprehension level estimated from the agent's facial expressions and utterances. The experimental results from investigating the interaction between two IAs showed that both IAs can acquire efficient strategies according to their own initial knowledge. The actions of IAs are effectively selected by the strategies according to the estimated knowledge of the counterpart. Moreover, in the experiments of human–IA interaction, the acquired strategies of IAs are also effective for humans.

In a future work, in order to make IAs acquire both strategies of teaching and learning, we will conduct experiments in which initial knowledge is given to both IAs, as well as analyze the detailed human behavior in human–IA interaction and use the findings to study the IA's dialog strategy.

Acknowledgments

This research was supported by a 21st Century COE Program Grant for "Intelligent Human Sensing".

References

[1] D. Roy, "Integration of speech and vision using mutual information," in Proc. ICASSP, Vol. 4, pp. 2369-2372, 2000.
[2] N. Iwahashi, "Language acquisition through a human-robot interface by combining speech, visual, and behavioral information," Information Sciences, Vol. 156, pp. 109-121, 2003.
[3] S. Singh, M. Kearns, D. Litman, and M. Walker, "Empirical Evaluation of Reinforcement Learning Spoken Dialog System," in Proc. AAAI, pp. 645-651, 2000.

[4] E. Levin, R. Pieraccini, and W. Eckert, "A stochastic model of human-machine interaction for learning dialog strategies," IEEE Transactions on Speech and Audio Processing, Vol. 8(1), pp. 11-23, 2000.
[5] R. Taguchi, K. Katsurada and Tsuneo Nitta, "Automatic Acquisition of Dialog Strategies for Concept Learning through Interaction among Agents", Proc. of CIS'04, FM7.1, 2004.
[6] C.J.C.H. Watkins, P. Dayan, "Technical Note: Q-learning", Machine Learning 8, pp. 279-292, 1992.

Evolving Distributed Representations for Language with Self-Organizing Maps

Simon D. Levy[1] and Simon Kirby[2]

[1] Computer Science Department, Washington and Lee University,
Lexington VA 24450, USA
levys@wlu.edu
[2] Language Evolution and Computation Research Unit, School of Philosophy,
Psychology and Language Sciences, University of Edinburgh, 40, George Square,
Edinburgh, UK

Abstract. We present a neural-competitive learning model of language evolution in which several symbol sequences compete to signify a given propositional meaning. Both symbol sequences and propositional meanings are represented by high-dimensional vectors of real numbers. A neural network learns to map between the distributed representations of the symbol sequences and the distributed representations of the propositions. Unlike previous neural network models of language evolution, our model uses a Kohonen Self-Organizing Map with unsupervised learning, thereby avoiding the computational slowdown and biological implausibility of back-propagation networks and the lack of scalability associated with Hebbian-learning networks. After several evolutionary generations, the network develops systematically regular mappings between meanings and sequences, of the sort traditionally associated with symbolic grammars. Because of the potential of neural-like representations for addressing the symbol-grounding problem, this sort of model holds a good deal of promise as a new explanatory mechanism for both language evolution and acquisition.

1 Introduction

Neural networks hold a great deal of appeal as models of language evolution. As an alternative to traditional "symbol-crunching" systems like grammars, neural nets offer greater biological plausibility – especially with regard to the processing of temporal sequences, limits on structural complexity of meanings, and other "performance" phenomena of real human language. Harnad [1], among others, has argued for the use of neural network models as a solution to the symbol grounding problem, as posed by Searle's famous Chinese Room argument. [2]

A few researchers have successfully used neural networks in modeling language evolution. Typically this work has focused on the emergence of mappings between small, simple meanings and sequences, showing how systematic regularities can emerge in these mappings without using an explicit grammar. A common approach is to embed a neural network in each member of a population

P. Vogt et al. (Eds.): EELC 2006, LNAI 4211, pp. 57–71, 2006.
© Springer-Verlag Berlin Heidelberg 2006

of agents, who participate in a communication game over some number of iterations. Batali [3], showed how the back-propagation algorithm [4] can be used to train a population of recurrent neural networks to map from input sequences (abc, cda) to simple propositional meanings (you hungry, me scared). Eventually the agents developed communication systems with structural regularities reminiscent of those in human languages, with a given symbol or sequence of symbols being used to represent the same concept in different contexts.

In a more recent paper, Smith [5] shows how a variant of Hebbian (simple associative) learning can be used to evolve mappings between simple meanings and signals. Each meaning and signal is an unstructured bit vector orthogonal to all the others. By exploring the set of possible learning rules relating signal bit values to meaning bit values, Smith shows how the "innate endowment" and learning biases of communicative agents can result in optimal communication, through a purely cultural (non-genetic) process.

Both of these projects show how insight into language evolution can be gained from even a simple network model. With both projects, however, it is not clear whether or how these results can be extended to more complicated language structures. From a representational perspective, it is not clear how to extend simple binary coding schemes to more complex meanings – especially, how such schemes could represent hierarchical, recursive structures of the sort that appear to underly language and thought. [6]. From an algorithmic perspective, both back-propagation and Hebbian learning pose problems. In addition to being criticized as biologically implausible [7], back-propagation is a computationally intensive, iterative algorithm whose ability to scale up to larger languages is questionable. As for Hebbian learning, the limitations created by the requirement of mutually orthogonal vectors [8] make it unlikely that these sorts of networks would scale up to more realistic, structured representations of meanings and signals.[1]

In the remainder of this paper, we describe a model using a neurally plausible representation of meanings and sequences, and a neural network algorithm for mapping between them, that has the potential to overcome these limitations. We conclude by with some experimental results that validate the ability of this model to learn rule-like mappings, without recourse to grammar.

2   Distributed Representations

In contrast to the the "atomic" or "localist" representations employed in traditional cognitive science, a *distributed representation* is one in which "each entity is represented by a pattern of activity distributed over many computing elements, and each computing element is involved in representing many different entities". [10] Most commonly, the pattern of activity is represented by a vector of real values in some fixed interval, typically $[0, 1]$ or $[-1, 1]$. Proponents of

---

[1] Subsequent work by Smith *et al.* [9] uses Hebbian associative networks to map structured meanings to structured signals; however, the representation scheme used in that work makes the size of the networks grow explosively as more structure is added, making it impractical for more than very simple structures.

this sort of representations have cited several advantages over traditional symbolic representation. These include robustness to noise ("graceful degradation") and content-addressability (the ability to retrieve items by some feature of their content, rather than an arbitrary address), which are properties of human intelligence seen as lacking in traditional symbolic models. [8]

Distributed representations of meaning have appeared in a variety of contexts in contemporary AI and cognitive science. Most commonly they are used to model the meanings of individual words. In a widely cited paper, Elman [11] demonstrated the ability of a simple recurrent neural network to form richly structured distributed representations of word meaning, based on the task of predicting the next word in a sentence. More recently, the method of Latent Semantic Analysis [12] has used distributed representations successfully in a wide variety of practical AI tasks. On a more theoretical level, Gärdenfors [13] has elaborated a framework in which conceptual meanings are analyzed as regions in a vector space. A very useful feature of all such models is that the vector representations of similar structures end up close together in the vector space, as determined by a common metric like Euclidean distance, dot product, or cosine.

Although these sorts of distributed representations can be seen as encoding structure, it is structure of a categorical, rather than propositional or sentential, nature. As pointed out by Steedman [14], such structure corresponds more to part-of-speech information than to the propositional structures used in AI, logic, and linguistics. For example, given distributed representations of the concepts man, tiger, and chases, simply adding or multiplying the representations together gives no way to extract the difference between the propositions chases(man,tiger) and chases(tiger,man); but these propositions contrast in the assignment of the agent and patient roles to each of the two arguments.

Partly in response to such criticisms, several researchers have developed distributed representations of structured meaning. These include the Holographic Reduced Representations (HRR) of Plate [15], the Binary Spatter Codes of Kanerva [16], the Context-dependent Thinning Networks of Rachkovskij [17], and the Multiplicative Binding Networks of Gayler. [18] All these architectures use vectors of real (or binary) values with high dimensionality (typically 1000 or more dimensions), a binding operation to join vectors representing roles (agent, patient) with those representing fillers (man, tiger), and a combinatory operation to build meaningful structures out of the bound elements.[2] Crucially, these operations do not increase the size of the representations, which was a problem in earlier distributed representation binding schemes. [20]

In Plate's HRR framework, used in our experiments reported below, the binding operation is circular convolution: given vectors $\tilde{c}$ and $\tilde{x}$ of dimension n, their circular convolution "trace vector" $\tilde{t} = \tilde{c} \circledast \tilde{x}$ is defined as

$$t_j = \sum_{k=0}^{n-1} c_k x_{j-k} \qquad (1)$$

---

[2] Pollack's Recursive Auto-Associative Memory [19] is a close cousin of such representations, using relatively low-dimensional vectors for fillers, and matrices for roles.

for $j = 0$ to $n - 1$, subscripts modulo-n. A noisy version $\tilde{y}$ of $\tilde{x}$ can be recovered by circular correlation: $\tilde{y} = \tilde{c} \oplus \tilde{t}$,defined as

$$y_j = \sum_{k=0}^{n-1} c_k t_{k+j} \tag{2}$$

for $j = 0$ to $n - 1$, subscripts modulo-n. The distributed vector representation of a proposition like chases(tiger,man) can then be computed as

$$R(\text{chases(tiger, man)}) = R(\text{chases}) + R(\text{tiger}) \circledast R(\text{agent}) + R(\text{man}) \circledast R(\text{patient}) \tag{3}$$

where $R(symbol)$ is the distributed representation of $symbol$. The representation in (3) encodes both the fact that the proposition is about chasing (first term) and the fact that it is the tiger doing the chasing and the man being chased (last two terms). To query, $e.g.$, who did the chasing in this representation, we correlate the sum in (3) with $R(\text{agent})$, and compare the noisy result with each of the original symbol vectors, to see which is closest (the so-called "cleanup" operation). As long as the original vectors are chosen randomly (zero mean, variance $1/n$), and given a sufficiently large n, this scheme can be used to encode arbitrarily complex structures like knows(man, believes(woman, chases(tiger, man))).

For language evolution research, we also need a way of representing symbol sequences. Plate [15] describes several ways of representing sequences with HRR. In the work described below, we use the method of positional cues, in which a separate set of vectors $\tilde{p}_i$ encodes the position of each element in the sequence by means of the convolution operation:

$$R(\langle \text{a,b,c} \rangle) = \tilde{p}_1 \circledast R(\text{a}) + \tilde{p}_2 \circledast R(\text{b}) + \tilde{p}_3 \circledast R(\text{c}) \tag{4}$$

A noisy version of the ith sequence element can be recovered from the distributed representation of the sequence by circular correlation with $\tilde{p}_i$. For example:

$$R(\text{a}) \cong \tilde{p}_1 \oplus R(\langle \text{a,b,c} \rangle) \tag{5}$$

As with the distributed representations of concepts discussed in the previous section, HRR and related coding schemes have the feature that the vector representations of similar structures (chases(tiger,man), chases(lion,man)) end up close together in the vector space. This fact is illustrated in Table 1, for a set of simple propositions containing a predicate (arbitrarily denoted by p, q, and r) and one argument (arbitrarily denoted by x, y, and z) . The same property holds for the vector representations of similar sequences.

With efficient distributed representations of arbitrarily complex meanings and signals, we arrive at the question of how to evolve mappings between the two. An obvious approach would be to train a three-layer backpropagation network to perform the mapping. This approach would however suffer from the problems described in relation to backprop network earlier: training times can grow arbitrarily long, and the algorithm itself lacks biological plausibility. The following section reviews the Kohonen Self-Organizing Map, the neural-net architecture that we ended up choosing for this task.

Table 1. Cosines between 1000-dimensional HRR's of simple propositions

	p(x)	p(y)	p(z)	q(x)	q(y)	q(z)	r(x)	r(y)	r(z)
p(x)	1.00								
p(y)	0.32	1.00							
p(z)	0.31	0.28	1.00						
q(x)	0.71	0.04	0.03	1.00					
q(y)	0.01	0.69	-0.01	0.32	1.00				
q(z)	0.01	0.00	0.70	0.21	0.31	1.00			
r(x)	0.72	0.06	0.04	0.70	0.03	0.02	1.00		
r(y)	0.04	0.71	0.01	0.04	0.69	0.01	0.35	1.00	
r(z)	0.04	0.02	0.71	0.03	0.01	0.70	0.33	0.32	1.00

3 Kohonen's Self-Organizing Map

The Self-Organizing Map (SOM) of Kohonen [21] is an unsupervised neural network learning method that can be used to reveal patterns of organization in a data set. The data set X consists of vectors of a fixed dimensionality. The network is typically organized into a two-dimensional grid $U_{i,j}, 1 \leq i \leq m, 1 \leq j \leq n$ of nodes, each of which is associated with an initially random weight vector $\tilde{w}^{i,j}$ of the same dimensionality as the members of X. On each learning iteration, a vector $\tilde{x}$ is randomly chosen from the data set, and the node whose weight vector is closest to this vector is considered the "winner" for that iteration. The winning node's weight vector is updated to move it closer to the vector picked from the data set, as are the weight vectors of the winner's grid neighbors. By decreasing the neighborhood size with increasing iterations, the weight vectors eventually settle into a reasonable representation of the data set.

Figure 1 shows a simple example of SOM learning. Here, the data set is two-dimensional, so each grid point is associated with a two-dimensional weight vector. The data set consists of points sampled uniformly from a ring shape. Each grid node is plotted at the point corresponding to its weight vector, and is connected to its north, south, east, and west neighbors by a line segment. The figure shows that no matter how close together or far apart the weight vectors are initially, they end up distributing themselves (and their associated nodes) uniformly within the space enclosing the ring shape.

A common application of SOM is dimensionality reduction for data visualization in two dimensions. There is, however, no restriction on the dimensionality of the nodes U. In fact, the grid of nodes is itself a special case (discrete, two-dimensional) of a continuous metric space, and the algorithm will work with any U for which a neighborhood (distance) metric is defined. The $U_{i,j}$ are replaced with vectors $\tilde{u}^i, 1 \leq i \leq n$, and the index k of the winner $\tilde{u}^k$ is defined as

$$k = \arg\min_i |\tilde{w}^i - \tilde{x}| \tag{6}$$

where $\tilde{w}^i$ is the weight vector associated with $\tilde{u}^i$, and $|\tilde{x} - \tilde{y}|$ is the distance between $\tilde{x}$ and $\tilde{y}$. Instead of updating the winner and the nodes in its neighborhood, all nodes in the network are updated, with the size of the update determined by distance from the winner:

$$\tilde{w}^i_{t+1} \leftarrow \tilde{w}^i_t + \mu_t f(i,k,t)(\tilde{x} - \tilde{w}^i_t) \tag{7}$$

where μ_t is a learning rate parameter, f is the neighborhood function

$$f(i,k,t) = e^{-|\tilde{u}^i - \tilde{u}^k|^2 / 2\sigma_t^2} \tag{8}$$

and σ_t is a neighborhood parameter. Both parameters decrease with time, allowing the weights to settle into an approximate representation of the data set X. In short, the SOM forms a regular *topographic map* [22] from one vector space to another. Recent work in language evolution [23] has argued for the importance of such maps as a key to understanding the ways in which languages develop and change.

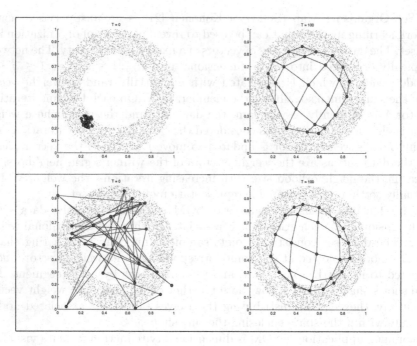

Fig. 1. Two-dimensional SOM learning a ring shape. Final (T=100) configurations are similar regardless of whether initial (T=0) weights are clustered close together (top) or far apart (bottom).

With this broader understanding of SOM, it becomes possible to develop efficient mappings between high-dimensional distributed representations of symbol sequences and high-dimensional distributed representations of meanings. Each meaning vector $\tilde{u}$ can be associated with a weight vector $\tilde{w}$. The sequence vector $\tilde{x}$ expressing $\tilde{u}$ is then chosen as the member of the vector space X of possible sequences that is closest to $\tilde{w}$. In the next section we describe an algorithm that uses this scheme to evolve systematic, grammar-like mappings.

4 Experiments

4.1 Learning a Simple Mapping

To explore the possibility of using an SOM to evolve systematic mappings between distributed representations of meanings and sequences, we started with a simple model not explicitly involving agents or communication. We used the small predicate/argument propositional meanings from Table 1, and symbol sequences of length two over the alphabet {a, b, c}. Meanings were represented as 1000-dimensional HRR trace vectors, and sequences as 1200-dimensional HRR trace vectors. (These sizes were chosen arbitrarily, to show that the meaning traces and sequence traces need not agree in size.) Each 1000-dimensional meaning trace was associated with an initially random 1200-dimensional weight vector, which was modified according to Equations 6 - 8, with the meaning vectors being the U, the sequence vectors the X, and the weights between them the W. The learning rate μ_t was scaled linearly from 0.5 to 0.1, and the neighborhood value σ_t from 3.0 to 0.1. Our goal was to see what sorts of meaning-sequence mappings emerged.

Table 2 shows the results of eight different experimental runs of 500 SOM learning iterations each. In each row i, the first column shows the ith propositional meaning. The second column shows the "winning" sequence for that meaning at the start of the experimental run; *i.e.*, sequence j whose sequence trace $\tilde{x}^j$ is closest to the weights $\tilde{w}^i$ for that meaning:

$$j = \arg\min_k |\tilde{w}^i - \tilde{x}^k| \tag{9}$$

The remaining columns show the winning sequences at the end of eight different experimental runs. As Table 2 indicates, the meaning-sequence mappings changed from being highly non-systematic at the beginning of the experiment to maximally systematic at the end, for all but one of the eight runs reported. Each randomly initialized SOM learned to map from a given predicate (p, q, or r) to a single symbol (a, b, or c), and from a given argument (x, y, or z) to a single symbol. For example, the last column in the table shows a "verb-final" mapping in which the symbol corresponding to the predicate comes second, the

Table 2. Results of First Experiment

Meaning	Typical Initial Sequences	Final Sequences
p(x)	ac	bb ca cb cc ac cc ba ba
p(y)	ac	cb ba bb ac cc bb aa ca
p(z)	ac	ab aa ab bc bc ba ca aa
q(x)	ac	bc cc cc ca ab cc bc bc
q(y)	ac	cc bc bc aa cb bc ac cc
q(z)	ac	ac ac ac ba bb ca cc ac
r(x)	ca	ba cb ca cb aa ac bb bb
r(y)	ac	ca bb ba ab ca ab ab cb
r(z)	bc	aa ab aa bb ba aa cb ab

symbol corresponding to the argument comes first, and the systematic mappings are $(p/a, q/c, r/b)$ for predicates and $(x/b, y/c, z/a)$ for arguments. These results show that our approach can produce systematic mappings, for this small learning task at least.

4.2   Opening the Bottleneck

The mappings learned in the previous experiment are, for the most part, *compositional*: a given meaning component (predicate or argument) is always represented by the same symbol, independent of where it appears. No two predicates are represented by the same symbol, nor are any two arguments. This situation led us to ask whether our HRR/SOM learning model has a bias toward compositionality, or whether there is some other influence at work.

To examine this issue, we repeated the first experiment with an alphabet of six symbols instead of three. If our model were biased toward maximal compositionality, we would expect to end up with a one-to-one mapping between each meaning element and each sequence symbol. After trying a number of parameter settings, we were unable to obtain compositional mappings for this experimental setup. An example final, non-compositional sequence is shown in Table 3. A look

Table 3. Lack of Compositionality

Meaning	Typical Initial Sequences	Typical Final Sequences
p(x)	ee	af
p(y)	ee	fd
p(z)	ee	ed
q(x)	ee	ab
q(y)	ff	cc
q(z)	be	dd
r(x)	ee	ba
r(y)	de	cd
r(z)	be	dc

back at Figure 1 suggests a possible explanation for this lack of compositionality. This figure shows that, regardless of the initial weights, SOM learning produces a final weight configuration that is evenly distributed around the space defined by the input data. In the first experiment, the number of sequences was identical to the number of meanings. Hence, there was no "room" in the input space for the weights to expand, and this even distribution yielded a compositional mapping. In the second experiment, there were four times as many sequences (36) as meanings (nine). By distributing the meanings throughout the space of sequences, the SOM produced a highly non-compositional mapping for this data set.

This result may be seen as analogous to the *bottleneck* principle described by Kirby [24], in which the constraints of cultural transmission favor the emergence of languages describable by a small number of rules. The previous two experiments show how the constraint imposed by using a smaller number of symbols results in a similar outcome, using an entirely different computational substrate.

4.3 Evolving Word-Order Regularities

With this understanding of our HRR/SOM model in mind, we turned our attention to using the model to study specific phenomena. In a third experiment, we used the model to explore the emergence of word-order regularities among the subject, object, and verb in a simple model of sentence production. Based on a data set used by Kirby [24], we constructed simple proposition meanings of the form $predicate(argument1, argument2)$, where $predicate$ ranged over {loves, hates, admires, sees, detests}, and each argument ranged over {john, mary, gavin, bill, fred}. For the sake of clarity in comparing the relative order of subject and object, we avoided reflexives, yielding 100 ($5 \times 5 \times 4$) propositional meanings. Using the symbol set {l, h, a, s, d, j, m, g, b, f}, we constructed all six permutations of compositional three-symbol "sentences" for each such meaning; for example, the proposition loves(john,mary) yielded the possible sentences {ljm, lmj, jlm, jml, mjl, mlj}. Meanings and sequences were both represented by 2000-dimensional HRR trace vectors. Unlike the previous two experiments, this experiment associated the weight vectors to the *sequences*, rather than the meanings, resulting in a situation in which six possible sequences were competing for each meaning. The winner of each competition was chosen via Equation 6, after which the weights for all 600 sequences (not just the six competitors) were updated via Equation 7. For this experiment the learning rate μ_t decreased linearly from 0.125 down to 0.025.

The results of this experiment were quite consistent: over 500 iterations of the SOM learning algorithm, the astronomically large set of possible mappings quickly converged to one of the six possible word orders relating predicates and arguments to verbs, subjects, and objects (VSO, VOS, SVO, SOV, OSV, OVS). Figure 2 shows a sample experimental run, where the model converged to SVO word order. The figure shows the fraction per 10 iterations of each kind of mapping. Note that the SVO order becomes dominant before 50 iterations have

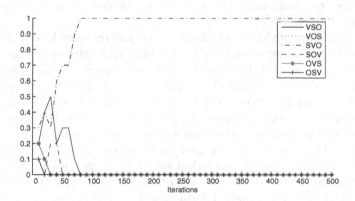

Fig. 2. Sample run for the third experiment, showing fraction of mappings with given word order against iterations, in steps of 10

passed, meaning that the model begins to generalize before fewer than half of the possible meanings have been presented to it.

4.4   An Agent-Based Approach

Several recent approaches to the evolution of language have used a population of agents as a basis for exploring the emergence of systematic communication. [3, 25, 26, 27]. Such models are based on the idea that language evolved to accommodate the transmission of information, which although not universally accepted [28], holds a great deal of intuitive appeal. This situation led us to wonder whether neural HRR/SOM model could be used as the computational "core" of an agent-based approach.

To explore this issue, we adapted a simple two-agent "Iterated Learning Model" (ILM) developed by on of the authors. [24] This model employs a *cultural transmission* paradigm [29] in which biological evolution – specifically, adaptive fitness – plays no role. In ILM, the population consists of an idealized speaker and an idealized learner. On each cultural "generation", the speaker must produce some pre-determined number of utterances. Each utterance consists of a propositional meaning (of the sort described above), and a symbol string generated on the basis the speaker's (initially empty) grammar. If the speaker's grammar cannot generate a string for that meaning, the speaker invents a string at random, and uses it as input to a grammar-induction algorithm that accommodates its current grammar to the new meaning/string pair. The learner "hears" the meaning/string utterance produced by the speaker, and behaves in a parallel fashion: if it cannot parse the string using its (initially empty) grammar, it uses the meaning/string as input to grammatical induction. At the end of each generation, the speaker "dies", the learner becomes the new speaker, and a new learner with an empty grammar is added to the simulation. As mentioned above, an important result of grammar-based ILM was that when the number of utterances per generation was constrained to be less than the total number possible, the resulting "transmission bottleneck" led to the emergence of compositional grammars.

In our adaptation of the model, the grammar was replaced by our HRR/SOM model, and grammar induction by SOM learning. To produce a string for a given meaning, the speaker used the string whose weight vector was closest to the HRR representation of that meaning (Equation 6). The weights for all strings were then modified using Equation 7. Unlike the original ILM work [24], there was no sense of invention or ability to generate/parse a given string; the speaker always used Equation 6 to generate a string for a given meaning, and the learner always accommodated this meaning/string pair via Equation 7. As in [24], however, the first speaker and each new learner lacked any "knowledge" of language, which in this new experiment meant random weights on each string. The identity of the meaning/string pair was the only information shared by the speaker and learner: the speaker's initial random weights and HRR vectors were not the same as any learner's, and each new learner was given a new set of random weights and HRR vectors.

The data set for this experiment was the same as for the previous one, consisting of 100 propositional meanings of the form *predicate(argument1, argument2)*, with six different length-three symbol strings possible for each. Again, and unlike [24], our goal was not to test for the emergence of compositionality. Instead, we wanted to see whether the emergence of consistent word order shown by our model would transfer to an agent-based, information-transmission paradigm. Following [24], each speaker produced 50 utterance per generation, meaning that the listener was exposed to less than the full range of possible meanings.

Like the previous experiment, the results of this experiment were quite consistent. After five to 10 generations, a single word order emerged for all meanings. [3] As in our previous experiment, the final word order began to dominate the others early on, typically by the end of the second generation. Like [5], these results show that grammars are not the only computational mechanism by which linguistic regularity can be acquired in an iterated cultural learning model.

4.5   Generalizing from Sparse Data

Perhaps the greatest challenge in modeling language emergence comes from the so-called "poverty of the stimulus" problem. The language learner, presented with a small, finite set of exemplars, must generalize to the patterns of the full language. [30] To explore the ability of our model to generalize based on sparse data, we conducted the following experiment.

Using the 100 utterances from the previous two experiments, we trained the SOM to map from a given meaning to the corresponding VSO sequence. For example, the meaning trace for loves(john,mary) was mapped to the sequence

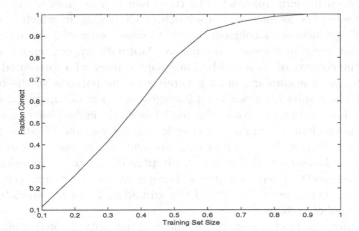

Fig. 3. Fraction of correct mappings versus training set size. Results for each condition are averaged over five trials.

---

[3] This is far fewer than the 1000 generations used in [24]; the difference is due to the much more constrained learning task employed here.

trace for ljm, detests(gavin,bill) to dgb, etc. The goal was to see what fraction of the total utterances would be correctly generalized, based on the fraction of training examples presented. Training examples were picked at random, starting with 10 percent of the training set and continuing up through 100 percent. Each example was presented to the network five times.

Figure 3 shows the results of this experiment, averaged over five trials for each training condition. Like Figure 2, this figure suggests that our model has the potential to generalize from incomplete information. After seeing 50 percent of the mappings, the model can generalize to another 30 percent, and it can generalize to the full set after seeing about 85 percent of the data. Although it would be premature to make any broad claims about this ability, the data from this experiment show that the model cannot simply be "memorizing" particular meaning/sequence mappings.

5   Discussion

The work described here represents a very preliminary attempt to provide a neurally plausible alternative to traditional grammars as a basis for research in language evolution and development. Our model learns to map between high-dimensional, distributed representations of propositional meanings and symbol sequences, without using a computationally expensive and biologically implausible algorithm like back-propagation.

Our goal is not to supplant existing approaches to explaining the development of language. Indeed, the very nature of our model, in which symbol sequences compete for the propositional meanings that they signify, is very much in the spirit of several modern approaches to these issues. The most recent and obvious of these is the evolutionary approach of Croft [31], in which individual "linguemes" (phonemes, morphemes, words, phrases, collocations) are viewed as competing for usage in a speech community. Alternatively, our model could be viewed in the context of an individual language learner who, presented with a small, finite set of exemplars, must generalize to the patterns of the full language. [30] The results from Section 4.5 suggest this sort of capability. Finally, as our fourth experiments shows, the model is easily embedded in an agent-based setting involving an explicit teacher/learner interaction. What we hope to add to these endeavors is a sense of how the symbolic representations used in all of them might be grounded in a neurally plausible model of representation. By using these sorts of representations throughout – instead of merely at the lowest sensory/motor level – we avoid the grounding problem associated with traditional symbol systems.

As with any new model, however, we have of necessity ignored a number of crucial issues. Most glaring of these is perhaps our treatment of sequences, in which we encode the absolute position of each symbol. A more psychologically realistic model would focus on the relative position of symbols, thereby supporting the kinds of phenomena found in serial-order experiments. [32] Nor have we dealt in any way with recursion, a property generally considered to be part of the minimally adequate characterization of human language. [33] As noted above, a desirable feature of the Holographic Reduced Representations employed here is their ability to encode recursive structures of arbitrary complexity. Another possible direction for this research would therefore involve exploring the kinds of mappings that emerge from the need to communicate recursive propositional meanings with symbol sequences, using the HRR/SOM model.

Finally, as with any model of evolution or acquisition, we arrive at the question of what exactly our model is learning. As we have shown in our experiments, the model is learning more than a simple mapping from representations of whole meanings to representations of whole sequences. Instead, it learns, for example, that a string beginning with a d corresponds to a proposition whose predicate is detests, and that a string with a j in the second position corresponds to a proposition whose first argument is john. As it stands, this sort of mapping is not much different from a mapping between two types of coding of sequences. It has been known for quite some time that mere sequence information is inadequate to capture the relationships among meaning-bearing elements of phrases and sentences [34]; hence the popularity of context-free grammars and other mechanisms for capturing dependencies over arbitrary distances. An important next step for our research would therefore be to come up with a more plausible HRR representation of word-order information. Following [35], Plate [15] presents a method of HRR sequence encoding that incorporates relative position as well as absolute position. Such a representation might allow the SOM to focus on relative, as opposed to absolute, order, thereby supporting long-distance dependencies.

Acknowledgments

The first author would like to thank: Washington and Lee University for support during the sabbatical leave in which the ideas in this paper were developed; Mark Steedman and the University of Edinburgh Informatics Department for sponsoring his visit; Jim Hurford, Kenny Smith, and the Language Evolution and Computation Research Unit at Edinburgh for discussion and criticism about the ideas presented here; and Tony Plate for help with the HRR model. The authors also thank three anonymous reviewers for their helpful comments.

References

[1] Harnad, S.: Grounding symbols in the analog world with neural nets. Think 2(1) (1993) 12–78
[2] Searle, J.: Minds, brains, and programs. Behavioral and Brain Sciences 3 (1980)
[3] Batali, J.: Computational simulations of the emergence of grammar. In Hurford, J., Studdert-Kennedy, M., Knight, C., eds.: Approaches to the Evolution of Language: Social and Cognitive Bases. Cambridge University Press, Cambridge (1998)
[4] Rumelhart, D., Hinton, G., Williams, R.: Learning internal representation by error propagation. In Rumelhart, D., McClelland, J., eds.: Parallel Distributed Processing: Explorations in the Microstructure of Cognition. Volume 1. MIT Press (1986)

[5] Smith, K.: The cultural evolution of communication in a population of neural networks. Connection Science **14**(1) (2002) 65–84

[6] Fodor, J.: The Language of Thought. Crowell, New York (1975)

[7] Grossberg, S.: Competitive learning: from interactive activation to adaptive resonance. In: Connectionist models and their implications: readings from cognitive science. Ablex Publishing Corp., Norwood, NJ, USA (1988) 243–283

[8] McClelland, J., Rumelhart, D., Hinton, G.: The appeal of parallel distributed processing. In Rumelhart, D., McClelland, J., eds.: Parallel Distributed Processing: Explorations in the Microstructure of Cognition. Volume 1. MIT Press (1986)

[9] Smith, K., Brighton, H., Kirby, S.: Complex systems in language evolution: the cultural emergence of compositional structure. Advances in Complex Systems **6**(4) (2003) 537–558

[10] Hinton, G.: Distributed representations. Technical Report CMU-CS-84-157, Computer Science Department, Carnegie Mellon University (1984)

[11] Elman, J.: Finding structure in time. Cognitive Science **14** (1990) 179–211

[12] Landauer, T.K., Dumais, S.T.: A solution to plato's problem: The latent semantic analysis theory of the acquisition, induction, and representation of knowledge. Psychological Review **104** (1997) 211–240

[13] Gärdenfors, P.: Conceptual Spaces: The Geometry of Thought. MIT Press (2000)

[14] Steedman, M.: Connectionist sentence processing in perspective. Cognitive Science **23**(4) (1999) 615–634

[15] Plate, T.A.: Holographic Reduced Representation: Distributed Representation for Cognitive Science. CSLI Publications (2003)

[16] Kanerva, P.: The binary spatter code for encoding concepts at many levels. In Marinaro, M., Morasso, P., eds.: ICANN '94: Proceedings of International Conference on Artificial Neural Networks. Volume 1., London, Springer-Verlag (1994) 226–229

[17] Rachkovskij, D.A., Kussul, E.M.: Binding and normalization of binary sparse distributed representations by context-dependent thinning. Neural Computation **13**(2) (2001) 411–452

[18] Gayler, R.: Multiplicative binding, representation operators, and analogy,. In Holyoak, K., Gentner, D., Kokinov, B., eds.: Advances in Analogy Research: Integration of Theory and Data from the Cognitive, Computational, and Neural Sciences. New Bulgarian University, Sofia, Bulgaria (1998) 405

[19] Pollack, J.: Recursive distributed representations. Artifical Intelligence **36** (1990) 77–105

[20] Smolensky, P.: Tensor product variable binding and the representation of symbolic structures in connectionist systems. Artificial Intelligence **46** (1990) 159–216

[21] Kohonen, T.: Self-Organizing Maps. 3 edn. Springer-Verlag, Secaucus, NJ (2001)

[22] VanHulle, M.: Faithful Representations and Topographic Maps. Wiley-Interscience, New York (1990)

[23] Brighton, H., Kirby, S.: Understanding linguistic evolution by visualizing the emergence of topographic mappings. Artificial Life **12**(2) (2006) 229–242

[24] Kirby, S.: Learning, bottlenecks and the evolution of recursive syntax. In Briscoe, T., ed.: Linguistic Evolution through Language Acquisition: Formal and Computational Models. Cambridge University Press (2002)

[25] MacLennan, B.: Synthetic ethology: An approach to the study of communication. In Langton, C., Taylor, C., Farmer, D., Rasmussen, S., eds.: Artificial Life II, Redwood City, CA, Addison-Wesley (1992) 631–658

[26] Werner, G., Dyer, M.: Evolution of communication in artificial organisms. In Langton, C., Taylor, C., Farmer, D., Rasmussen, S., eds.: Artificial Life II, Redwood City, CA, Addison-Wesley Pub. (1992) 659–687

[27] Briscoe, T.: Grammatical acquisition: Inductive bias and coevolution of language and the language acquisition device. Language **76**(2) (2000) 245–296

[28] Chomsky, N.: Language and Mind. Harcourt Brace Jovanovich, San Diego (1972)

[29] Smith, K.: Natural selection and cultural selection in the evolution of communication. Adaptive Behavior 10(1) (2002) 25–44

[30] Chomsky, N.: Rules and Representations. Basil Blackwell, Oxford (1980)

[31] Croft, W.: Explaining language change: an evolutionary approach. Longman, Harlow, Essex (2000)

[32] Lewandowsky, S., Murdock, B.: Memory for serial order. Psychological Review **96**(1) (1989) 25–27

[33] Hauser, M.D., Chomsky, N., Fitch, W.T.: The faculty of language: What is it, who has it, and how did it evolve? Science **298** (2002) 1569–1579

[34] Chomsky, N.: Three models for the description of language. IRE Transactions on information theory **2** (1956) 113–124

[35] Murdock, B.B.: Serial order effects in a distributed-memory model. In Gorfein, D.S., Hoffman, R.R., eds.: MEMORY AND LEARNING: The Ebbinghaus Centennial Conference, Lawrence Erlbaum Associates (1987) 277–310

How Do Children Develop Syntactic Representations from What They Hear?

Elena Lieven[1,2]

[1] Max Planck Institute for Evolutionary Anthropology, Leipzig
[2] School of Psychological Sciences, University of Manchester

Children learn language from what they hear. In dispute is what mechanisms they bring to this task. Clearly some of these mechanisms have evolved to support the human speech capacity but this leaves a wide field of possibilities open. The question I will address in my paper is whether we need to postulate an innate _syntactic_ module that has evolved to make the learning of language structure possible. I will suggest that more general human social and cognitive capacities may be all that is needed to support the learning of syntactic structure.

I start by briefly discussing precursors to language development that are developing in the first year of life: some of these are probably primate-wide skills, for instance, the capacity for distributional learning (e.g., [1]), others are probably in large part, human-specific, for instance the highly sophisticated socio-cognitive skills that one-year-olds already show (e.g., [2]).

Next, I outline an approach to language development that involves the learning of constructional schemas, both specific and abstract. Children are thought to start out with concrete pieces of language and to gradually develop more schematic constructions. All constructions are mappings between the form of the construction and a meaning, though this may not be either the full meaning or the full construction of the adult grammar. For instance a child may say Whats that? for months, perhaps as a request for the name of an object or perhaps as a way of getting attention without connecting the clitic -s to any representation of the verb, to BE. As their language develops children (1) learn more constructions (2) develop slots in constructions as they notice variation (3) abstract a more schematic meaning for each slot, making the constructions more abstract (4) add more slots to constructions making them more complex and (5) relate constructions to each other through distributional and analogical processes.

Many previous studies of language development have argued that children could not learn from the input because there is no surface guide to underlying constituency. In support of this, they claim that there is empirical evidence that childrens grammars are abstract from the outset. There are two major problems with assessing such claims. First, until recently, most empirical studies of language development have been conducted on very thinly sampled data. This makes it difficult to know whether either relatively infrequent utterances or the complete absence of an utterance is due to chance sampling or is really indicative of development [3]. In what follows, I report research that has largely been

P. Vogt et al. (Eds.): EELC 2006, LNAI 4211, pp. 72–75, 2006.

conducted using dense database corpora that are orders of magnitude greater than most previous corpora.

The second problem with assessing nativist-linguistic claims is that childrens language (and that of the adults speaking to them) is often analysed in terms of the abstract categories of grammar, rather than in terms of the frequency and contexts of particular forms (morphemes, words or strings). I will demonstrate that if the utterances of children and adults are analysed at a lexically specific level there are extremely strong relationships between the input and childrens own development and that satisfactory accounts can be given for many phenomena in language acquisition research (for instance, systematic errors) that have previously been explained in terms of pre-existing abstract syntactic knowledge.

The presentation of data falls into four parts. The first part is concerned with how children might build novel utterances from what they hear. Using a methodology that we have developed which we call Traceback, I assess the ways in which children could build utterances out of previously learned strings [4,5] and show how, with development, slots in constructions start to become more abstract. In this section I also present a study showing that English Child Directed Speech is very lexically restricted and that this is likely to be where childrens early lexically-based schemas come from [6]. I report briefly some current research on German and Russian CDS which, contrary to what one might expect from formal grammatical descriptions, also shows high degrees of lexical restrictiveness at the beginnings of maternal utterances [7].

However, it is important to note that while childrens language development depends crucially on the nature of the input, it is not a simple mapping from the input (for instance, the frequency of each construction) to the childs linguistic representations. This is because children build up an inventory of constructions, each a mapping of form to meaning. Childrens communicative needs and cognitive understanding play a part in this as the learning process identifies emergent forms in constructions and seeks to attach meaning to them. In the second empirical part of the paper I will demonstrate this by reference to a dense database study of the development of negation [8] and a study of auxiliary development [9].

Another reason why children are not simple frequency matchers is because constructions interconnect in ways that mean that the developing system will not be a proper subset of the adult system, but one with its own transitory states and developmental trajectory. In the third empirical section, I discuss two studies that illustrate this, one on the development of verb argument structure [10] and the other a dense database study of the development of German passive constructions [11].

In the final empirical part of the paper, I discuss data relevant to two criticisms often levelled at the usage-based approach. Firstly, it is correctly pointed out that the results come largely from English-speaking childrens acquisition and English is a very untypical language with highly restrictive syntactic word order and virtually no inflectional morphology. There are a number of reports in the literature of early and relatively error-free acquisition of morphology in morphologically-richer languages. However recent research by Aguado-Orea [12] shows that if Spanish childrens verbal morphology is analysed at the level of specific inflections, it shows high error rates in some parts of the system and that this is closely related to the frequency of these forms in the input. A second criticism is that the dependence of the usage-based approach on frequency means that it cannot explain the sorts of systematic errors that children make with syntactically complex constructions such non-inversion and double tense marking errors in English. If children were learning the correct strings from what they hear, why would they make these errors? A recent study by Rowland [13] has shown that, in fact, these errors can be explained as a function of the frequency with which particular questions occur in the input if these are analysed lexically: highly frequent lexical strings in the input are protected from error in the childs system; errors occur when the child has less evidence as to what the correct string should be.

I conclude the paper by suggesting that the usage-based approach is by far the most promising way of making the study of language development a tractable scientific problem but that there is still a long way to go. I briefly raise some of the major challenges. These include the learning of complex morphological systems and the mechanisms underlying generalisation. Solving these problems will require considerable scientific ingenuity as well as contributions from modelling and artificial language research and the continued development of naturalistic and experimental methodologies.

In language development children build their novel utterances and their more advanced linguistic representations out of old parts [14] — here indeed is a parallel with how the evolution of language must have proceeded.

References

1. Jusczyk, P.: The discovery of spoken language. Cambridge, MA: The MIT Press (1997)
2. Tomasello, M., Carpenter, M., Call, J., Behne, T., Moll, H.: Understanding and sharing intentions: The origins of cultural cognition. Behavioral and Brain Sciences **28** (2005) 675–735
3. Tomasello, M., Stahl, D.: Sampling children's spontaneous speech: how much is enough? Journal of Child Language **31** (2004) 101–121
4. Lieven, E., Behrens, H., Speares, J., Tomasello, M.: Early syntactic creativity: A usage-based approach. Journal of Child Language **30** (2003) 333–370
5. Dabrowska, E., Lieven, E.: Towards a lexically specific grammar of childrens question constructions. Cognitive Linguistics **16** (2005) 437–474
6. Cameron-Faulkner, T., Lieven, E., Tomasello, M.: A construction based analysis of child directed speech. Cognitive Science **27** (2003) 843–873
7. Stoll, S., Abbot-Smith, K., Lieven, E.: (Lexically restricted utterances in russian, german and english child directed speech) submitted.
8. Cameron-Faulkner, T., Lieven, E., Theakston, A.: (What part of no do children not understand? a usage-based account of multiword negation) submitted.
9. Theakston, A., Lieven, E., Pine, J., Rowland, C.: The acquisition of auxiliary syntax: Be and have. Cognitive Linguistics **16** (2005) 247–277

10. McClure, K., Pine, J., Lieven, E.: Investigating the abstractness of children's early knowledge of argument structure. Journal of Child Language (2006) in press.
11. Abbot-Smith, K., Behrens, H.: How known constructions influence the acquisition of other constructions: the german passive and future constructions. Cognitive Science **30** (2006) in press.
12. Aguado-Orea, J.: The acquisition of morpho-syntax in Spanish: implications for current theories of development. PhD thesis, University of Nottingham (2004)
13. Rowland, C.: Explaining errors in children's questions. Cognition (2006) in press.
14. Bates, E., Benigni, Bretherton, Camaioni, Volterra: The emergence of symbols: Cognition and communication in infancy. New York: Academic Press (1979)

How Grammar Emerges to Dampen Combinatorial Search in Parsing

Luc Steels[1,2] and Pieter Wellens[2]

[1] SONY Computer Science Laboratory - Paris
[2] Vrije Universiteit Brussel, Artificial Intelligence Laboratory
Pleinlaan 2, B-1050 Brussel

Abstract. According to the functional approach to language evolution (inspired by cognitive linguistics and construction grammar), grammar arises to deal with issues in communication among autonomous agents, particularly maximisation of communicative success and expressive power and minimisation of cognitive effort. Experiments in the emergence of grammar should hence start from a simulation of communicative exchanges between embodied agents, and then show how a particular issue that arises can be solved or partially solved by introducing more grammar. This paper shows a case study of this approach, focusing on the issue of search during parsing. Multiple hypotheses arise in parsing when the same syntactic pattern can be used for multiple purposes or when one syntactic pattern partly overlaps with another one. It is well known that syntactic ambiguity rapidly leads to combinatorial explosions and hence an increase in memory use and processing power, possibly to a point where the sentence can no longer be handled. Additional grammar, such as syntactic or semantic subcategorisation or word order and agreement constraints can help to dampen search because it provides information to the hearer which hypotheses are the most likely. The paper shows an operational experiment where avoiding search is used as the driver for the introduction and negotiation of syntax. The experiment is also a demonstration of how Fluid Construction Grammar is well suited for experiments in language evolution.

1 Introduction

The research reported in this paper is part of a growing body of research that tries to show through careful computational and robotic experiments how communication systems with properties similar to those of human natural languages may emerge in populations of agents. (See recent overviews in [1], [2], and others) Many aspects of language are being studied, ranging from the origins of sound systems, the origins of lexicons, the co-evolution of lexicons with ontologies usable for categorisation, etc. In this paper we focus on issues related to grammar.

We will adopt a functional view on the evolution of language, compatible with cognitive linguistics approaches [3] and construction grammar [4], as opposed to a structuralist view, familiar from generative grammar [5]. Broadly speaking,

P. Vogt et al. (Eds.): EELC 2006, LNAI 4211, pp. 76–88, 2006.

the functional view argues that syntax is motivated by attempts to solve some aspect of the communication problem, whereas in a structuralist view, syntax is not motivated by communicative function. These two views lead to different models of language evolution. Genetic and cultural transmission models such as those of Nowak, et.al. [6] or most models based on the Iterated Learning framework [7] illustrate a structuralist view. Agents introduce hierarchical structure as they induce (or inherit after mutation) the language of their parent, and this structure is reused when they produce language themselves. But the structure is not motivated by issues that arise when attempting to communicate. Indeed communication itself is not modeled, only the transmission process. The nature of the resulting grammar is therefore solely due to the nature of the learning algorithm (e.g. induction based on minimal description length) and chance factors. Although this is probably a reasonable model for language transmission it makes it hard to understand why language is the way it is and how the intricate structure we observe might have arisen.

In this paper we explore a functional view on language evolution, which means that features of grammar are supposed to emerge because they deal with a particular issue that embodied communicating agents necessarily have to solve. This implies that we must first create situations in which embodied agents encounter certain difficult issues which prevent them from communicating successfully with reasonable cognitive effort, and then formulate repair strategies for dealing with these issues that lead to increased grammaticality and a better communication system.

Our team has already reported several very concrete operational examples of this approach. Steels [8] argued that grammar is needed to link partial meanings introduced by different lexical items and showed computational simulations which use the damping of equalities between variables (which arise when partial meanings are only implicitly linked to each other) as main driver for introducing case grammar [9]. De Beule and Bergen [10] showed how compositional coding (as opposed to holistic coding) emerges when there is a sufficiently large fraction of structured meanings that need to be expressed. When agents reuse existing expressions, communicative success increases more rapidly and cognitive load decreases as they need smaller lexicons. Steels and Loetzsch [11] argued that embodied communication involving spatial relations (like left or right) requires recruiting the ability to adopt different perspectives and communicating explicitly the perspective from which a scene is described because it substantially increases communicative success and decreases the cognitive effort of the agents.

In this paper, we report on another case study, now focusing on the issue of combinatorial explosions in parsing. Multiple hypotheses in parsing arise unavoidably as soon as the same syntactic pattern is re-used as part of a bigger structure. Moreover natural languages re-use the same syntactic pattern with different levels of detail. For example, it is possible to build a noun phrase with just an article and a noun ("the box") but also with an article, an adjective and a noun ("the big box"), or two noun phrases combined with a preposition ("a small box next to the orange ball"), and so on. Unless there is additional syntax, "a" or "the" in the latter example can both be combined with either "box" or "ball", and "big" or "orange" can equally be combined with both nouns and the phrase can also be parsed as "the orange ball next to a small box". Clearly languages introduce syntactic means to restrict the set of possible combinations which otherwise would quickly run out of hand. In English, this additional syntax is usually based on word order, but other languages may use other syntactic devices such as agreement between number and gender.

This suggests that detection of parsing ambiguity can be used as a motor that drives the introduction of syntax. The speaker can re-enter the utterance that he has just produced to detect ambiguity and then add additional constraints if there is a risk of combinatorial explosion. The hearer can parse the utterance produced by the speaker, 'bite the bullet' to arrive at an interpretation even if it involves search, but then use the syntactic sugar that the speaker might have introduced as a way to avoid that search in the future. This is precisely the repair strategy that we have implemented and report on in this paper.

The rest of the paper describes the experimental set-up, how failure or cognitive strain is detected, the repair strategies, and the effect of their application on the communicative success and cognitive effort of language users. The experiments rest on highly sophisticated technical tools contributed by many other members of our team (see acknowledgement). Lexicon and grammar use the Fluid Construction Grammar (FCG) framework, which is a new HPSG-style implementation of construction grammar [12]. An implementation on a LISP substrate has been released for free download through http://arti.vub.ac.be/FCG/. The technical part of this paper assumes some familiarity with FCG, and in particular the way that hierarchy is handled using the J-operator (see [13]). Finally, semantic aspects are handled through grounded procedural semantics based on a constraint language called the Incremental Recruitment Language (IRL) (see [14]).

2   Modeling Communication

It has been well documented that the ability to establish a joint attention frame is an important prerequisite for human-like communication [15]. A joint attention frame is only possible when agents share motives and communicative goals and find themselves in the same (physical) situation in which they can establish joint attention to the same objects or aspects of the situation. We achieve these prerequisites by carefully constructing a language game, which is highly constrained routinised interaction between agents. The game takes place in a physically shared environment and shared motives and communicative goals are part of the scripts through which these robots interact with each other in this environment. For example, two robots are both paying attention to an orange ball that is pushed around by an experimenter and they describe how the current movement of the ball is different from previous events [11] (see figure 1 bottom).

To achieve a communicative goal, the speaker must first conceptualise what to say and this must be based on a perception of the world as experienced through

Fig. 1. Typical experimental setup in our language game experiments. The bottom shows two robots moving around in an environment that contains balls and boxes. The robots are equipped with a complex sensory-motor system, able to detect the objects and build an analog world model of their location and trajectories. The top shows objects being detected (left) and a ball trajectory (right) as seen by the robot on the right.

the agent's sensori-motor system. The agent's world models in our experiments are analog and based on direct output of sensors and actuators (as shown in figure 1 top). Often it is assumed that there is a simple straightforward way to transform a non-symbolic world model into a categorical situation model, which is a representation of the world in the form of facts in some variant of predicate calculus however we believe that this assumption is not realistic. Instead we have adopted a 'procedural semantics' view [16] in which the meaning of a phrase is not an expression to be matched against a situation model, but a program to perform the necessary categorisations and conceptualisations in order to achieve specific communicative goals like reference. Conceptualising what to say then becomes a planning process and interpretation is equal to running the programs reconstructed from parsing a sentence. We call these meanings 'semantic programs'.

To operationalise this procedural semantics, our team has designed and implemented a constraint propagation language IRL (Incremental Recruitment Language) [14]. The primitive constraints are cognitive operations like filtering the set of objects in the world model with an image schema, taking the intersection of two sets, checking whether a certain event fits with the dynamical behavior of the objects in a particular situation, etc. A simple example of a constraint network in IRL-notation is as follows (no control flow is expressed):

```
1. (external-context ?s1)       ; ?s1 is the current context
2. (filter-set-prototype ?s2 ?s1 ?p1); retain elements of ?s2 matching ?p1
3. (prototype ?p1 [box])        ; introduce prototype to be used
4. (unique-element ?o1 ?s2)     ; ?o1 is the unique element from s2
```

All symbols preceded by question marks are variables. ?o1 will be bound to an object in the world model, ?s1 and ?s2 will be bound to sets of objects, and ?p1 is bound to a prototype or image schema that is used to filter the set of objects in the context (?s1). The resulting set (?s2) is assumed to contain only a unique element (?o1).

Constraints are exercised until the possible bindings of variables are restricted as much as possible, ideally to single choices. The constraint networks operate in different directions for conceptualisation and for interpretation. For example, in the phrase "the box" the hearer is given a prototype [box] and uses it to classify the objects in the world model, perhaps by a nearest neighbor match with the prototype. But in conceptualising, the speaker must find a suitable prototype, so that if this prototype is used, the hearer will be able to find back a set containing the referent. The constraints are not only able to perform a particular operation over the world model, such as categorising a set of visual stimuli in terms of color categories, but also extend the available repertoire (the ontology) of the agent. In other words, constraints can invent new categories, adjust categories, introduce new prototypes, etc. This way the acquisition of a conceptual repertoire is completely integrated in the process of conceptualising and interpreting language and it is therefore possible to have a strong interaction between the two. IRL features mechanisms to find a network that is adequate for achieving a particular communicative goal and chunking found solutions so that they can be reused later. In multi-agent experiments, each agent builds up his own repertoire of composite constraints and ontologies and they get coordinated due to alignment.

The next task of the speaker is to transform a constraint network into a language utterance using the lexical and grammatical constructions available in his inventory. We have adopted the perspective of construction grammar [17], [18] and our team has designed and implemented a new formalism known as Fluid Construction Grammar (FCG). Construction grammar assumes that every rule in the grammar has both a semantic and a syntactic pole. This contrasts with a (generative) constituent structure grammar that specifies only syntax, and semantics is supposed to be defined separately by translation rules. The semantic pole of a construction specifies how meaning has to be built up in parsing or decomposed in production, and the syntactic pole how the form has to be analysed in parsing or built in production. An important feature of FCG is that rules are truly bi-directional. The same rule can be used both for parsing and production, even if it involves hierarchy ([13]). The syntactic and semantic structure being built during parsing and production takes the form of feature structures and unify and merge are the basic operations that are used for expanding these feature structures through the application of rules, similar to widely used HPSG frameworks [19].

There is a systematic correspondence between constraint networks and grammar (explained in more detail in [20]) in the sense that (1) lexical items introduce the semantic objects used by constraints (for example prototypes, relations, categories, etc.), (2) first order constructions specify how these items are used, and

(3) higher order constructions combine these and establish linking of variables between them. We illustrate this with hand-coded examples because they make it easier to understand the underlying ideas, but the agents invent their own words, their own syntactic categories, etc.

The following FCG rule is an example of a lexical rule that associates a semantic object (the prototype [box]) with a stem.

```
(def-lex-stem rule [box]
  ((?top-unit
    (meaning (== (prototype ?prototype [box]))))
   ((J ?new-unit ?top-unit)
    (context (== (link ?prototype)))
    (sem-cat (prototype ?prototype))))
  <-->
  ((?top-unit
    (syn-subunits (== ?new-unit)))
   (?new-unit
    (form (== (stem ?new-unit "box"))))))
```

The left-pole contains a bit of semantic structure (introducing a prototype [box]) and a semantic category for it, and the right pole a bit of syntactic structure (introducing the stem "box" expressing this prototype).

A first order construction that uses prototypes is as follows.

```
(def-con-rule CommonNoun
  ((?top-unit
    (sem-subunits (== ?prototype-unit))
    (meaning (== (filter-set-prototype ?result-set ?context ?prototype))))
   (?prototype-unit
    (context (== (link ?prototype))))
   ((J ?new-unit ?top-unit (?prototype-unit))
    (context (== (link ?result-set ?context)))))
  <-->
  ((?top-unit
    (syn-subunits (== ?prototype-unit)))
   (?prototype-unit
    (syn-cat (== (lex-cat CommonNoun))))
   ((J ?new-unit ?top-unit (?prototype-unit))
    (syn-cat (== (constituent CommonNoun))))))
```

It handles another bit of meaning, namely a filter-set-prototype constraint and associates it with a Common Noun constituent. The context feature of a unit refers to variables that are linked from pending subunits to other subunits. Thus the ?prototype-unit introduces ?prototype which is used by the filter-set-prototype constraint to filter the set of objects bound to ?context and return a new set ?result-set. The syntactic pole requires that a unit is found whose lexical category is CommonNoun and it creates a CommonNoun constituent.

The next example is a higher order constraint which groups a CommonNoun constituent, as could have been built by the previous construction and an Adjective constituent, into a new CommonNoun constituent. The meaning pole of this construction does not add new meaning, except to link the appropriate variables coming from each of the subunits with each other. The J-operator creates a new unit that has the adjective and common noun units as its children and presents itself as having syntactic category 'constituent CommonNoun'. Therefore this new unit can recursively be combined as if it were a constituent CommonNoun.

```
(def-con-rule AdjNoun
  ((?top-unit
    (sem-subunits (== ?noun-unit ?adj-unit)))
   (?noun-unit
    (context (== (link ?filter-set ?input-set))))
   (?adj-unit
    (context (== (link ?target-set ?filter-set))))
   ((J ?new-unit ?top-unit (?noun-unit ?adj-unit))
    (context ((link ?target-set ?input-set)))))
  <-->
  ((?top-unit
    (syn-subunits (== ?noun-unit ?adj-unit)))
   (?noun-unit
    (syn-cat (== (constituent CommonNoun))))
   (?adj-unit
    (syn-cat (== (constituent Adjective))))
   ((J ?new-unit ?top-unit (?noun-unit ?adj-unit ))
    (syn-cat (== (constituent CommonNoun))))))
```

Constructions like these are systematically built up by agents, as explained in more detail in [20]. Whenever a construction for a semantic object or constructions for constraints that use them are missing, new ones are fabricated and the repertoire of each agent gradually expands. Note that these constructions so far contain virtually no syntax. They only contain very broad semantic subcategorisations (such as 'prototype') and basic syntactic categorisation (lexical categories and constituents).

When the speaker has produced an utterance that completely expresses the meaning, he first re-enters it, in other words he parses the utterance and checks whether the meaning is the same one as he wanted to express and whether no other problems come up (such as combinatorial explosions). Suppose that the speaker is entirely satisfied, then the utterance is transmitted to the hearer. The hearer attempts to parse the utterance and reconstruct a constraint network that can run over his own sensory world model. Both the parser and the constraint network are 'fluid' in the sense that they attempt to arrive at an interpretation even if there are unknown words, rules missing, etc. Based on feedback in the language game and on constraints coming from the language, the hearer reconstructs as well as possible the meanings that are compatible with the joint attention frame (the shared motives, communicative goal, and physical situation) and uses that to reconstruct missing rules. Because speaker and hearer invent new constructions all the time, incompatibilities are bound to arise, but these are flushed out by the lateral inhibition dynamics that we use in all our experiments. It is based on increasing success of winning inventory items (concepts, constraint networks, words, grammatical constructions, etc.) while decreasing competing solutions. The current experiment is based on an operational implementation of all this (reported in more detail in [20]) and we now move beyond these capabilities to focus on the problem of combinatorial explosions.

The bootstrapping of a language system is an extraordinarily difficult undertaking for a group of agents and it is greatly aided if they start simple and then increase complexity as they master basics. This growth in complexity can be regulated by the agents themselves, who monitor success and then increase challenge (based on the 'autotelic principle' described in [21]). In the language game implemented for the current experiment the speaker has to talk about an object in the shared context between the speaker and the hearer. Assume the speaker wishes to talk about a particular object in the context, e.g. a ball. Depending on the shared context the required utterance can range from very simple (e.g. "ball" when there is only one ball) to more complex (e.g. "big ball" when there are multiple balls but it is the only big one). Even spatial relation may need to be expressed to discriminate the object. The most complex utterances that can be construed in the current experiment are combinations of a spatial relation and Adjective-Noun constructions rendering utterances like "big ball next-to red box". It is this complexity that the agents can regulate, so they won't start talking about " big ball next to red box" until they are confident in talking about more simple scenes.

3   From a Lexical to a Grammatical Language

We now start by considering a lexical language, which is one where no grammatical constructions are built at all. When words are missing, agents execute repair strategies to invent new words (as speaker) or adopt them (as hearer). In the language game constructed for these experiments we speak of communicative success when the speaker can produce an utterance so that the hearer can infer the exact same meaning by interpreting this utterance. In the first experiment as meanings become more complex, lexical items are built for the total meaning as in holistic coding. Results for experiments for 5 runs with 5 agents playing 4000 games are shown in figure 2. We see that quite quickly agents reach a high level of communicative success and the lexicon becomes optimal after about 1500 games. Since there are about 13 basic semantic objects (prototypes, categories, relations) in the example domain, an optimal lexicon just for the semantic objects is around 13 words.

But challenge is increasing steadily and communicative success starts to drop. In response, the lexicons of the agents begin to increase as they use holistic coding to cope with the more complex meanings. If we continue the experiment we see

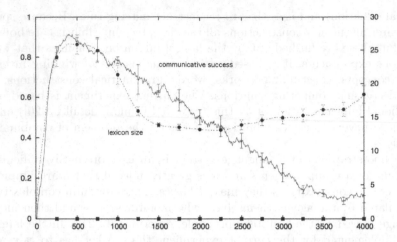

Fig. 2. Experiments where 5 agents use a purely lexical language to bootstrap a communication system. It is initially successful but cannot cope when the complexity of meanings begins to increase.

that communicative success climbs back up, but only at the expense of a much larger lexicon that is slower to get off the ground, more difficult to learn, and requiring more memory. Clearly it would be better if agents recruit strategies based on exploitation of grammar.

This happens in the second experiment (figure 3). In this experiment agents build grammatical constructions, for example to combine adjective-like semantic objects (categories) and noun-like predicates (prototypes) as in "big ball". The constructions are triggered by the need to express explicitly equalities between variables (as explained in [2]). The lexicon shows the same overshoot in the beginning and then stabilisation around 13 words as competing words are resolved and lexical coherence reached. The necessary grammatical constructions are built early on. They are similar to the Adj-Noun constructions above, i.e. without significant syntax. Only two constructions are needed so far and agents quickly reach agreement on them. The figure also shows 'grammaticality', this is the running average of number of utterances that make use of grammatical constructions. We see that the agents are able to cope with increasing complexity but it comes again at a price. The search space consisting of all applicable grammatical constructions steadily increases during parsing because there are multiple ways in which constructions can be applied. Because the interpretation is no longer guaranteed to be deterministic this also creates the possibility that the hearer has multiple interpretations at the end of the game. In this case we speak of communicative success only when the hearer is able to pick the correct one by inspecting his world model. It is however the growth of the search space that in the current experiment creates the need to recruit mechanisms to dampen the search as shown in the next experiment.

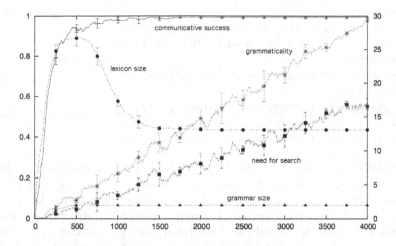

Fig. 3. Experiments where 5 agents use grammatical constructions in addition to a lexicon. They are now able to maintain communicative success even as complexity of meanings increases. But this again comes at a price because the agents have to search through the space of applicable grammatical constructions. This is expressed by the 'need for search', which is a running average of the number of utterances that couldn't be interpreted deterministically. In other words, that required search.

4   Diagnosing and Repairing Combinatorial Explosions

After the speaker produced an utterance he does not immediately utter it for interpretation by the hearer but instead interprets his own utterance himself. The difference with normal interpretation being that the speaker however knows the intended meaning and therefore has a much easier task interpreting his own utterance then the hearer will. We call this special kind of interpretation "re-entrance" [22]. During re-entrance the speaker builds new constructions if his interpreted meaning contains variables that should have been equal but are not. But re-entrance can also be used to diagnose whether search would be taking place in the hearer. For example, for "big small ball box", the Adjective-Noun construction triggers twice, creating a search space with two different possible interpretations: (1) "big box - small ball", and (2) "small box - big ball". The speaker knows which interpretation is intended. He can therefore analyse the choice point where a particular construction could match more than once and introduce additional syntax so as to avoid such choice in the future. In the present experiment, the speaker remedies the situation by imposing word order.

Concretely if a conflict arises between two Adjective-Noun constructions, the speaker knows that the syntactic pole of this construction is not specific enough and chooses (randomly) an order between the noun and adjective units and expands the syntactic pole to become as follows:

```
((?top-unit
  (syn-subunits (== ?noun-unit ?adj-unit))
  (form (== (meets ?noun-unit ?adj-unit))))
 (?noun-unit
  (syn-cat (== (constituent CommonNoun))))
 (?adj-unit
  (syn-cat (== (constituent Adjective))))
 ((J ?new-unit ?top-unit (?noun-unit ?adj-unit ))
  (syn-cat (== (constituent CommonNoun)))))
```

The only difference with the old Adjective-Noun construction is the addition of a form constraint in the top-unit. This form constraint requires that the noun unit 'meets' the adjective unit, i.e. has to come right before it. After the speaker has diagnosed and repaired his own inventory of constructions he restarts production. Because he added the form constraint, the speaker can no longer choose any combination of the four lexical entries but can only choose between "box big ball small" or "ball small box big" which both have the same meaning and therefore pose no real conflict.

Because there is no telepathy the hearer is not aware of the diagnosing and repairing the speaker went through. The hearer will parse the utterance and (if all goes well) still arrive at two possible interpretations for "box big ball small". However, to disambiguate, he can check against his world model which one of these is valid in the current situation. Having recovered the 'correct' interpretation, the hearer goes back to the constructional choice point that gave rise to search and takes the syntactic features used in the speaker's utterance (i.e. the word order) as a clue to tighten up the construction himself. In a community

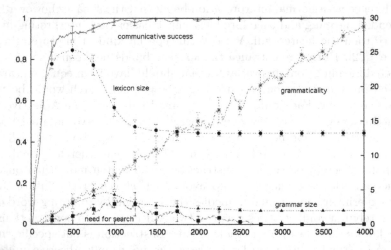

Fig. 4. Experiments where 5 agents now tighten grammatical constructions with additional syntax in order to avoid combinatorial search. We see a drastic reduction in search needed, even till the point (after the 2700th game) that parsing becomes deterministic in all cases.

of agents there will be different word-orders competing but the mechanism of lateral inhibition also used to drive the lexicon towards coherence will eliminate those that are less successful and grammatical coherence self-organises.

These repair strategies are seen at work in the next experiment (figure 4). We see again a rapid climb of communicative success in the beginning and overshoot in lexicon size, which becomes optimal. At the same time we see emergence of grammatical constructions. There is also an overshoot (in the sense of more constructions circulating in the population than strictly needed) because there are different ways to add syntax to a construction (e.g. Adj-Noun versus Noun-Adj order). The competing syntax is however flushed out due to lateral inhibition. The most important point, seen in the bottom graph, is that the search space is now completely under control and the grammar becomes deterministic.

5   Conclusion

This paper has argued that grammar is not imposing arbitrary structure on lexical items but that it is motivated by the need to solve certain issues that arise in communication among embodied autonomous agents. One obvious issue is that combinatorial explosions occur during parsing which need to be dampened as fast as possible, otherwise memory and processing time may reach such a level that the hearer has to give up. Additional syntactic constraints help because they provide cues that the hearer can use to cut down parse avenues that are not intended by the speaker. Syntactic constraints can take the form of word order constraints, agreement, or semantic and syntactic subcategorisation. The paper has substantiated this argument by showing a working implementation based on Fluid Construction Grammar.

Acknowledgment

The research reported here has been conducted at the Artificial Intelligence Laboratory of the Vrije Universiteit Brussel (VUB) and at the Sony Computer Science Laboratory in Paris. Partial funding for the Sony CSL work has come from the EU FET-ECAgents project 1940. We are very much indebted to Joachim De Beule for help in the technical foundations for the experiments reported here.

References

1. Minett, J. W. and Wang, W. S-Y. (2005) Language Acquisition, Change and Emergence: Essays in Evolutionary Linguistics. City University of Hong Kong Press: Hong Kong.
2. Steels, L. (2005) The emergence and evolution of linguistic structure: from lexical to grammatical communication systems. Connection Science, 17(3-4):213–230.
3. Langacker, R. (1990) Concept, Image, and Symbol: The Cognitive Basis of Grammar. Berlin and New York: Mouton de Gruyter.
4. Goldberg, A. (2006) Constructions at Work. Oxford University Press, Oxford.

5. Jackendoff, R. (1996) The Architecture of the Language Faculty. The MIT Press, Cambridge Ma.
6. Nowak, M.A., N. Komarova, P. Niyogi (2001) Evolution of universal grammar. Science, 291:114-118, 2001
7. Smith, K., Kirby, S., and Brighton, H. (2003). Iterated Learning: a framework for the emergence of language. Artificial Life, 9(4):371-386.
8. Steels, L. (2005) What triggers the emergence of grammar? A. Cangelosi and C.L. Nehaniv (ed.) (2005) Proceedings of the Second International Symposium on the Emergence and Evolution of Linguistic Communication (AISB 2005 Convention, University of Hertfordshire, Hatfield, UK). AISB.
9. Steels, L. (2002) Simulating the evolution of a grammar for case. Fourth International Conference on the Evolution of Language, Harvard University.
10. De Beule, J. and B. Bergen (2006) On the Emergence of Compositionality. Cangelosi, A., K. Smith and W.Smith (eds.) Sixth Conference on Evolution of Language Conference, World Scientific Pub. New York.
11. Steels, L. and M. Loetzsch (2006) Perspective Alignment in Spatial Language. In: K. Coventry, J. Bateman, and T. Tenbrink (eds.) Spatial Language in Dialogue. Oxford University Press, Oxford.
12. Steels, L. (2004) Constructivist Development of Grounded Construction Grammars Scott, D., Daelemans, W. and Walker M. (eds) (2004) Proceedings Annual Meeting Association for Computational Linguistic Conference. Barcelona. p. 9-19.
13. De Beule, J. and Steels, L. (2005) Hierarchy in Fluid Construction Grammar. In Furbach U., editor, Proceedings of KI-2005, pages 1-15. Lecture Notes in Computer Science. Springer-Verlag, Berlin.
14. Steels, L. and J. Bleys (2005) Planning What To Say: Second Order Semantics for Fluid Construction Grammars. In: Proceedings of CAEPIA 2005, Santiago. LNAI Springer-Verlag, Berlin.
15. Tomasello (1995). Joint attention as social cognition. In Moore, C. and Dunham, P., (Eds.), Joint attention : its origins and role in development. Lawrence Erlbaum Associates.
16. Johnson-Laird, P.N. (1977) Procedural Semantics. Cognition, 5 (1977) 189-214.
17. Croft, William A. (2001). Radical Construction Grammar: Syntactic Theory in Typological Perspective. Oxford: Oxford University Press.
18. Bergen, B.K. and Chang, N.C.: Embodied Construction Grammar in Simulation-Based Language Understanding. In: Ostman, J.O. and Fried, M. (eds): Construction Grammar(s): Cognitive and Cross-Language Dimensions. John Benjamin Publ Cy., Amsterdam (2003)
19. Pollard, C. and I. Sag (1994) Head-Driven Phrase Structure Grammar. University of Chicago Press (1994)
20. Steels, L. and J. De Beule (2006) The Emergence of Hierarchy in Fluid Construction Grammar. submitted.
21. Steels, L. (2004b) The Autotelic Principle. In Fumiya, I. and Pfeifer, R. and Steels,L. and Kunyoshi, K., editor, Embodied Artificial Intelligence, Lecture Notes in AI (vol. 3139), pages 231-242, Springer Verlag. Berlin, 2004.
22. Steels, L. (2003) Language-reentrance and the 'Inner Voice'. Journal of Consciousness Studies, 10(4-5), pages 173-185.

Implementation of Biases Observed in Children's Language Development into Agents

Ryo Taguchi, Masashi Kimura, Shuji Shinohara, Kouichi Katsurada,
and Tsuneo Nitta

Graduate School of Engineering, Toyohashi University of Technology
1-1 Hibariga-oka, Tempaku-cho, Toyohashi-city, 441-8580 Japan
{taguchi, kimura, shinohara, katurada, nitta}
@vox.tutkie.tut.ac.jp
http://www.vox.tutkie.tut.ac.jp/

Abstract. This paper describes efficient word meaning acquisition for infant agents (IAs) based on learning biases that are observed in children's language development. An IA acquires word meanings through learning the relations among visual features of objects and acoustic features of human speech. In this task, the IA has to find out which visual features are indicated by the speech. Previous works introduced stochastic approaches to do this, however, such approaches need many examples to achieve high accuracy. In this paper, firstly, we propose a word meaning acquisition method for the IA based on an Online-EM algorithm without learning biases. Then, we implement two types of biases into it to accelerate the word meaning acquisition. Experimental results show that the proposed method with biases can efficiently acquire word meanings.

1 Introduction

The demand for language-mediated natural communication with PDAs, navigation systems, and robots is increasing in line with the development and spread of IT technologies. In the study of communication, an important problem has been how to handle the meanings of symbols such as words and gestures and transfer them without misunderstanding. In classical AI such as the Semantic Net and Physical Symbol System, the meaning of each symbol is defined by another symbol, so some external systems are needed to connect the meaning with real objects in such schemes. This is called the "Symbol Grounding Problem" [1, 2]. One of the solutions to this problem is to give a computer, or an agent, the capability to acquire symbols representing the relations among visual features of objects and acoustic features of human speech through interactions with the real world. Moreover, in language-mediated natural communication between a human and an agent, the two parties need to share the symbols held by each other in order to correctly understand what the other party wants to say.

Recently, studies on word meaning acquisition, in which a human teaches words to an agent through human–agent interaction, have begun. Akaho et al. [3], Roy et al. [4] and Iwahashi et al. [5] respectively proposed mechanisms to acquire the word meanings that represent relations among visual features of objects and acoustic features of

P. Vogt et al. (Eds.): EELC 2006, LNAI 4211, pp. 89–99, 2006.

human speech using a machine learning method. By applying these mechanisms, agents can learn and understand word meanings in the real world.

Such studies are divided into two types: (1) an object has a name [4], and (2) an object has some features which have corresponding words and the words are taught [3, 5]. For example, suppose that a human shows an agent a picture of a rabbit: in type (1) the human speaks "rabbit", while in type (2) the human speaks "rabbit" together with "white" or "big". Type (2) is a more difficult task than type (1) because the agent has to find out which visual features are represented by a word. In studies [3] and [5], the features are identified by using stochastic methods, however, these methods need a lot of examples. To overcome this problem, we propose a word meaning acquisition mechanism with two types of learning biases, the mutual exclusivity bias [8] and the shape bias [9], which are observed in children's language development. When the agent with learning biases watches an object and listens to an unknown word at the same time, the agent can guess its word meaning based on the meanings of other known words. Therefore, the biases are expected to make the word meaning acquisition more efficient than a stochastic only approach.

In section 2, we propose a basic word meaning acquisition mechanism using an Online-EM algorithm without biases. In section 3, we discuss formulations and implementation of the biases. In section 4, we conduct experiments to test the effectiveness of the bias. Lastly, in section 5, we describe the conclusions of this paper.

2   Word Meaning Acquisition Mechanism

2.1   Infant Agent

A human infant learns language mainly based on the triadic relationship among him/herself, his/her parent, and an object. This relationship is also important in natural communication between a human and an agent because the agent can directly sense the object's features, share them with the human, and acquire word meanings on the basis of them. For this reason, we have developed Infant Agents (IAs) that are modeled after the language acquisition process of human infants. In the learning process of an IA, a human, who is a teacher, shows an object to the IA and speaks a word that represents certain features of the object. The IA perceives both human speech and the object's features through its audio-visual sensors, and acquires the relationship between visual information and auditory information. The IA regards this relationship as a meaning of the word.

2.2   IA's Sensory Information

(1) Visual Information (see Fig. 1)
When a human shows an object, an IA receives it as a bitmap image and extracts the visual features from it. These features are divided into three types of attributes (shape, hue and lightness) by the difference of extraction procedures. Hue and lightness features are obtained by converting RGB signals of the image into HSV colors that contain hue, saturation and value (lightness). The shape feature is

obtained by the following process. First, three monochrome images with different resolutions (100%, 50%, 25%) are generated from the original image. Then, contour exaction is applied to each image. Lastly, 25-dimensional Higher-order Local Auto-Correlation (HLAC) features are calculated for each image [6], and the total of 75 (25×3) dimensional features is used as the shape feature.

(2) Auditory Information

In this paper, words from keyboard input are used as auditory information to avoid experimental complexity caused by recognition errors.

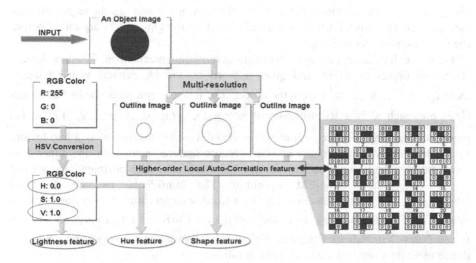

Fig. 1. Visual Information of an IA

2.3 Word Meaning Acquisition

In our approach, a human teaches a word related to the IA's sensory information such as "circle", "red", "dark", etc. For example, the word "circle" represents a set of specific shapes or a specific range of shape features. Note that it does not represent other attributes such as hue and lightness. However, at this point, the IA is not taught which features of objects are represented by each word. Therefore, the IA has not only to learn the range, but also to identify the target attributes represented by each word.

Learning the range is easier than identifying the target attributes because an IA can calculate the range by counting co-occurrence frequency between a word and visual features. In this paper, we express this co-occurrence frequency by probability distributions of the frequency with respect to each attribute. We apply the Online-EM algorithm [7] for calculating probability distributions in which probability distributions are generated, modified, and sometimes deleted through the E-steps and M-steps of the EM algorithm.

Identifying the target attributes needs more complex calculation. If an attribute is a target of a word, its probability distribution will be different from the ones obtained from other words because the distribution is calculated from the specific objects that are to be distinguished from others by the attributes. For example, when an IA learns the word "circle", the probability distribution of the shape attribute will be learned from shape features of only circle objects. On the other hand, the probability distribution of the hue attribute will not show any specific difference from the one obtained from "square" or "dark", because they are not the targets of each word and will be similarly learned from various hue features. Therefore, in this paper, we use the difference between the probability distribution of an attribute and that obtained from all objects (we call this distribution the Basis Distribution) to identify the target attribute (see Fig. 2). The Basis Distribution is calculated by the Online-EM algorithm before the word meaning acquisition.

Here, we formalize our word meaning acquisition mechanism. When a human shows an object to an IA and gives a word w, the IA extracts visual features $\mathbf{X} = (\mathbf{x}^1, \mathbf{x}^2, ..., \mathbf{x}^i, ..., \mathbf{x}^I)$ from the object. The index i represents one of I attributes (I=3) and each $\mathbf{x}^i$ is a J(i)-dimensional vector ($\mathbf{x}^i = (x_1^i, x_2^i, ..., x_j^i, ...x_{J(i)}^i)$). In this paper, $\mathbf{x}^1$ is a shape feature vector with seventy five dimensions, $\mathbf{x}^2$ is a hue feature vector with one dimension, and $\mathbf{x}^3$ is a lightness feature vector with one dimension. Then the IA calculates probability distribution $P(\mathbf{x}^i|w)$ for each attribute i and a word w by using the Online-EM algorithm. The confidence measure $Conf(i,w)$ ($0 \leq Conf(i, w) \leq 1$) that indicates whether a word w targets attribute i or not, is calculated. $Conf(i,w)$ is given by using the correlation $Corr(i,w)$ ($0 \leq Corr(i, w) \leq 1$) between Basis Distributions $P(\mathbf{x}^i)$ and $P(\mathbf{x}^i|w)$. The correlation $Corr(i,w)$ and the confidence measure $Conf(i,w)$ are calculated as follows.

$$Corr(i, w) = \left(\frac{1}{J(i)}\right) \sum_{j=1}^{J(i)} \int P(x_j^i) P(x_j^i|w) dx_j^i \qquad i = 1, 2, 3 \tag{1}$$

$$Conf(i, w) = 1 - Corr(i, w) \qquad i = 1, 2, 3 \tag{2}$$

If $Conf(i,w)$ is less than a threshold Th_i, the attribute i is determined as a non-target attribute of a word w. When an object is shown to an IA, the occurrence probability of a word w $P(w | \mathbf{X})$ is calculated by the next equation.

$$P(w|\mathbf{X}) = P(w) \prod_{i \in \text{arg}[Conf(i,w) > Th_i]} \frac{P(\mathbf{x}^i | w)}{P(\mathbf{x}^i)} \tag{3}$$

where $P(w)$ is probability of a word w.

If a word w has a higher value of $P(w | \mathbf{X})$ than those of the other words that have the same set of target attributes as w, the IA considers the word w as a word representing the features of the object.

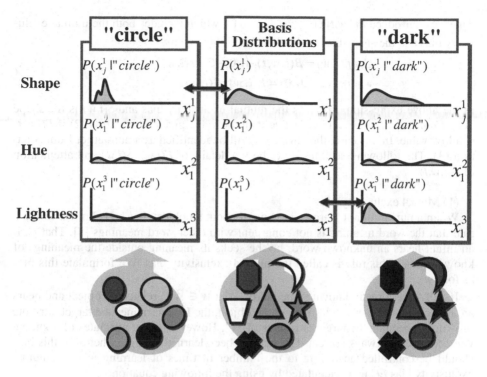

Fig. 2. Word meaning acquisition using stochastic methods

3 Implementation of Learning Bias

3.1 Learning Bias Observed in Children's Language Development

The philosopher Quine pointed out the following problem. If an unknown word is given to a child in some context, it is very difficult to determine the referent indicated by the word because there are huge amounts of candidate hypotheses to be a referent. However, when a child hears a word for the first time, he/she does not test these hypotheses completely but understands the referent of the word quickly with few errors. This is called fast mapping. Currently, many psychologists consider that fast mapping is executed based on some learning biases which children have inherently [8,9,10,11]. These biases may also be important for the agent that acquires word meanings in the real world. In this paper, we incorporate two biases, the mutual exclusivity bias and the shape bias, into an IA to acquire word meanings efficiently.

3.2 Formulations and Implementation

In our framework, the above hypotheses correspond to combinations of attributes. To test these hypotheses (combinations of attributes), our IAs use the confidence measure $Conf(i,w)$. Therefore, biases should be some parameters that inhibit $Conf(i,w)$. In this paper, we introduce $B(i,w,t)$ ($0 \le B(i,w,t) \le 1$), which includes both the mutual exclusivity bias and the shape bias, to inhibit $Conf(i,w)$.

$$Conf(i,w) = B(i,w,t) \cdot (1.0 - Corr(i,w)) \qquad (4)$$
$$where \quad B(i,w,0) = E(i,w) \cdot S(i,w)$$

In the above expression, $E(i,w)$ is the mutual exclusivity bias and $S(i,w)$ is the shape bias. $Conf(i,w)$ becomes a lower value than the value given by equation (2) if $B(i,w,t)$ is a low value. In this case, the attribute i will be identified as a non-target from equation (3). The following sections describe the details of $E(i,w)$, $S(i,w)$ and attenuation of $B(i,w,t)$.

(1) Mutual exclusivity bias

When a human infant learns a new word about an object, he/she is known to use a rule that the word meaning is not congruent with other word meanings [8]. That is, if an infant hears an unknown word, he/she seeks its meaning outside the meanings of known words. This rule is called the mutual exclusivity bias. We formulate this bias as follows.

If an IA has already known some words **W'** ($w' \in W'$) related an object and hears an unknown word w when looking at the object, the IA determines the target attribute of w not to become the target attributes of **W'**. However, target attributes of a known word w' are not always correct if w' has not been learned enough. Therefore this bias should be controlled according to the number of times of learning w'. The mutual exclusivity bias $E(i,w)$ is calculated by using the following equation.

$$E(i,w) = \begin{cases} 1.0 & (\Theta_i \leqq Th_i) \\ 0.5 & (\Theta_i > Th_i) \end{cases} \qquad (5)$$
$$where \quad \Theta_i = \max_{w' \in W'} \left[\frac{Conf(i,w)}{1.0 + \exp\{-\alpha(t^{w'} - \beta)\}} \right]$$

Here, α and β are the parameters of the sigmoid function, and $t^{w'}$ represents the number of times learning w'.

(2) Shape bias

Human infants use another rule. When they hear a new word about an object, they tend to interpret the word as indicating the shape of the object. This is called the shape bias [9]. This bias can be formulated by inhibiting each $Conf(i,w)$ for non-shape attributes of the word as shown in equation (6). However, it is not used if the shape attribute has already been inhibited by the mutual exclusivity bias.

$$S(i,w) = \begin{cases} 1.0 & (i = 1 \, or \, E(i,w) < 1.0) \\ 0.5 & (i \neq 1) \end{cases} \qquad (6)$$

(3) Attenuation of bias

The above two biases may decrease the efficiency of word meaning acquisition depending on the order of teaching words. For example, if a human teaches a word representing color (hue or lightness) of an object first, the IA will assume that the word represents the shape of the object due to the shape bias. To avoid this problem, we attenuate $B_i^w(t)$ according to the number of learning t as follows.

$$B(i, w, t) = B(i, w, t-1) + \gamma[1.0 - B(i, w, t-1)] \qquad (7)$$

where γ is an attenuation rate ($0 < \gamma < 1$).

4 Experiments

4.1 Experimental Setup

In the experiments, we prepared 1,080,000 objects with different features (Fig. 3 shows a part of them). Each object has one of 108 shape features, one of 100 grada-tions of hue features, and one of 100 levels of lightness features. We assume that each attribute is represented by 7 words, and so an IA is taught a total of 21 words such as "circle", "square", "red", and so on. Note that each word targets only an attribute and does not have duplicated meanings. We taught the words according to the following three types of teaching sequence.

Table 1. Parameters used in the experiments

Th_1	0.2
Th_2	0.4
Th_3	0.4
α	0.5
β	20
γ	0.1

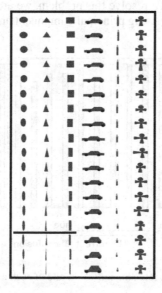

Fig. 3. Objects used in the experiments

TS1: Taught words are chosen randomly.

TS2: Seven shape words are taught first. After that, seven hue words are taught and then seven lightness words.

TS3: Seven hue words are taught first. After that, seven lightness words are taught and then seven shape words.

We evaluate the word meanings acquired by the IA each time we teach one word. In the evaluation, we show the IA 200 objects chosen randomly, and the IA speaks the words that represent the features of those objects. When the spoken words correctly represent the features of the object and their target attributes are correct, we consider that the IA has acquired correct word meanings. Table 1 shows parameters used in word meaning acquisition.

4.2 Evaluation of Word Meaning Acquisition Mechanism Without the Biases

We calculate correct rates and confusion rates to evaluate our basic word meaning acquisition mechanism without the biases. The confusion rate was calculated from the frequency that an IA had correctly identified the target attribute of a word but the IA used the word as having a different meaning. Figure 4 shows the correct rates and confusion rates of the word meanings that were acquired by the IA after 2,000 iterations of teaching according to the teaching sequence TS1.

The average of the correct rates was more than 90%, showing that the IA correctly acquired word meanings. However, the confusion rates of shape words were higher than those of hue and lightness concepts. Figure 5 shows the difficulty of correctly acquiring shape words (the horizontal axis represents the number of teaching while the vertical axis represents the correct rate). Shape words are more complex than hue and lightness because they are represented by 75-dimensional features. Moreover, the feature ranges of shape words are also narrower than others, and some parts of them overlap, causing confusion. To resolve this problem, we are now considering reducing the number of dimensions by using principal component analysis.

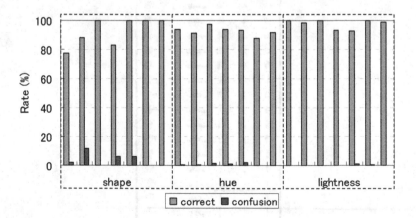

Fig. 4. Correct rate and confusion rate of each acquired word

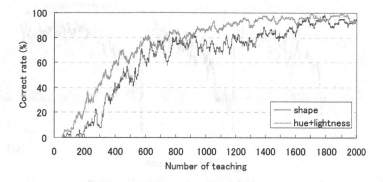

Fig. 5. Correct word rate of shape words and other words in the learning stage

4.3 Evaluation of the Biases

Figures 6 to 8 show the results of comparing between the presence and absence of the biases in the above condition TS1 to TS3. The horizontal axis represents the number of teaching while the vertical axis represents the correct word rate (%). These graphs show that the IA with the biases is able to learn word meanings more efficiently than without biases. When shape words are taught first (TS2), improvement of the correct word rate is quicker than the other conditions, because the shape bias is applied to the initial shape words and the mutual exclusivity bias is applied to subsequent words (see Fig. 7). On the other hand, when words are chosen randomly (TS1) or shape words are taught at the end (TS3), the shape bias is incorrectly applied to the hue and lightness words. However, in actuality, this was not found to have adverse influences and acquisition of shape words became faster because the IA was able to correctly determine target attributes by attenuating incorrect biases according to the number of learning. However, the most efficient word meaning acquisition is achieved by teaching shape words first.

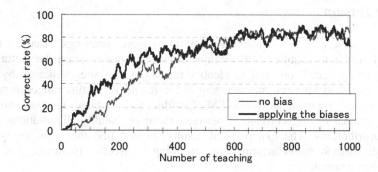

Fig. 6. Effectiveness of the biases in TS1

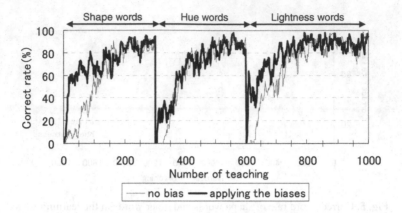

Fig. 7. Effectiveness of the biases in TS2

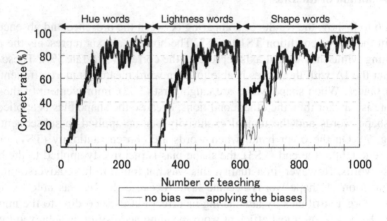

Fig. 8. Effectiveness of the biases in TS3

5   Conclusion

This paper described the efficient acquisition of word meanings based on learning biases. In order to acquire word meanings, an agent has to learn the feature range represented by each word and to identify the target attributes indicated by it. Our stochastic method for word meaning acquisition learns the feature ranges as probability distributions by using an Online-EM algorithm, and the target attributes are identified by comparing the correlation between these probability distributions and the Basis Distributions. The experimental results showed that the agent applying our stochastic method could acquire word meanings correctly. However, this method needs many examples.

In order to resolve this problem, we formulated two biases which are observed in children's language development, and implemented them into the agent. Although the effects of these biases depend on the teaching sequence, the results of comparative experiments showed that this has few adverse influences and the most efficient learning is achieved by teaching shape words first.

In a future work, we will implement the principle of contrast [10]; this is a widely-known bias which is expected to make the acquisition of hierarchical meanings more efficient.

Acknowledgments

This research was supported by a 21st Century COE Program Grant for "Intelligent Human Sensing".

References

[1] S. Harnad, The symbol grounding problem, Physica D 42, 1990, 335-346.
[2] R. Pfeifer and C. Scheier, Understanding Intelligence. The MIT Press, Cambridge, MA, 1999.
[3] S. Akaho et al., Concept acquisition from multiple information sources by the EM algorithm, IEICE Trans, J80-A(9), 1997, 1546-1553.
[4] D. Roy, Integration of speech and vision using mutual information, in Proc. ICASSP, Vol. 4, 2000, 2369-2372.
[5] N. Iwahashi, Language acquisition through a human-robot interface by combining speech, visual, and behavioral information, Information Sciences, Vol. 156, 2003, 109-121.
[6] N. Otsu and T. Kurita, A new scheme for practical, flexible and intelligent vision systems, Proc. IAPR Workshop on Computer Vision, 1988, 431-435.
[7] M. Sato and S. Ishii, On-line EM algorithm for the normalized Gaussian network, Neural Computation, 12(2), 2000, 407-432.
[8] E.M. Markman, Categorization and naming in children, MIT Press, 1989.
[9] B. Landau et al., The importance of shape in early lexical learning, Cognitive Development, 3, 1988, 299-321.
[10] E. Clark, The principle of contrast: A constraint on language acquisition. In B. MacWhinney (Ed.), Mechanisms of language acquisition, Hillsdale, NJ: Lawrence Erlbaum Assoc, 1987, 1-33.
[11] M. Imai and E. Haryu, The nature of word learning biases: From a cross linguistic perspective, In D.G. Hall & S. Waxman, (Eds.), Weaving a lexicon. MIT Press, 2004, 411-444.

Lexicon Convergence in a Population With and Without Metacommunication

Zoran Macura and Jonathan Ginzburg

Department of Computer Science,
King's College, London
The Strand, London WC2R 2LS
{zoran.macura, jonathan.ginzburg}@kcl.ac.uk

Abstract. How does a shared lexicon arise in population of agents with differing lexicons, and how can this shared lexicon be maintained over multiple generations? In order to get some insight into these questions we present an ALife model in which the lexicon dynamics of populations that possess and lack metacommunicative interaction (MCI) capabilities are compared. We suggest that MCI serves as a key component in the maintenance of a linguistic interaction system. We ran a series of experiments on mono-generational and multi-generational populations whose initial state involved agents possessing distinct lexicons. These experiments reveal some clear differences in the lexicon dynamics of populations that acquire words solely by introspection contrasted with populations that learn using MCI or using a mixed strategy of introspection and MCI. Over a single generation the performance between the populations with and without MCI is comparable, in that the lexicon converges and is shared by the whole population. In multi-generational populations lexicon diverges at a faster rate for an introspective population, eventually consisting of one word being associated with every meaning, compared with MCI capable populations in which the lexicon is maintained, where every meaning is associated with a unique word.

1 Introduction

A key feature of natural language is metacommunicative interaction (MCI)—utterance acts in which conversationalists acknowledge understanding or request clarification. The need to verify that mutual understanding among interlocutors has been achieved with respect to any given utterance—and engage in discussion of a clarification request if this is not the case—is one of the central organising principles of conversation [1,2]. However, hitherto there has been little work on the emergence and significance of MCI meaning. Communicative interaction is fundamental to evolution of grammar work, since it is interactions among communicating agents that leads an initial 'agrammatical' system to evolve into a grammar (with possible, concomitant phylogenetic modification; see e.g. [3,4]).

P. Vogt et al. (Eds.): EELC 2006, LNAI 4211, pp. 100–112, 2006.

However, given an I-language[1] perspective, the communicative aspect as such is not internalised in the grammar (though see [6]). Consequently, such models of evolution of grammar cannot explain the existence of forms whose meaning is intrinsically MCI oriented.

What significance does MCI have for linguistic interaction within a community? Pretheoretically, MCI is redundant in so far as the communication channel, i.e. that which mediates between speaker and addressee, is perfect or close to that. The need for MCI not only arises when the communication channel is noisy, it also arises when there is ambiguity in the referents of the communicative interaction.

Moreover, languages are ever changing. Utterances used in slightly various contexts can rapidly lead the language itself to change so much as to become unrecognisable in only a few generations [7].

Given this, acknowledgements, clarification requests (CRs) and corrections are a key communicative component for a linguistic community. They serve as devices for allaying worries about miscommunication (acknowledgements) or for reducing mismatches about the linguistic system among agents (CRs and corrections). That is, they serve as a device for ensuring a certain state of equilibrium or lack of divergence gets maintained within a linguistic community. The plausibility of this speculation can be assessed by converting it into more concrete questions such as the following:

(1) Given a community A where clarification requests do not get expressed, and community B where they do, how do the two communities evolve with respect to vocabulary drift. How does this vocabulary drift change once a gradual turnover of community members is introduced?

In previous work, we have shown how language converges for different types of populations in a mono-generational model [8]. In this paper we modify the set up in two significant ways: (a) the lexicon is continually dynamic (in our previous set up once a word is acquired, its meaning does not change) (b) there is generational turnover. As will become evident, this changes the results in a dramatic and quite unexpected way.

In the next section we describe the computational model, including how gradual turnover of agents is implemented. In Sect. 3 we present the experiments and assess the validity of the proposed model. Finally, in Sect. 4, we conclude.

2   The Model

The model we propose here is an extension of the model described in [8], with the main extensions being the introduction of a dynamic lexicon, and the implementation of a gradual turnover of agents. In our previous work we have shown how

---

[1] Following Chomsky (as clarified by Hurford), a distinction is sometimes made between 'I language' — language as represented in the brains of the population and 'E-language' — language that exists as utterances in the arena of use. Ginzburg and Sag [5] dispute the dichotomy particularly given the need for a view of language that accommodates MCI.

language converges for different types of populations within a single generation. In this type of model as there is no generational turnover of agents the transmission of language is horizontal, where the communication is between adult agents of the same generation (e.g. [6]). In multi-generational models such as the iterated learning model (e.g. [9,10]) language is vertically transmitted from one generation to the next, where the adult agents are allowed to speak to the child agents only. So in these models there is no horizontal communication (i.e. between adults of the same generation).

We present a model which implements both horizontal (adult-adult) and vertical (adult-child) language transmission (see [11] for a similar approach). The model contains an ALife environment in which the lexicon dynamics of populations that possess and lack MCI capabilities are compared. The environment is modelled loosely after the Sugarscape environment [12], in that it is a spatial grid containing different plants. This environment is resemblant to the mushroom environment in [13]. Plants can be perceived and disambiguated by the agents. Unlike the environments in [12,13], plants are not used as a food resource but only as topics for conversations. Agents walk randomly in the environment and when proximate to one another engage in a brief conversational interaction concerning plants visible to them.[2]

In the next section we look at the communication protocol in more detail, followed by a closer look at the implementation of generational agent turnover.

2.1 Communication

Agents can talk about the plants in the environment by making syntactically simple utterances—essentially one consisting of a single word. Every agents has an internal lexicon which is represented by an association matrix (see [10,14] for similar approaches). The lexicon stores the association scores for every meaning–representation pair (i.e. plant–word) based on individual past experiences. Agents don't have an invention capability therefore are only able to talk about the plants that they have a representation for.

Communication is a two sided process involving an intrinsic asymmetry between speaker and addressee: when talking about a plant in his field of vision, the speaking agent necessarily has a lexical representation of the plant (a word with the highest association score for the plant chosen as the topic), which he sends to the hearing agent. There is no necessity, however, that the addressee agent is able to interpret this utterance. If unable to do so (meaning that the hearing agent doesn't have the word in her lexicon, or that the plant it associates with the word is not in her context) the way that the agent tries to ground it depends on the agent's type.

Three types of communicative agents exist in the model; agents capable of making a clarification request (CR agents), agents incapable of doing so (introspective agents), and hybrid agents that use both CRs and introspection.

---

[2] An agent's field of vision consists of a grid of fixed size originating from his location. Hence proximate agents have overlapping but not identical fields of vision.

An introspective agent learns the meanings of words through disambiguation across multiple contexts. Upon hearing a word the agent looks around her and for every plant in her context (field of vision) she increases its association score with the word heard. This strategy is akin to the cross-situational statistical learning strategy used by inferential agents in [10], and to selfish learners in [14].

A CR agent on the other hand can resort to a clarification request upon hearing a word. If hearing the word for the first time (no associations with the word in her lexicon) or if there are no plants in her context, a clarification request is raised. Otherwise the agent checks the plants in her context and if there is a mismatch between her internal state and the context (agent thinks that the word heard refers to a plant not in her context) she again resorts to raising a clarification request. The speaking agent answers this clarification request by pointing to the plant intended, after which the hearing agent increases the association score of the word heard with the pointed plant. However, if the perceived plant is in her context then the hearing agent only reinforces its association score with the word heard without resorting to a clarification request.

A hybrid agent has a capability of either using the CR strategy or the introspective strategy. The agent only resorts to a clarification request if she cannot ground the word heard (there are no plants in her context or there is a mismatch between her internal state and the context). When hearing an unknown word and having some plants in the context the agent follows the introspective strategy.

After updating her lexicon[3] the hearing agent chooses the plant with the highest association score for the word heard. If this perceived plant matches with the speakers intended plant then the conversational interaction is deemed as a success. Neither agent is given any feedback on the outcome of their conversational interaction (see [10] for a similar approach). Note that there is no lateral inhibition of all competing associations after a conversational interaction, as is the case for guessing game models such as [6,14]. Another significant difference, specifically between a guessing game strategy (e.g. [14]) and the CR strategy, is in the way feedback is provided. In a guessing game, agents verify whether the intended and perceived meanings match by evaluating 'corrective feedback' provided to them by the system. On the other hand, in our model, feedback is given only on the initiative of the hearing agent. In other words, a hearing agent is given feedback only when it explicitly asks for it (by raising a clarification when there is an uncertainty in the meaning of the word heard).

2.2 Generational Turnover

A typical approach when modelling a multi-generational population is the introduction of agent turnover. The iterated learning model [9] is an example of a multi-generational model where the language transmission is vertical (i.e. from one generation to the next). In such models the adult agents are always the speakers and child agents are always the hearers. The agents play a number of

---

[3] Only the hearing agents update their lexicons after a conversational interaction.

language games, which defines the length of a generation. At the end of a generation, the adults are removed from the model, the children become the new adults, and new children are introduced. This way of implementing generational turnover in the iterated learning model and other multi-generational models (e.g. [15]) is very rigid.

We propose a multi-generational model which is more realistic and resembles closer a human community (e.g. a tribe). In order to extend the mono-generational model described in [8] into a multi-generational model, there is a need to introduce a gradual agent turnover. This is done by introducing mortality. Every agent has a maximum age which is set randomly when the agent is born, and it lies in the range of ±20% from agent to agent. Upon reaching his maximum age the agent dies. Thus it is very unlikely that the whole adult population dies out at the same time, as the adult agents are of different ages and have different maximum ages.

In order to keep the population size stable, we also introduce natality. So for every agent that dies a new infant agent is born to a random adult agent in the model. The infant agent inherits the parent's type (introspective, CR or hybrid). Infants have an empty lexicon, with no knowledge of the meaning space or the word space. Each infant follows the parent around and is only able to listen to the parent's dialogues with other agents. In fact an infant only hears the dialogues in which her parent is the speaker. So the assumption here is that an infant learns only the words uttered by her parent. An infant cannot be a speaker and learns exclusively by introspection. The reason for this restriction is that infants start without any knowledge of language, and before they can actively engage in conversations they need to have at least some knowledge of the language. Every infant agent has an adulthood age which is set randomly and is about a sixth of the agent's lifespan. The adulthood age was experimentally determined and it gives the infant enough time to reach a good enough grasp of the language, enabling her to actively participate in conversations with other agents. When reaching the adulthood age an infant stops following her parent and becomes an adult, meaning that she is able to walk around independently, engage in conversations with other adult agents and become a parent. An infant can die only if her parent reaches the maximum age and dies.

This multi-agent model implements both vertical and horizontal language transmission as adult agents can communicate with each other as well as parent agents can communicate with their children. There is no clear distinction of when a generation starts and ends, like in the other multi-generational models, because there is continual agent turnover which makes calculating the results more intricate (see Sect. 3).

3   Experimental Results

This section describes different setups and experiment results for the model described in Sect. 2. In order to test the questions raised in (1) we ran several experiments in which agents posses distinct lexicons, and clarification requesting (CR) and introspective capabilities.

Before creating a population of agents, the environment is created containing 20 different plants (which represent 20 different meanings). There are six instances of every plant and they are randomly distributed in the environment.

The population in the simulations described here is made up of 40 agents that are also randomly distributed in the environment at the start. 20% of the initial population is made up of infants (i.e. 8 infant agents). Agents form two different communities each of whose members initially share a common lexicon. The initial community lexicons are distinct from each other (in that no meaning has the same representation associated with it). Agents can be either of the same or different type within the community. Apart from the differences in the initial lexicons and types between the agents, all other properties are the same.

Once the simulation starts the agents begin walking randomly in the environment. At every tick (time step) an agent's age increase and the agent walks one step in a random direction. After moving an agent looks for other agents (that fall into his field of vision). If he sees another agent then two of them enter a dialogue where the 'see-er' is the speaker and the 'seen' is the addressee. After a dialogue the agent continues walking in a random direction. In one tick every agent goes through this process. When an agent reaches his maximum age he dies and a new infant is born.

The performance of the model is based upon these behaviours which are collected at regular intervals in a simulation run:

- *Lexical Accuracy*: the population average of correctly acquired words. A word is said to be correctly acquired if it is associated with the same meaning as in either of the two initial lexicons.
- *Meaning Coverage*: the average number of meanings expressible by the overall population. There is no requirement that the meanings have correct associations.
- *Word Coverage*: the average number of words expressible by the population (correctness not taken into account).
- *Communicative Success*: the percentage of successfully completed conversations. A successful conversation is when the intended meaning by the speaker matches the perceived meaning by the hearer.
- *Method of Acquisition*: the percentage of conversational interactions that follow the introspective strategy or the CR strategy.
- *Distinct Lexicons*: the total number of distinct lexicons in the population. A lexicon is distinct only if there is no other lexicon in the population with which it shares all plant-word associations, so even if two or more lexicons have 19 out of 20 same plant-word associations they are regarded as distinct.
- *Lexical Convergence*: the percentage of agents sharing a lexicon. Agents share a lexicon if and only if all the plant-word associations are the same in their respective lexicons. Lexical convergence of 1 implies that all the agents use the same words for every plant in their lexicons.

We ran four types of experiments with different population make-ups, namely introspective populations, CR populations, hybrid populations and mixed populations (made up of both introspective and CR agents in a 1:1 ratio). For all different experiments, 10 trial runs were carried out for statistical analysis.

Firstly, mono-generational experiments were carried out (Sect. 3.1) in order to see how lexicon changes within a single generation with infant agents and no mortality. Then multi-generational experiments (Sect. 3.2) were carried out to view the lexicon change on a longer timescale with a gradual turnover of agents.

3.1   Mono-generational Experiments

Mono-generational experiments were ran to see how the introduction of infant agents into the model affects the performance of different populations based on the behaviours described above. In these experiments the population was made up of 40 agents in total, 20% of which were infants. There was no mortality and the experiments were stopped after 100,000 ticks. Results were collected at every 1,000 ticks.

As can be seen in Fig. 1(a) the lexical accuracy for every population raises rapidly and reaches nearly 100% by 20,000 ticks. What this means is that out of 40 possible words[4] the populations are correctly acquiring around 99% of them. Communicative success (Fig. 1(b)) also rises similarly to the lexical accuracy. As agents acquire and strengthen their plant-word associations their lexicons become more similar and their communications more successful. The introspective population is slower than the others as learning less frequent words takes more time, but performancewise doesn't differ much from the CR or hybrid populations.

The meaning and word coverage for each population reaches 100% and there is no difference in the time it takes between the different populations. The graphs are very similar to the graphs in Fig. 1, thus not shown here.

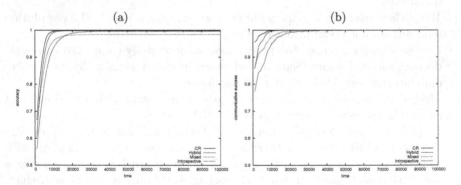

Fig. 1. (a) Lexical accuracy against time for mono-generational populations. There is a sharp initial increase in accuracy as new words are acquired correctly. (b) Communicative success also increases sharply and eventually reaches 100%.

---

[4] There are two initial communities, each with a distinct lexicon—for every plant the two communities are using a distinct word. As there are 20 different plants in the environment, the total number of distinct words in the population is 40.

The percentage of conversational interactions where introspective or clarification strategy have been used can be seen in Fig. 2(a). In an introspective population all the interactions follow the introspective strategy. In CR and hybrid populations clarifications are raised 45% of the time while 55% of the time they use introspection. In a mixed population the level of clarifications drops down to around 25% as half of the population is made up of introspective agents.

Figure 2(b) shows the number of distinct lexicons in the population. There is a sharp increase initially in the number of distinct lexicons. At the beginning of the simulation there are two distinct lexicons. As the agents speak they acquire novel plant-word associations so their lexicons diverge and the number of lexicons increases. Between 10,000 and 20,000 ticks there is a peak of 38 distinct lexicons indicating that only two agents in the population share a lexicon while everyone else has a distinct lexicon. As the time increases, agents have more conversations and the plant-word associations in their lexicons are strengthened, thus more and more agents use the same word for a given plant. This increases the lexical similarities between agents so the number of distinct lexicons starts to decrease. Eventually one lexicon becomes predominant in the population, where every agent uses the same word for a given plant. The CR and hybrid populations are fastest in converging to a shared lexicon, while it takes considerably longer for an introspective population to achieve this. A mixed population is a bit slower than the CR and hybrid, but the peak of distinct lexicons is smaller than in other populations (i.e. 35 distinct lexicons).

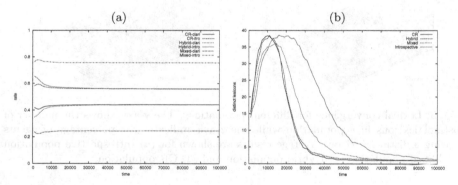

Fig. 2. (a) Percentage of conversational interactions that follow either the introspective or the CR strategy. (b) Number of distinct lexicons in the populations raise sharply reaching a peak of nearly one distinct lexicon per agent. As more dialogues occur within the population so does the number of lexicons drop, eventually stabilising at a single lexicon that is shared by the whole population.

The lexical convergence of different populations is shown in more detail by Fig. 3. The general trend is similar for different populations, where at the beginning there are many distinct lexicons shared by few agents (represented by peaks on the right side of the graphs). As time increases more and more agents start sharing a lexicon (represented by smaller peaks going from right to left), up to the point where every agent shares a single common lexicon (represented by peaks on the left side). What can be seen from Fig. 3(d) is that in a CR population there are considerably fewer peaks in the middle of the graph. This means that there are fewer competing lexicons, and that the convergence is faster than in other populations. Introspective population shown by Fig. 3(a) is on the other hand much slower in reaching a shared lexicon. The convergence of hybrid (Fig. 3(c)) and mixed (Fig. 3(d)) populations are similar.

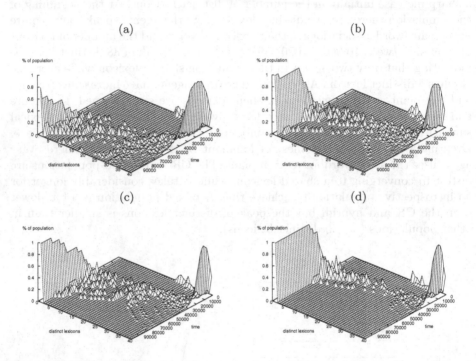

Fig. 3. Lexical convergence for different populations. The y-axis shows the number of distinct lexicons in a population while the z-axis indicates the percentage of agents sharing a distinct lexicon. Average results are shown for (a) Introspective population (b) Mixed population (c) Hybrid population and (d) CR population.

3.2   Multi-generational Experiments

The population in these experiments is kept constant to around 40 agents at any moment in time and the ratio of adults to infants is roughly 3:1. The agent life span is limited to around 30,000 ticks (±20%). This should reduce convergence and raise issues of generational variation. Results were taken at every 20,000 ticks. The simulation is stopped when it reaches 2 million ticks, which means after around 70 generations.

There are some clear differences between the mono-generational results and the multi-generational ones. The lexical accuracy initially drops very sharply for every population (Fig. 4(a)). At the beginning of the simulation there are a total of 40 words in the population (20 words from each community). As the words compete with one another there is a point when one word becomes dominant for a given plant and the majority of agents start using it. Thus the other competing words for the same meaning are used less frequently. The fact that the infant agents only learn the words uttered by their parents makes it very unlikely that the infrequently uttered words will pass to the next generation. After around three generations (100,000 ticks) the lexicon stabilises for every population except for the introspective.

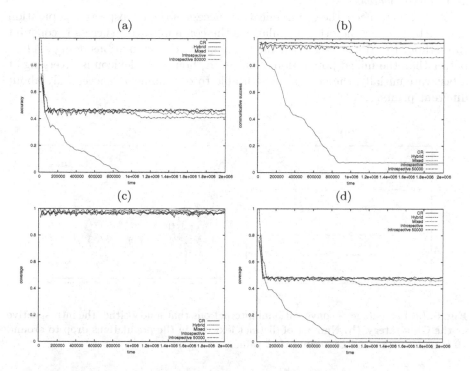

Fig. 4. Results for multi-generational populations showing (a) Lexical accuracy, (b) Communicative success, (c) Meaning coverage (d) Word coverage

The reason for this stabilisation can be explained by looking at Fig. 4(c) and Fig. 4(d). Fig. 4(c) shows that the meaning coverage for different populations is stable (all of them are able to express nearly every meaning). The word coverage however drops rapidly along with the lexical accuracy, as seen in Fig. 4(d). This is an indication that only the dominant words are surviving. Once the word coverage drops to 50% the lexicon stabilises. Around 20 different plants (Fig. 4(c)) and 20 different words (Fig. 4(d)) are expressible by the population at this stage, so every plant is associated with one word. These words can be successfully passed on to the next generation as they are used with greater frequency, causing the lexicon to stabilise.

This is not the case for the introspective population. The lexicon keeps diverging very rapidly and eventually reaches nearly 0% convergence (meaning that very few words have the association with the same plants as in the initial lexicon). Looking again at Fig. 4(c) and Fig. 4(d) explains why this happens. The word coverage also drops very sharply, where in the end only one word is known by the whole population. As the meaning coverage is comparable with other populations it can be derived that every plant in the population is associated with the single word expressible by the population, causing the lexical accuracy to decrease.

This in turn affects the communicative success of the introspective population (Fig. 4(b)). As for the other populations the communicative success is constant throughout the simulation, with the CR and hybrid populations doing slightly better than the mixed population. Thus even though the lexicon is diverging at a fast rate initially, the agents are still able to communicate successfully about different plants.

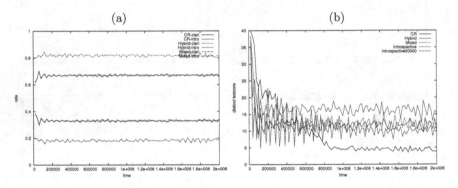

Fig. 5. (a) Percentage of conversational interactions that follow either the introspective or the CR strategy. (b) Number of distinct lexicons in the populations drop to around 10 lexicons then oscillate around that value.

The percentage of conversational interactions where introspective or CR strategy has been employed in shown by Fig. 5(a). The results are similar to monogenerational results with the clarification frequencies for all populations (except introspective populations) being slightly lower. The ascending order of CR frequency is: introspective 0%, mixed 20%, hybrid and CR 32%. It can be seen in Fig. 4 that the populations in which CRs can be expressed (CR, hybrid and mixed) perform much better than the ones in which CRs can't be expressed (introspective populations).

None of the populations converge to a single common shared lexicon as was the case in the mono-generational model (Fig. 5(b)). The reason is that infants make up around 20% of the population. As infant agents tend to have incomplete lexicons which differ form other agents, the number of distinct lexicons is higher than in mono-generational experiments.

Figure 6(b) shows a high degree of convergence to a common lexicon on the
adult part in a CR population. The infant lexicons are represented by peaks on
the right side of the graph and are used by about 20% of the population. The
majority of the population shares a common lexicon represented by the peaks
on the left side of the graph (between 20 and 35 agents). As for the introspective
population (Fig. 6(a)) it looks as the population has converged to a common
lexicon. This is true, but as we have shown one word is used for representing
every plant so the majority of agents converge to the same lexicon containing
only this single word.

(a)   (b)

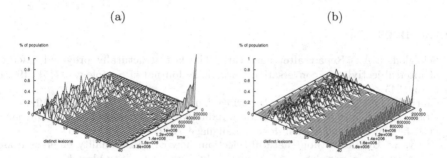

Fig. 6. Lexical convergence for (a) Introspective population and (b) CR population.
Results for hybrid and mixed populations are similar to those of CR populations thus
not shown here.

4   Conclusions and Future Work

In this paper we have discussed how metacommunicative interaction (MCI)
serves as a key component in the maintenance of a linguistic interaction system.
We ran a series of experiments on mono-generational and multi-generational populations in which lexicon dynamics of the populations that posses and lack MCI
capabilities were compared. We have shown that in a mono-generational model
all the populations converge to a common lexicon, although the introspective
population was the slowest to achieve this.

Limiting life span of agents in the multi-generational model raised some clear
differences in the lexicon dynamics between the MCI capable and incapable populations. The main effect demonstrated is that in the introspective populations
the lexicon diverges continually, ending up with a situation where every agent in
the population uses the same word to represent every plant in the environment.
On the other hand MCI capable populations are able to maintain the lexicon,
and the adult agents converge to a common lexicon.

While this confirms our initial theorising, much work remains to butress it as
a fundamental dividing line between MCI-ful and MCI-less populations. In our
current experiments we are seeing that increasing the maximum age of agents
in introspective populations to 50,000 improves the lexicon stability and convergence (see *Introspective 50000* results in Fig. 4). Another issue concerns the

influence of topography (e.g. variety of plants in the environment), as increasing the variety affects the performance of all populations. Further work needs to be done in order to get more insight into both of these issues. A more far reaching goal is to see whether using a syntactically complex language where the meaning space is potentially unbounded changes the results.

Acknowledgements

This work is supported by an EPSRC quota award to Macura. We would like to thank three reviewers for EELC06 for their very helpful comments.

References

1. Schegloff, E.A.: Repair after next turn: The last structurally provided defense of intersubjectivity in conversation. American Journal of Sociology **97**(5) (1992) 1295–1345
2. Clark, H.H.: Using Language. Cambridge University Press, Cambridge (1996)
3. Briscoe, E.J.: Grammatical acquisition: Inductive bias and coevolution of language and the language acquisition device. Language **76**(2) (2000) 245–296
4. Kirby, S.: Syntax without natural selection: how compositionality emerges from vocabulary in a population of learners. In Knight, C., Studdert-Kennedy, M., Hurford, J.R., eds.: The Evolutionary Emergence of Language: Social Function and the Origins of Linguistic Form. Cambridge University Press, Cambridge (2000) 303–323
5. Ginzburg, J., Sag, I.A.: Interrogative Investigations: the form, meaning and use of English Interrogatives. Number 123 in CSLI Lecture Notes. CSLI Publications, Stanford: California (2000)
6. Steels, L.: The origins of ontologies and communication conventions in multi-agent systems. Autonomous Agents and Multi-Agent Systems **1**(2) (1998) 169–194
7. Deutscher, G.: The Unfolding of Language: an evolutionary tour of mankind's greatest invention. Metropolitan Books, New York (2005)
8. Ginzburg, J., Macura, Z.: Lexical acquisition with and without metacommunication. In Lyon, C., Nehaniv, C.L., Cangelosi, A., eds.: Emergence of Communication and Language. Springer Verlag, London (in press)
9. Kirby, S., Smith, K., Brighton, H.: From ug to universals: linguistic adaptation through iterated learning. Studies in Language **28**(3) (2004) 587–607
10. Smith, A.D.M.: The inferential transmission of language. Adaptive Behavior **13**(4) (2005) 311–324
11. Vogt, P.: On the acquisition and evolution of compositional languages: Sparse input and the productive creativity of children. Adaptive Behavior **13**(4) (2005) 325–346
12. Epstein, J.M., Axtell, R.: Growing Artificial Societies: Social science from the bottom up. MIT Press (1996)
13. Acerbi, A., Parisi, D.: Cultural transmission between and within generations. Journal of Artificial Societies and Social Simulation **9**(1) (2006)
14. Vogt, P., Coumans, H.: Investigating social interaction strategies for bootstrapping lexicon development. Journal of Artificial Societies and Social Simulation **6**(1) (2003)
15. Vogt, P.: Stability conditions in the evolution of compositional languages: issues in scaling population sizes. In: Proceedings of the European Conference on Complex Systems. (in press)

Operational Aspects of the Evolved Signalling Behaviour in a Group of Cooperating and Communicating Robots

Elio Tuci[1], Christos Ampatzis[1], Federico Vicentini[2], and Marco Dorigo[1]

[1] IRIDIA, CoDE, Université Libre de Bruxelles,
Avenue F. Roosevelt 50, CP 194/6, 1050 Bruxelles, Belgium
{etuci, campatzi, mdorigo}@ulb.ac.be
http://iridia.ulb.ac.be/
[2] Robotics Lab, Mechanics Dept., Politecnico di Milano
P.zza Leonardo da Vinci 32, 20133 Milan, Italy
federico.vicentini@polimi.it

Abstract. This paper complements the results and analysis shown in current studies on the evolution of signalling and cooperation. It describes operational aspects of the evolved behaviour of a group of robots equipped with a different set of sensors, that navigates towards a target in a walled arena. In particular, analysis of the sound signalling behaviour shows that the robots employ the sound to remain close to each other at a safe distance with respect to the risk of collisions. Spatial discrimination of the sound sources is achieved by exploiting a rotational movement which amplifies intensity differences between the two sound sensors.

1 Introduction

In recent years, various types of agent-based simulation models have been employed to look at issues concerning communication in natural organisms and human language which can hardly be investigated with classic analytical models [1,2]. With respect to analytical and other simulation models, agent-based models do not require the designer to make strong assumptions about the essential features on which social interactions are based—e.g, assumptions concerning what communication is and about the requirement of individual competences in the domain of categorisation and naming. This is particularly true in models in which evolutionary computation algorithms are used to design artificial neural networks as agent's controllers. These models appear to be a valuable tool to study how semantics and syntax originate from the evolutionary and ontogenetic history of populations of autonomous agents [3,4]. In other words, the question is how the evolution and the development of perceptual, cognitive and motor capabilities relates to the emergence of a communicative system and possibly language in a population of agents.

By using evolutionary computation and neural network controllers, Tuci et al. [5] described an agent-based model which shows that communication, based

P. Vogt et al. (Eds.): EELC 2006, LNAI 4211, pp. 113–127, 2006.

on a simple sound signalling system and infrared sensors, evolves in a group of physically different robots required to cooperate in order to achieve a common goal. This paper complements the results and analysis shown in [5] by describing operational aspects of the communication system employed by the robots to perform that task. The experiment we considered is the following: three robots are placed in an arena, as shown in Figure 1. The arena is composed of walls and a light that is always turned on. The light can be situated at the bottom left corridor (*Env. L*) or at the bottom right corridor (*Env. R*). The robots are initialised with their centre anywhere on an imaginary circle of radius 12 cm centred in the middle of the top corridor, at a minimum distance of 3 cm from each other. Their initial orientation is always pointing towards the centroid of the group. By centroid we refer to the geometric centroid of the triangle formed by the centres of the three robots. The goal of the robots is to (i) navigate towards the light whose position changes according to the type of environment they are situated in, and (ii) avoid collisions.

The peculiarity of the task lies in the fact that the robots are equipped with different sets of sensors. In particular, two robots are equipped with infrared and sound sensors but they have no ambient light sensors. These robots are referred to as R_{IR} (see Figure 2a). The other robot is equipped with ambient light and sound sensors but it has no infrared sensors. We refer to this robot as R_{AL} (see Figure 2b). Robots R_{IR} can perceive the walls and other agents through infrared sensors, while the robot R_{AL} can perceive the light. Therefore, given the nature of the task, the robots are forced to cooperate in order to accomplish their goal. In principle, it would be infeasible for each of them to solve the task solely based on their own perception of the world. R_{AL} can hardly avoid collisions; R_{IR} can hardly find the light source. Thus, the task requires cooperation and coordination of actions between the different types of robots. Notice that the reason why we chose the group to be composed of two R_{IR} and one R_{AL} robot is that this intuitively seems to be the smallest group capable of spatially arranging itself adaptively in order to successfully navigate the world. Although the robots differ with respect to their sensory capabilities, they are homogeneous with respect to their controllers. That is, the same controller, synthesised by artificial evolution,

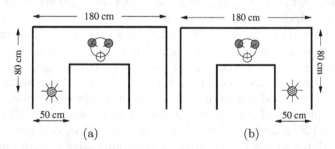

(a)   (b)

Fig. 1. (a) *Env. L*; (b) *Env. R*. The white circle represents robot R_{AL} and the grey circles represent the robots R_{IR}. The thick lines represent the walls, and the filled circles with spikes at the bottom left and right represents the light in each environment.

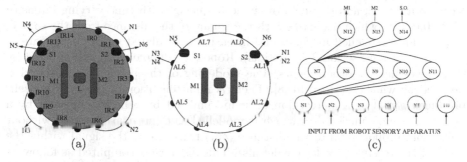

Fig. 2. (a) The simulated robots R_{IR}; (b) The simulated robots R_{AL}; (c) the network architecture. Only the connections for one neuron of each layer are drawn. The input layer of R_{IR} takes readings as follows: neuron N_1 takes input from the infrared sensors $\frac{IR_0+IR_1+IR_2}{3}$, N_2 from $\frac{IR_4+IR_5+IR_6}{3}$, N_3 from $\frac{IR_8+IR_9+IR_{10}}{3}$, N_4 from $\frac{IR_{12}+IR_{13}+IR_{14}}{3}$, N_5 from sound sensor S_1, and N_6 from sound sensor S_2. The input layer of R_{AL} takes readings as follows: N_1 and N_2 take input from ambient light sensors AL_1, N_3 and N_4 take input from AL_2, N_5 from S_1, and N_6 from S_2. M_1 and M_2 are respectively the left and right motor. L is the loud-speaker (i.e., the sound organ).

is cloned in each member of the group. Both types of robots are equipped with a sound signalling system (more details in Section 1.1). However, contrary to other studies (see [6,7]) we do not assume that the agents are capable of distinguishing their own sound from that of the other agents. The sound broadcasted into the environment is perceived by the agent through omnidirectional microphones. Therefore, acoustic signalling is subject to problems such as the distinction between own sound from those of others and the mutual interference due to lack of turn-taking (see [8]).

The goal of this paper is to try to reveal operational aspects of the communication system (e.g., causal relationships between sound signals and behaviour) used by the robots (i) to remain close to the others without colliding, and (ii) to make actions which bring the group closer to the target.

1.1 The Simulated Agents

The controllers are evolved in a simulation environment which models some of the hardware characteristics of the real *s-bots*. The *s-bots* are small wheeled cylindrical robots, 5.8 cm of radius, equipped with a variety of sensors, and whose mobility is ensured by a differential drive system (see [9] for details). Robot R_{IR} makes use of 12 out of 15 infrared sensors (IR_i) of an *s-bot*, while robot R_{AL} uses the ambient light sensors (AL_1) and (AL_2) positioned at $\pm 67.5°$ with respect to the orientation of the robot (see Figure 2a and 2b). The signal of the infrared sensor is a function of the distance between the robot and the obstacle. Light sensor values are simulated through a sampling technique (see [10]).

All robots are equipped with a loud-speaker (L) that is situated in the centre of the body of the robot, and with two omnidirectional microphones (S_1 and S_2), placed at $\pm 45°$ with respect to the robot's heading. Sound is modelled as an instantaneous, additive field of single frequency with time-varying intensity ($\eta_i \in [0.0, 1.0]$) which decreases with the square of the distance from the source, as previously modelled in [8]. Sound intensity is regulated by the firing rate of neuron $N14$ (see Section 2 for details). Robots can perceive signals emitted by themselves and by other agents. The modelling of the perception of sound is inspired by what described in [8]. There is no attenuation of intensity for self-produced signal. The perception of sound emitted by others is affected by a "self-shadowing" mechanism which is modelled as a linear attenuation without refraction, proportional to the distance (δ_{sh}) travelled by the signal within the body of the receiver (see [8] for details). This distance is computed as follows:

$$\delta_{sh} = \delta_{sen}(1 - A), \qquad 0 \leq A < 1, \qquad A = \frac{\delta^2 - R^2}{\delta_{sen}^2} \tag{1}$$

where δ_{sen} is the distance between the sound source and the sensor and δ is the distance between the sound source and the centre of the body of the receiver, and R is the robot's radius (see also Figure 3). The "self" component of the sound signal is simply equal to η_i. In order to calculate the "non-self" component, we firstly scale the intensity of sound emitted by the sender (η_j) by applying the inverse square law with respect to the distance between the sound source and the microphones of the receiver. Subsequently, we multiply the scaled intensity with an attenuation factor ψ which ranges linearly from 1 when $\delta_{sh} = 0$ to 0.1 when $\delta_{sh} = 2R$. To summarise, the reading $\hat{S}_{is}$ of each sound sensor s of robot i is computed as follows:

$$\hat{S}_{is} = \text{self} + \text{non-self}; \qquad \begin{array}{l} \text{self} = \eta_i \\ \text{non-self} = \sum_{\substack{j \in [1,3] \\ j \neq i}} \eta_j \frac{R^2}{\delta_{sen}^2} \psi \end{array} \tag{2}$$

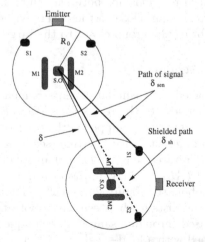

Fig. 3. This picture has been adapted from [8]. It shows the working principles of the self-shadowing mechanism.

The auditory receptive field of each microphone is bounded within the following interval $\hat{S}_{is} \in [0, 1]$. Therefore, the sound receptor can be saturated by the "self" emitted sound in case a robot emits at its highest intensity ($\eta_i = 1.0$). If the sound sensor is saturated by the "self" component, it is not possible for this robot to perceive sound signals emitted by others. Concerning the function that updates the position of the robots within the environment, we employed the Differential Drive Kinematics equations, as presented in [11]. 10% uniform noise was added to all sensor readings, the motor outputs and the position of the robot. The characteristics of the agent-environment model are explained in detail in [12].

2   The Controller and the Evolutionary Algorithm

The agent controller is composed of a network of five inter-neurons and an arrangement of six sensory neurons and three output neurons (see Figure 2c). The sensory neurons receive input from the agent sensory apparatus. Thus, for robots R_{IR}, the network receives the readings from the infrared and sound sensors. For robots R_{AL}, the network receives the readings from the ambient-light and sound sensors. The inter-neuron network (from N_7 to N_{11}) is fully connected. Additionally, each inter-neuron receives one incoming synapse from each sensory neuron. Each output neuron (from N_{12} to N_{14}) receives one incoming synapse from each inter-neuron. There are no direct connections between sensory and output neurons. The network neurons are governed by the following state equation:

$$\frac{dy_i}{dt} = \begin{cases} \frac{1}{\tau_i}(-y_i + gI_i) & i \in [1,6] \\ \frac{1}{\tau_i}\left(-y_i + \sum_{j=1}^{k} \omega_{ji}\sigma(y_j + \beta_j) + gI_i\right) & i \in [7,14]; \ \sigma(x) = \frac{1}{1+e^{-x}} \end{cases} \quad (3)$$

where, using terms derived from an analogy with real neurons, y_i represents the cell potential, τ_i the decay constant, g is a gain factor, I_i the intensity of the sensory perturbation on sensory neuron i, ω_{ji} the strength of the synaptic connection from neuron j to neuron i, β_j the bias term, $\sigma(y_j + \beta_j)$ the firing rate. The cell potentials y_i of the 12th and the 13th neuron, mapped into [0,1] by a sigmoid function σ and then linearly scaled into $[-6.5, 6.5]$, set the robot motors output. The cell potential y_i of the 14th neuron, mapped into [0,1] by a sigmoid function σ, is used by the robot to control the intensity of the sound emitted η. The following parameters are genetically encoded: (i) the strength of synaptic connections ω_{ji}; (ii) the decay constant τ_i of the inter-neurons and of neuron N_{14}; (iii) the bias term β_j of the sensory neurons, of the inter-neurons, and of the neuron N_{14}. The decay constant τ_i of the sensory neurons and of the output neurons N_{12} and N_{13} are set to 0.1. Cell potentials are set to 0 any time the network is initialised or reset, and circuits are integrated using the forward Euler method with an integration step-size of $dt = 0.1$.

A simple generational genetic algorithm is employed to set the parameters of the networks [13]. The population contains 80 genotypes. Generations following the first one are produced by a combination of selection with elitism, recombination and mutation. More details on the characteristics of the evolutionary algorithm employed and on the genotypes' component values can be found in [5].

3   The Fitness Function

During evolution, each genotype is translated into a robot controller, and cloned in each agent. Then, the group is evaluated eight times, four trials in *Env. L*, and four trials in *Env. R*. The sequence order of environments within the eight trials has no bearing on the overall performance of the group since each robot controller is reset at the beginning of each trial. Each trial (e) differs from the others in the initialisation of the random number generator, which influences the robots' starting position and orientation, and the noise added to motors and sensors. Within a trial, the robot life-span is 400 s (4000 simulation cycles). In each trial, the group is rewarded by an evaluation function f_e which seeks to assess the ability of the team to approach the light bulb, while avoiding collisions and staying within the range of the robots' infrared sensors.

Taking inspiration from the work of Quinn et al. [14], the fitness score is computed as follows:

$$f_e = KP \sum_{t=i}^{T} [(d_t - D_{t-1})(\tanh(S_t/\rho))]; \tag{4}$$

The simulation time steps are indexed by t and T is the index of the final time step of the trial. d_t is the Euclidean distance between the group location at time step t and its location at time step $t = 0$, and D_{t-1} is the largest value that d_t has attained prior to time step t. S_t is a measure of the team's dispersal beyond the infrared sensor range $\rho = 24.6$ cm at time step t. If each robot is within ρ range of at least another, then $S_t = 0$. Otherwise, the two shortest lines that can connect all three robots are found and S_t is the distance by which the longest of these exceeds ρ.

$P = 1 - \sum_{i=1}^{3} c_i/c_{max}$ if $\sum_{i=1}^{3} c_i \leq c_{max}$ reduces the score in proportion to the number of collisions which have occurred during the trial. c_i is the number of collisions of the robot i and $c_{max} = 4$ is the maximum number of collisions allowed. $P = 0$ if $\sum_{i=1}^{3} c_i > c_{max}$. The team's accumulated score is multiplied by $K = 3.0$ if the group moved towards the light bulb, otherwise $K = 1.0$. Note that a trial was terminated early if (a) the team reached the light bulb (b) the team distance from the light bulb exceeded an arbitrary limit set to 140 cm, or (c) the team exceeded the maximum number of allowed collisions c_{max}. More details on the characteristics of the fitness function can be found in [5].

4   Results

Ten evolutionary simulations, each using a different random initialisation, were run for between 2500 and 3600 generations of the evolutionary algorithm. The termination criterion for each run was set to a time equal to 86400 seconds of CPU time. Experiments were performed on a cluster of 32 nodes, each with 2 AMD Opteron244^{TM} CPU running GNU/Linux Debian 3.0 OS. Recall that the robots of a successful group should be capable of coordinating their movement and of cooperating, in order to approach the target without collisions. A trial is successfully terminated when the centroid of the group is closer than 10 cm to the the light bulb. Cooperation is required since no robot of the group can potentially acquire, through its sensors, sufficient "knowledge" of the environment to accomplish the task. The results of these simulations and of some preliminary post-evaluation tests are illustrated and discussed in [5]. To summarise, we post-evaluated each of the best evolved controllers at the last generation of each evolutionary run. Two of them had a success rate higher than 90% in both environments; two displayed a performance over 80%, while the performance of the remaining six controllers was not sufficiently good in both environments. This paper complements these results by providing an operational analysis of the system, in terms of the mechanisms employed by the robots to achieve their goal. In particular, we focus on the analysis of the behaviour of a group controlled by the best evolved controller run n. 9, that, at the re-evaluation test, had a success rate higher than 90% in both environments.

For the sake of clarity, we recall that during a post-evaluation test, the group is subject to a set of 1200 trials in both environments. The number of post-evaluation trials per type of environment (i.e., 1200) is given by systematically varying the initial positions of the three robots according to the criteria illustrated in [5]. During post-evaluation, the robot life-span is more than two times longer than during evolution (i.e., 1000 s, 10000 simulation cycles). This should give the robots enough time to compensate for possible disruptive effects induced by initial positions never or very rarely experienced during evolution. At the beginning of each post-evaluation trial, the controllers are reset (see Section 2). All the post-evaluation tests illustrated in this paper are carried out by following the criteria mentioned above and detailed in [5]. In all the tests in which different types of alterations are applied to the system to disclose operational principles, the disruptions are applied after 10 s (i.e., 100 simulation cycles) from the beginning of each trial. This should give time to the controllers to reach a functional state different from the initial one, arbitrarily chosen by the experimenter, in which the cell potential of the neurons is set to 0.

4.1   The Group's Behaviour

In this section we provide a qualitative description of the individual and group motion of the best evolved simulated agents as observed through a simple graphical interface. First of all, we noticed that the systematic variation of the initial positions of the robots during post-evaluation brings about contingencies in

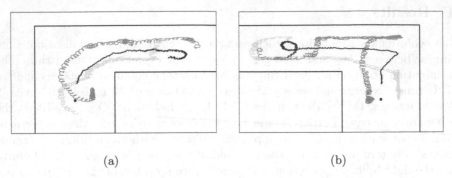

(a)   (b)

Fig. 4. Trajectories of the agents during a successful trial (a) in an *Env. L*, and (b) in an *Env. R*. The black lines refer to the trajectories of robot R_{AL} while the other lines refer to the trajectories of robots R_{IR}. The horizontal and vertical segments represent the walls. In each figure, we depict only the side of the corridor where the light—i.e., the small black dot—is located.

which the coordination of movements of the group toward the target requires an initial effort of the robots in re-arranging their relative positions. During this initial phase of a trial a dynamic process guided by the nature of the flow of sensation (i.e., infrared sensors reading versus ambient light reading) induces the specialisation of the controllers with respect to the physical characteristics of the robots, and to the relative role that they play in the group. This phase is followed by the navigation phase in which the group seems to maintain a rather regular spatial configuration; that is, the two robots R_{IR} place themselves in between the target and the robot R_{AL}. However, note that while *Env. L* requires the group to make a left turn, *Env. R* requires the group to make a right turn. This asymmetry in the environmental structures corresponds to differences in behavioural strategies employed by the group to reach the target as shown in Figure 4. While in *Env. L* the robots simply turn towards the light keeping their relative positions in the group, in *Env. R* we firstly observe an alignment of the agents along the far right wall (see Figure 4b). Subsequently, the agent close to the corner (see the dark gray line) overcomes the other two and the group starts moving towards the target once the classical configuration of the two robots R_{IR} in between the target and the robot R_{AL} is re-established.

Another important qualitative element is that each of the members of the group is characterised by a movement with a strong angular component (anti-clockwise). In other words, the robots proceed toward the light by rotating on the spot. The evolution of the rotational movement is not particularly surprising if we think about its effect of the perception of sound. First of all, we should remind the reader that the intensity of sound perceived at each microphone results from the summation of two components—the "self" and the "non-self"—and the noise. The "self" component (i.e., the agent's own signal) is only determined by the intensity of the sound emitted by the robot itself. The "non-self" component is determined by the intensity at which the sound is emitted from the loud-speaker of a sender as well as by the relative distance and orientation of the loud-speaker with respect to the receiver's microphones. Although the agents have no means to distinguish between the "self" and "non-self" component of the perceived sound, they can act in a way to determine patterns in the flow of sensations which are informative on their spatial relationships. In particular, spatial discrimination of sound sources can be achieved by the receiver through intensity differences between the sound perceived in each ear. In our model, these differences come about from the "simulated" physics of the propagation of sound, including the shadowing effect (see Section 1.1). The rotational movement may introduce rhythm in perception of an amplitude bigger than the oscillations manifested in signalling behaviour. The oscillations of perceived sound, amplified by the rotational movement, may provide the robots the cues to adjust their positions relative to each other, since intensity differences between the two microphones can be a valuable mechanism for spatial discrimination of sound sources. This issue will be extensively investigated in the next section. Notice that, within a trial, pure linear movement replaces the rotational behaviour only sporadically and for a very short interval. This can happen to avoid an imminent danger of collision or if required by the navigational strategy of the group.

Two of the phenomena above mentioned (i.e., the effect of the starting position and the rotational movement) have a strong effect on the time it takes to the group to reach the target. Indeed, as resulted from the post-evaluation test shown in [5], most of the successful trials of the best evolved group of robots last longer than the 400 s given to the groups to complete the task during the evolutionary phase. In the following, we try to clarify the role of sound signalling for the achievement of the group phototaxis and collision avoidance behaviour.

4.2 Coordinated Motion Through Sound Signalling

Each robot of the group is required to coordinate its actions in order (i) to remain close to the other two agents without incurring into collisions, and (ii) to make actions which bring the group closer to the target. How are these two objectives achieved? An answer to this question may be provided by showing the relationship between the sensor readings and the actions they trigger in the robots. How the robots sensations influence the way in which they move? In this section we focus on the analysis of the role of the sound with respect to the achievement of the group's coordination of motion. In Table 1 the reader can find some statistics concerning the intensity of "self" and "non-self" component of the sound as perceived by each agent through its microphones. This Table shows that on average more than 92% of the sound perceived by each agent comes from the "self" component (see Table 1 columns 2 and 8). Moreover, the small standard deviation suggests that each agent is emitting sound at a rather fixed intensity with very small oscillations that are not enough to saturate the auditory channels (see Table 1 columns 3 and 9). Given the high intensity of the "self" component, the "non-self" component can only induce changes in the perception of sound that are less than 10% of the sensors' receptive-field. However, by looking at the average intensity of the "non-self" component (see Table 1 columns 4,

6, 10, and 12) we notice that, the latter is already very "weak", possible due to the relatively "long" robot-robot distances. Despite this, we noticed that, if not affected by the shadowing effect, the "non-self" plus the "self" component may be sufficient to saturate the sensors' receptive field of the receiver. If we combine this data with the fact that the robots rotate on the spot while moving towards the target, we may deduce that, during navigation, the readings of the sound sensors of each robot may go through oscillations constrained between an upper and a lower bound. The upper bound corresponds to the saturation value (1.0) that is reached when the "non-self" component is not attenuated by the shadowing effect. The lower bound corresponds to the intensity of the "self" component that is reached when the "non-self" component is strongly attenuated by the shadowing effect. These oscillations are very small since they concern less than 10% of the auditory receptive field, and certainly not very regular since the random noise applied to the sensors reading may be large enough to disrupt the regularity of the oscillations determined by the contingencies. However, in spite of being small and noisy, these oscillations seem to be the only phenomenon related to the perception of sound that may play a significant role in the coordination of action of the group. In fact, given a controller sufficiently sensitive to capture them, they may represent a valuable perceptive cue for the receiver to spatially discriminate sound sources and consequently relative position and orientation of the emitter/s. Our hypothesis is that this phenomenon is exploited by the robots to remain close to each other while avoiding collisions and moving towards the target. The tests that follow further investigate our hypothesis on the significance of sound for spatial discrimination and coordination of actions. We run two series of post-evaluation tests. In the first series, we interfere with the propagation of sound in the environment by disrupting the orientation of the robot emitter with respect to the heading of the receiver. We refer to this as the *orientation test*. In the second series, we interfere with the propagation of sound in the environment by disrupting the the sender-receiver distance. We refer to this as the *distance test*. In each of these tests, the robots undergo a set of 1200 trials in each type of environment. For all the simulation cycles following the first 10 seconds of each trial, the sound sensors reading of each agent are computed with respect to a hypothetical state of the system in which the senders are supposed to be:

Table 1. This table shows average and standard deviation of the "self" and "non-self" component of the intensity of the sound perceived by the robots at each of their microphone—$S1$ and $S2$—during 1200 trials in each environment. Recall that the "self" component does not differ between the microphones of the emitter.

	Env. L						Env. R					
	self		non-self				self		non-self			
			S1		S2				S1		S2	
	avg	std	avg	std	avg	std	avg	std	avg	std	avg	std
R_{IR}	0.935	0.027	0.059	0.0574	0.054	0.046	0.936	0.028	0.067	0.063	0.060	0.048
R_{IR}	0.934	0.028	0.063	0.061	0.0571	0.047	0.936	0.028	0.064	0.062	0.0571	0.048
R_{AL}	0.925	0.012	0.061	0.058	0.061	0.055	0.922	0.017	0.063	0.059	0.063	0.059

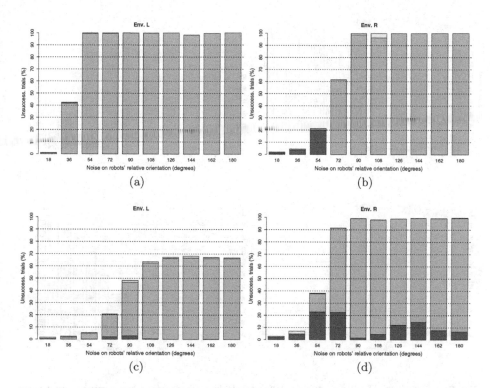

Fig. 5. Percentage of failure during 1200 trials in each type of environment in post-evaluation tests with alterations applied to the relative orientation of the robots during the computation of the perceived sound. In (a) and (b) the robots R_{IR}, during all the simulation cycles following the first 10 seconds of any trial, are considered to be re-oriented with respect to the heading of robot R_{AL} by applying the angular displacement indicated on the horizontal axis and randomly choosing the direction of displacement (i.e., clockwise or anti-clockwise). In (c) and (d) the robot R_{AL} is re-oriented with respect to the heading of each robot R_{IR} as explained above. (a) and (c) refer to tests in *Env. L*; (b) and (d) refer to tests in *Env. R*. The black area of the bars refers to the percentage of trials terminated without collisions and with the group not having reached the target. The light grey area of the bars refers to the percentage of trials terminated due to robot-robot collisions. The dark grey area of the bars refers to the percentage of trials terminated due to robot-wall collisions.

orientation test: re-oriented by a fixed angular displacement, ranging from a minimum of 18° to a maximum of 180°, with a randomly chosen direction (clockwise or anti-clockwise) with respect to the heading of the receiver.

distance test: at a fixed distance to the receiver, ranging from a minimum of 2 cm to a maximum of 32 cm.

Note that, the hypothetical states are taken into account only as far as it concerns the updating of the sound sensors' reading of one type of robot at the time. That is, during a set of trials, the sound perceived by robot R_{AL} is computed with

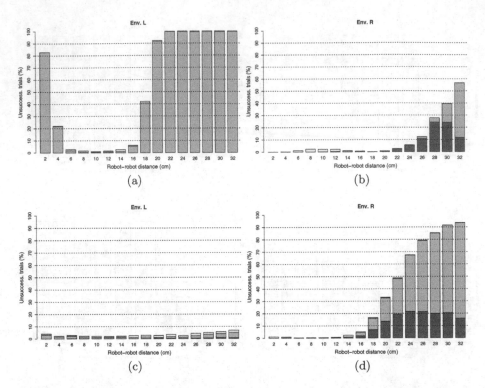

Fig. 6. Percentage of failure during 1200 trials in each type of environment in post-evaluation tests with alterations applied to the robot-robot distance during the computation of the sound perceived by the receiver. In (a) and (b) the robots R_{IR}, during all the simulation cycles following the first 10 seconds of any trial, are both considered to be at the distance to robot R_{AL} indicated on the horizontal axis. In (c) and (d) the robot R_{AL} is considered to be at the distance to robots R_{IR} indicated on the horizontal axis as explained above. (a) and (c) refer to tests in *Env. L*; (b) and (d) refer to tests in *Env. R*. The black area of the bars refers to the percentage of trials terminated without collisions and with the group not having reached the target. The light grey area of the bars refers to the percentage of trials terminated due to robot-robot collisions. The dark grey area of the bars refers to the percentage of trials terminated due to robot-wall collisions.

reference to a hypothetical state in which the orientation/position of both robots R_{IR} is changed in order to meet the angular displacement/distance requirements. In this type of tests no disruptions are applied to update the sound perceived by robots R_{IR}. For the *orientation test* the results are shown in Figure 5a and 5b. For the *distance test*, the results are shown in Figure 6a and 6b. In a different set of tests, the sound perceived by the robots R_{IR} is computed with reference to a hypothetical state in which the orientation/position of robot R_{AL} is changed in order to meet the angular displacement/distance requirements. In this type of tests no disruptions are applied to update the sound perceived by robot R_{AL}.

For the *orientation tests* the results are shown in Figure 5c and 5d. For the *distance test*, the results are shown in Figure 6c and 6d.

Generally speaking, by varying the sender-receiver orientation/distance, we indirectly increase/decrease the magnitude of the "non-self" component. In particular, those hypothetical states in which the sender-receiver distances tend to be decreased with respect to normal conditions, produced an increase of the magnitude of the "non-self" component and consequently an increase of the proportion of time in a trial the sound sensors are saturated. The same effect is obtained by applying angular displacements which increase the attenuation factor ψ. On the contrary, those hypothetical states in which the sender-receiver distances tend to be increased, produce a decrease of the magnitude of the "non-self" component and consequently a decrease of the proportion of time in a trial the sound sensors are saturated. The same effect is obtained by applying angular displacements which decrease the attenuation factor ψ. However, while the *distance test* preserves the intensity differences between the sound perceived in each ear due to the relative orientation of the sender with respect to the receiver, the *orientation test* disrupts any kind of regularities in the perception of sound which are linked to sender-receiver relative orientation. Therefore, a drop in performance at the *orientation test* can be a sign of the significance of binaural perception for spatial discrimination and behavioural coordination. Contrary to the *orientation test*, the *distance test* informs us on the robustness of the mechanisms that exploit binaural perception with respect to a general increase/decrease of the intensity of the "non-self" component.

The results of the tests shown in Figure 5 and 6 are very informative. First, the performance of the group is significantly disrupted by alterations which concern the orientation of the sender with respect to the heading of the receiver. Figure 5 shows that the bigger the magnitude of the disruption the higher the percentage of failure of the system. This proves that intensity differences between the sound perceived in each ear have a bearing on the development of effective navigational strategies as hypothesised above. In particular, regularities in the oscillation of the sound sensors' reading linked to the environmental contingencies and to the "variation" of the "non-self" component, are important perceptual cues exploited by the agents to coordinate their movements. The majority of failure are due to robot-wall collision. In particular, by looking at the behaviour of the group in these conditions, we noticed that, under the effects induced by the disruptions, the robots are not capable of remaining close to each other—i.e., within the infrared sensors' range. When the distances becomes too high, the robots start wandering around the arena, and the trial terminates due to a collision of the robot R_{AL} with the arena walls. Only in few circumstances the robots do not lose contact to each other but they are not capable of reaching the target within the time-limits (see Figure 5 black area of the bars).

The results shown in Figure 6 tell us that the mechanisms which exploit binaural perception for spatial discrimination and behavioural coordination are quite robust to a general increment of the sound intensity. An exception is the case in which the robots R_{IR} are placed very close to robot R_{AL} in an environment

Env. L (see Figure 6a). By looking at the behaviour of the group in these conditions, we noticed that contrary to what observed in the *orientation test*, in the unsuccessful trial the robots manage to remain close to each other—i.e., within the infrared sensors' range. However, the robot R_{AL} is not capable of making the left turn hitting the walls close to the corner. This is a quite general problem in these type of tests. That is, the robots manage to approach the turn (left or right) relatively close to each other but they fail due to the lack of behavioural coordination of robot R_{AL} during the turn. Another significant result is that the robustness with respect to this type of disruptions is not the same for both types of robots. In general, the most disruptive effects are recorded in those tests in which discrepancies are artificially induced between the current state of the system and the perception of sound of robot R_{AL}. Disruptions on the perception of sound of robots R_{IR} when the group is located in *Env. L* do not alter the performance of the system with respect to the normal conditions (see Figure 6c). This suggests that, in *Env. L* robots R_{IR} "favour" infrared over sound sensors to coordinate their actions.

5   Conclusion

The paper described operational aspects of the behaviour of a group of robots equipped with a different set of sensors, that navigates towards a target in a walled arena. The results of our analysis suggest that the robots use sound to regulate the inter-robot distances. Movements towards a zone of higher/lower intensity of sound keep the robots close to each other at a safe distance. The robots R_{IR} tend to place themselves in between the robot R_{AL} and the target. Owing to this spatial displacement, the motion toward the target of robot R_{AL} is secured from collision against the walls. Rotational movement introduces rhythm in perception which is an important cue to spatially discriminate the sound source. Implementation details, such as the homogeneity of the controllers, or the mechanism employed to regulate the sound intensity, may have precluded our system the possibility to develop a more articulated signalling behaviour. Future work will explore solutions that allow the agents to develop more complex communication through mechanisms which favour the recognition of "self/non-self" sound, and help minimise the interference between simultaneous production.

Acknowledgements

E. Tuci and M. Dorigo acknowledge European Commission support via the *ECAgents* project, funded by the Future and Emerging Technologies programme (grant IST-1940), and by COMP2SYS, a Marie Curie Early Stage Training Site (grant MEST-CT-2004505079). The authors thank their colleagues at IRIDIA for stimulating discussions and feedback during the preparation of this paper, and the two anonymous reviewers for their helpful comments. M. Dorigo acknowledges support from the Belgian FNRS, of which he is a Research Director, and from the "ANTS" project, an "Action de Recherche Concertée" funded by the Scientific Research Directorate of the French Community of Belgium. The information provided is the sole responsibility of the authors and does not reflect the Community's opinion. The Community is not responsible for any use that might be made of data appearing in this publication.

References

1. Cangelosi, A., Parisi, D., eds.: Simulating the Evolution of Language. Springer Verlag, London, UK (2002)
2. Vogt, P.: Language acquisition and evolution. Adaptive Behavior **13** (2005) 265–268
3. Quinn, M.: Evolving communication without dedicated communication channels. In Kelemen, J., Sosik, P., eds.: Advances in Artificial Life: 6th European Conf. on Artificial Life, Springer Verlag, Berlin, Germany (2001) 357–366
4. Cangelosi, A.: Approaches to grounding symbols in perceptual and sensorimotor categories. In Cohen, H., Lefebvre, C., eds.: Handbook of Categorization in Cognitive Science. Elsevier (2005) 719–737
5. Tuci, E., Vicentini, C.A.F., Dorigo, M.: Evolved homogeneous neuro-controllers for robots with different sensory capabilities: coordinated motion and cooperation. Technical Report TR/IRIDIA/2006-015, IRIDIA, Université Libre de Bruxelles (2006) Technical report available at http://iridia.ulb.ac.be/IridiaTrSeries.
6. Marocco, D., Nolfi, S.: Emergence of communication in embodied agents: Co-adapting communicative and non-communicative behaviours. In Cangelosi, A., Bugmann, G., Borisyuk, R., eds.: Modeling language, cognition and action: 9th Neural Computation and Psychology Workshop, World Scientific (2005)
7. Baldassarre, G., abd D. Parisi, S.N.: Evolving mobile robots able to display collective behaviour. Artificial Life **9** (2003) 255–267
8. Paolo, E.D.: Behavioral coordination, structural congruence and entrainment in a simulation of acoustically coupled agents. Adaptive Behavior **8** (2000) 27–48
9. Mondada, F., Pettinaro, G., Guignard, A., Kwee, I., Floreano, D., Deneubourg, J.L., Nolfi, S., Gambardella, L., Dorigo, M.: SWARM-BOT: A new distributed robotic concept. Autonomous Robots **17** (2004) 193–221
10. Miglino, O., Lund, H., Nolfi, S.: Evolving mobile robots in simulated and real environments. Artificial Life **2** (1995) 417–434
11. Dudek, G., Jenkin, M.: Computational Principles of Mobile Robotics. Cambridge University Press, Cambridge, UK (2000)
12. Vicentini, F., Tuci, E.: *Swarmod*: a 2d *s-bot*'s simulator. Technical Report TR/IRIDIA/2006-005, IRIDIA, Université Libre de Bruxelles (2006) Technical report available at http://iridia.ulb.ac.be/IridiaTrSeries.
13. Goldberg, D.E.: Genetic Algorithms in Search, Optimization and Machine Learning. Addison-Wesley, Reading, MA (1989)
14. Quinn, M., Smith, L., Mayley, G., Husbands, P.: Evolving controllers for a homogeneous system of physical robots: Structured cooperation with minimal sensors. Phil. Trans. of the Royal Soc. of London, Series A **361** (2003) 2321–2344

Propositional Logic Syntax Acquisition*

Josefina Sierra-Santibáñez

Departamento de Lenguajes y Sistemas Informáticos
Universidad Politécnica de Barcelona, Spain
jsierra@lsi.upc.edu

Abstract. This paper addresses the problem of the acquisition of the syntax of propositional logic. An approach based on general purpose cognitive capacities such as invention, adoption, parsing, generation and induction is proposed. Self-organisation principles are used to show how a shared set of preferred lexical entries and grammatical constructions, i.e., a *language*, can emerge in a population of autonomous agents which do not have any initial linguistic knowledge.

Experiments in which a population of autonomous agents constructs a language that allows communicating the formulas of a propositional language are presented. This language although simple has interesting properties found in natural languages, such as compositionality and recursion.

1 Introduction

Recent work in linguistics and artificial intelligence [1,2,3,4,5,6,7,8] has described interesting experiments showing the emergence of compositional and recursive syntax in populations of agents without initial linguistic knowledge. This paper combines general purpose cognitive capacities (e.g., invention, adoption, parsing, generation and induction) and self-organisation principles in order to address the problem of the acquisition of the syntax of propositional logic.

The important role of logic in knowledge representation and reasoning [9] is well known in artificial intelligence. Much of the knowledge used by artificial intelligent agents today is represented in logic, and linguists use it as well for representing the meanings of words and sentences. This paper differs from previous approaches in using the syntax of logic as the subject of learning. Some could argue that it is not necessary to learn such a syntax, because it is built in the internal knowledge representation formalism used by the agents. We'd argue on the contrary that logical connectives and logical constructions are a fundamental part of natural language, and that it is necessary to understand how an agent can both conceptualise and communicate them to other agents.

The research presented in this paper assumes previous work on the conceptualisation of logical connectives [10,11]. In [12] a grounded approach to the acquisition of logical categories (connectives) based on the discrimination of a "subset

---

* This work is partially funded by the DGICYT TIN2005-08832-C03-03 project (MOISES-BAR).

of objects" from the rest of the objects in a given context is described. The "subset of objects" is characterized by a logical formula constructed from perceptually grounded categories. This formula is satisfied by the objects in the subset and not satisfied by the rest of the objects in the context. In this paper we only focus on the problem of the acquisition of the syntax of propositional logic, because it is a necessary step to solve the complete problem of the acquisition of a grounded logical language (encompassing the acquisition of both the syntax and the semantics of propositional logic) and to our knowledge it has not been addressed before.

The emergence of recursive communication systems in populations of autonomous agents has been studied by other authors[1]. The research presented in [6] differs from the work described in the present paper by focusing on learning exemplars rather than grammar rules. These exemplars have costs, as our grammar rules do, and their costs are reinforced and discouraged using self-organization principles as well. The main challenge for the agents in the experiments described in [6] is to construct a communication system that is capable of naming atomic formulas and, more importantly, marking the identity relations among the arguments of the different atomic formulas that constitute the meaning of a given string of characters. This task is quite different from the learning task proposed in the present paper which focusses on categorizing propositional sentences and connectives, and marking the scope of each connective using the order of the constituents of a string of characters.

The most important difference between our work and that presented in [7] is that the latter one focusses on language transmission over generations. Rather than studying the emergence of recursive communication systems in a single population of agents, as we do, it shows that the bottleneck established by language transmission over several generations favors the propagation of compositional and recursive rules because of their compactness and generality. In the experiments described in [7] the population consists of a single agent of a generation that acts as a teacher and another agent of the following generation that acts as a learner. There is no negotiation process involved, because the learned never has the opportunity to act as a speaker in a single iteration. We consider however populations of three agents which can act both as speakers and hearers during the simulations. Having more than two agents ensures that the interaction histories of the agents are different from each other, in such a way that they have to negotiate in order to reach agreements on how to name and order the constituents of a sentence.

The induction mechanisms used in the present paper are based on the rules for chunking and simplification in [7], although we extend them so that they can be applied to grammar rules which have costs and usage counters attached to them. In particular we use the approach proposed in [8] for adding costs to the grammar rules, and computing the costs of sentences and meanings from the costs of the rules used for generating such sentences or meanings.

Finally the meaning space used in [7] (a restricted form of atomic formulas of second order logic) is different as well from the meaning space considered in the

---

[1] We review the work of the authors mentioned in this introduction in section 5.

present paper (arbitrary formulas from a propositional logic language), although both of them require the use of recursion.

The rest of the paper is organised as follows. First we present the formalism used for representing the grammars constructed by the agents. Then we describe in some detail the language games played by the agents, focusing on the main cognitive processes they use for constructing a shared lexicon and grammar: invention, adoption, induction and self-organisation. Next we report the results of some experiments in which a population of autonomous agents constructs a shared language that allows communicating propositional logic formulas. Finally we summarize some related work and the contributions of the paper.

2   Grammatical Formalism

We use a restricted form of definite-clause grammar in which non-terminals have three arguments attached to them. The first argument conveys semantic information. The second is a *score* in the interval $[0, 1]$ that estimates the usefulness of that association in previous communication. The third argument is a counter that records the number of times the association has been used in previous language games.

Many grammars can be used to express the same meaning. The following holistic grammar can be used to express the propositional formula $right \land light^2$.

$$s([and, right, light]), 0.01) \rightarrow andrightlight \qquad (1)$$

This grammar consists of a single rule which states that 'andrightlight' is a valid sentence meaning $right \land light$.

The same formula can be expressed using the following compositional, recursive grammar: s is the start symbol, $c1$ and $c2$ are the names of two syntactic categories associated with unary and binary connectives, respectively. Like in Prolog, variables start with a capital letter and constants with a lower case letter.

$$s(light, 0.70) \rightarrow light \qquad (2)$$
$$s(right, 0.25) \rightarrow right \qquad (3)$$
$$s(up, 0.60) \rightarrow up \qquad (4)$$
$$c1(not, 0.80) \rightarrow not \qquad (5)$$
$$s([P, Q], S) \rightarrow c1(P, S1), s(Q, S2), \{S \ is \ S1*S2*0.10\} \qquad (6)$$
$$c2(or, 0.30) \rightarrow or \qquad (7)$$
$$c2(and, 0.50) \rightarrow and \qquad (8)$$
$$c2(if, 0.90) \rightarrow if \qquad (9)$$
$$c2(iff, 0.60) \rightarrow iff \qquad (10)$$
$$s([P, Q, R], S) \rightarrow c2(P, S1), s(Q, S2), s(R, S3), \{S \ is \ S1 * S2 * S3 * 0.01\} \qquad (11)$$

---

[2] Notice that we use Prolog grammar rules for describing the grammars. The semantic argument of the rules uses Lisp like (prefix) notation for representing propositional formulas (e.g., the Prolog list $[and, [not, right], light]$ is equivalent to $\neg right \land light$). The third argument (the use counter) of non-terminals is not shown in the examples.

This grammar breaks down the sentence 'andrightlight' into subparts with independent meanings. The whole sentence is constructed concatenating these subparts. The meaning of the sentence is composed combining the meanings of the subparts using the variables P, Q and R.

The *score of a lexical rule* is the value of the second argument of the left hand side of the rule (e.g., the score of rule 8 is 0.50). The *score of a grammatical rule* is the last number of the arithmetic expression that appears on the right hand side of the rule[3] (e.g., the score of rule 11 is 0.01). The score of a sentence generated using a grammatical rule is computed using the arithmetic expression on the right hand side of that rule (e.g., the score of sentence *andrightlight* is 0.50*0.25*0.70*0.01=0.00875).

3   Language Games

Syntax acquisition is seen as a collective process by which a population of autonomous agents constructs a *grammar* that allows them to communicate some set of meanings. In order to reach such an agreement the agents interact with each other playing language games. In the experiments described in this paper a particular type of *language game* called *the guessing game* [13,14] is played by two agents, a *speaker* and a *hearer*:

1. The speaker chooses a formula from a given propositional language, generates a sentence that expresses it and communicates that sentence to the hearer.
2. The hearer tries to interpret the sentence generated by the speaker. If it can parse the sentence using its lexicon and grammar, it extracts a meaning which can be equal or not to the formula intended by the speaker.
3. The speaker communicates the meaning it had in mind to the hearer and both agents adjust their grammars in order to become successful in future language games.

In a typical experiment hundreds of language games are played by pairs of agents randomly chosen from a population. The goal of the experiment is to observe the evolution of: (1) the communicative success[4]; (2) the internal grammars constructed by the individual agents; and (3) the external language used by the population.

3.1   Invention

In the first step of a language game the speaker tries to generate a sentence that expresses a propositional logic formula.

---

[3] The Prolog operator *"is"* allows evaluating the arithmetic expression at its right hand side.

[4] The *communicative success* is the average of successful language games in the last ten language games played by the agents. A language game is *successful* if the hearer can parse the sentence generated by the speaker, and the meaning interpreted by hearer is equal to the meaning intended by the speaker.

The agents in the population start with an empty lexicon and grammar. It is not surprising thus that they cannot generate sentences for some meanings at the early stages of a simulation run. In order to allow language to get off the ground, the agents are allowed to invent new words for those meanings they cannot express using their lexicons and grammars[5].

The invention algorithm is a recursive procedure that invents a sentence E for a meaning M. If M is atomic (not a list), it generates a new word E. If M is a list of elements (i.e., a unary or binary connective followed by one or two formulas, respectively), it tries to generate an expression for each of the elements in M using the agent's grammar. If it cannot generate an expression for an element of M using the agent's grammar, it invents an expression for that element calling itself recursively on that element. Once it has generated an expression for each element in M, it concatenates these expressions randomly in order to construct a sentence E for the whole meaning M.

As the agents play language games they learn associations between expressions and meanings, and induce linguistic knowledge from such associations in the form of grammatical rules and lexical entries. Once the agents can generate sentences for expressing a particular meaning using their own grammars, they select the sentence with the highest score out of the set of sentences they can generate for expressing that meaning, and communicate that sentence to the hearer. The algorithm used for calculating the score of a sentence from the scores of the grammatical rules applied in its generation is explained in detail later.

3.2   Adoption

The hearer tries to interpret the sentence generated by the speaker. If it can parse the sentence using its lexicon and grammar, it extracts a meaning which can be equal or not to the formula intended by the speaker.

As we have explained earlier the agents start with no linguistic knowledge at all. Therefore they cannot parse the sentences generated by the speakers at the early stages of a simulation run. When this happens the speaker communicates the formula it had in mind to the hearer, and the hearer adopts an association between that formula and the sentence used by the speaker.

It is also possible that the grammars and lexicons of speaker and hearer are not consistent, because each agent constructs its own grammar from the linguistic interactions in which it participates, and it is very unlikely that speaker and hearer share the same history of linguistic interactions unless the population consists only of these two agents. When this happens the hearer may be able to parse the sentence generated by the speaker, but its interpretation of that sentence may be different from the meaning the speaker had in mind. In this case, the strategy used to coordinate the grammars of speaker and hearer is to decrement the score of the rules used by speaker and hearer in the processes of generation and parsing, respectively, and allow the hearer to adopt an association between the sentence and the meaning used by the speaker.

---

[5] New words are sequences from 1 to 3 letters randomly chosen from the alphabet.

The adoption algorithm used in this paper is very simple. Given a sentence E and a meaning M, the agent checks whether it can parse E and interpret it as meaning M. This may happen when the hearer can parse the sentence used by the speaker, but it obtains a different meaning from the one intended by the speaker. In a language game the hearer always chooses the interpretation with the highest score out of the set of all the interpretations it that can obtain for a given sentence. So it is possible that the hearer knows the grammatical rules used by the speaker, but the scores of these rules are not higher than the scores of the rules it used for interpretation. If the hearer can interpret sentence E as meaning M, the hearer does not take any action. Otherwise it adopts the association used by the speaker by adding a new holistic rule of the form $s(M, 0.01) \rightarrow E$ to its grammar. The induction algorithm, used to generalise and simplify the agents' grammars, compares this rule with other rules already present in the grammar and replaces it with more general rules whenever it is possible.

3.3   Induction

In addition to invent and adopt associations between sentences and meanings, the agents use some *induction rules* [7] to extract generalizations from the grammar rules they have learnt so far [15]. The induction rules are applied whenever the agents invent or adopt a new association, to avoid redundancy and increase generality in their grammars.

Simplification: *Let $r1$ and $r2$ be a pair of grammar rules such that the left hand side semantics of $r1$ contains a subterm $m1$, $r2$ is of the form $n(m1, S) \rightarrow e1$, and $e1$ is a substring of the terminals of $r1$. Then simplification can be applied to $r1$ replacing it with a new rule that is identical to $r1$ except that $m1$ is replaced with a new variable X in the left hand side semantics, and $e1$ is replaced with $n(X, S)$ on the right hand side. The second argument of the left hand side of $r1$ is replaced with a new variable SR. If the score of $r1$ was a constant value $c1$, an expression of the form $\{SR$ is $S * 0.01\}$ is added to the right hand side of $r1$. If the score of $r1$ was a variable, then the arithmetic expression $\{SR$ is $S1 * c1\}$ in the right hand side of $r1$ is replaced by $\{SR$ is $S * S1 * 0.01\}$.*

Suppose an agent's grammar contains rules 2, 3 and 4, which it has invented or adopted in previous language games. It plays a language game with another agent, and it invents or adopts the following rule.

$$s([and, light, right], 0.01) \rightarrow andlightright. \tag{12}$$

It could apply simplification to rule 12 (using rule 3) replacing it with rule 13.

$$s([and, light, R], S) \rightarrow andlight, s(R, SR), \{S \text{ is } SR * 0.01\} \tag{13}$$

Rule 13 could be simplified again using rule 2, replacing it with 14.

$$s([and, Q, R], S) \rightarrow and, s(Q, SQ), s(R, SR), \{S \text{ is } SQ * SR * 0.01\} \tag{14}$$

Suppose the agent plays another language game in which it invents or adopts a holistic rule for expressing the formula $[or, up, light]$ and applies simplification in a similar way. Then the agent's grammar would contain the following rules that are compositional and recursive, but which do not use syntactic categories for unary or binary connectives.

$$s([and, Q, R], S) \rightarrow and, s(Q, SQ), s(R, SR), \{S \ is \ SQ * SR * 0.01\} \quad (15)$$
$$s([or, Q, R], S) \rightarrow or, s(Q, SQ), s(R, SR), \{S \ is \ SQ * SR * 0.01\} \quad (16)$$

Chunk I. *Let $r1$ and $r2$ be a pair of grammar rules with the same left hand side category symbol. If the left hand side semantics of the two rules differ in only one position, and there exist two strings of terminals that, if removed, would make the right hand sides of the two rules the same, then chunking can be applied.*

Let $m1$ and $m2$ be the differences in the left hand side semantics of the two rules, and $e1$ and $e2$ the strings of terminals that, if removed, would make the right hand sides of the rules the same. A new category n is created and the following two new rules are added to the grammar.

$$n(m1, 0.01) \rightarrow e1 \qquad\qquad n(m2, 0.01) \rightarrow e2$$

Rules $r1$ and $r2$ are replaced by a new rule that is identical to $r1$ (or $r2$) except that $e1$ (or $e2$) is replaced with $n(X, S)$ on the right hand side, and $m1$ (or $m2$) is replaced with a new variable X in the left hand side semantics. The second argument of the left hand side of $r1$ is replaced with a new variable SR. If the score of $r1$ was a constant value $c1$, an expression of the form $\{SR \ is \ S * 0.01\}$ is added to the right hand side of $r1$. If the score of $r1$ was a variable, then the arithmetic expression $\{SR \ is \ S1 * c1\}$ in the right hand side of $r1$ is replaced by $\{SR \ is \ S * S1 * 0.01\}$.

For example the agent of previous examples, which has rules 15 and 16 for conjunctive and disjunctive formulas in its grammar, could apply chunking to these rules and create a new syntactic category for binary connectives as follows.

$$s([P, Q, R], S) \rightarrow c2(P, S1), s(Q, S2), s(R, S3), \{S \ is \ S1 * S2 * S3 * 0.01\} \ (17)$$
$$c2(and, 0.01) \rightarrow and \ (18)$$
$$c2(or, 0.01) \rightarrow or \ (19)$$

Rules 15 and 16 would be replaced with rule 17, which generalises them because it can be applied to arbitrary formulas constructed using binary connectives, and rules 18 and 19, which state that *and* and *or* belong to $c2$ (the syntactic category of binary connectives), would be added to the grammar.

Chunk II. *If the left hand side semantics of two grammar rules $r1$ and $r2$ can be unified applying substitution $X/m1$ to $r1$ and there exists a string of terminals $e1$ in $r2$ that corresponds to a nonterminal $c(X, S)$ in $r1$, then chunking can be applied to $r2$ as follows. Rule $r2$ is deleted from the grammar and a new rule of the following form $c(m1, 0.01) \rightarrow e1$ is added to it.*

Suppose the agent of previous examples adopts or invents the following rule[6].

$$s([\text{iff}, up, right], 0.01) \to \textit{iffupright}. \tag{20}$$

Simplification of rule 20 with rules 4 and 3 leads to replace rule 20 with 21.

$$s([\text{iff}, Q, R], S) \to \text{iff}, s(Q, SQ), s(R, SR), \{S \textit{ is } SQ * SR * 0.01\} \tag{21}$$

Then chunking could be applied to 21 and 17, replacing rule 21 with 22.

$$c2(\text{iff}, 0.01) \to \text{iff} \tag{22}$$

3.4   Self-organisation

The agent in the previous examples has been very lucky, but things are not always that easy. Different agents can invent different words for referring to the same propositional constants or connectives, and the invention process uses a random order to concatenate the expressions associated with the components of a given meaning. This has important consequences, because the simplification rule takes into account the order in which the expressions associated with the meaning components appear in the terminals of a rule. Imagine an agent invented/adopted the following holistic rules for expressing [and,light,right] and [if,light,right].

$$s([and, light, right], 0.01) \to \textit{andlightright}$$
$$s([if, light, right], 0.01) \to \textit{ifrightlight}$$

The result of simplifying these rules using rules 2 and 3 would be the following pair of rules which cannot be used for constructing a syntactic category for binary connectives, because they do not satisfy the preconditions of chunking.

$$S([and, X, Y], SC) \to and, s(X, SX), s(Y, SY), \{SC \textit{ is } SX * SY * 0.56\}$$
$$S([if, X, Y], SC) \to \text{if}, s(Y, SY), s(X, SX), \{SC \textit{ is } SX * SY * 0.56\}$$

The agents must therefore reach agreements on how to name propositional constants and connectives, and on how to order the expressions associated with the different components of non-atomic meanings. Self-organisation principles help to coordinate the agents' grammars in such a way that they prefer to use the rules that are used more often by other agents [16,6,3]. The set of rules preferred by most agents for naming atomic meanings and for ordering the expressions associated with the components of non-atomic meanings constitutes the *external language* spread over the population.

The goal of the self-organisation process is that the agents in the population be able to construct a shared external language and that they prefer using the rules in that language over the rest of the rules in their individual grammars.

---

[6] Notice that the scores of all rules created using invention, adoption or induction are initialised to 0.01. The use counters (not shown in the examples) are initialised to 0.

Coordination takes place at the third stage of a language game, when the speaker communicates the meaning it had in mind to the hearer. Depending on the outcome of the language game speaker and hearer take different actions. We have talked about some of them already, such as invention or adoption, but they can also adjust the scores of the rules in their grammars to become more successful in future games.

First we consider the case in which the speaker can generate a sentence for the meaning using the rules in its grammar. If the speaker can generate several sentences for expressing that meaning, it chooses the sentence with the highest score, the rest are called *competing sentences*.

The *score of a sentence* (or a *meaning*) is computed at generation (parsing) multiplying the scores of the rules involved [8]. Consider the generation of a sentence for expressing the meaning $[and, right, light]$ using the following rules.

$$s(light, 0.70) \rightarrow light \quad (23)$$
$$s(right, 0.25) \rightarrow right \quad (24)$$
$$c2(and, 0.50) \rightarrow and \quad (25)$$
$$s([P, Q, R], S) \rightarrow c2(P, S1), s(Q, S2), s(R, S3), \{S \text{ is } S1 \cdot S2 \cdot S3 \cdot 0.01\} \quad (26)$$

The score S of the sentence *andrightligth*, generated by rule 26, is computed multiplying the score of that rule (0.01) by the scores of the rules 25, 24 and 23 which generate the substrings of that sentence. The *score of a lexical rule* is the value of the second argument of the left hand side of the rule (e.g., the score of rule 25 is 0.50). The *score of a grammatical rule* is the last number of the arithmetic expression that appears on the right hand side of the rule[7] (e.g., the score of rule 26 is 0.01). The score of a sentence generated using a grammatical rule is computed using the arithmetic expression on the right hand side of that rule (e.g., the score of sentence *andrightlight* is 0.50*0.25*0.70*0.01=0.00875).

Suppose the hearer can interpret the sentence communicated by the speaker. If the hearer can obtain several interpretations for that sentence, the meaning with the highest score is selected, the rest are called *competing meanings*.

If the meaning interpreted by the hearer is the same as the meaning the speaker had in mind, the game succeeds and both agents adjust the scores of the rules in their grammars. The speaker increases the scores of the rules it used for generating the sentence communicated to the hearer and decreases the scores of the rules it used for generating competing sentences. The hearer increases the scores of the rules it used for obtaining the meaning the speaker had in mind and decreases the scores of the rules it used for obtaining competing meanings. This way the rules that have been used successfully get reinforced, and the rules that have been used for generating competing sentences or competing meanings are inhibited to avoid ambiguity in future language games.

The rules used for *updating the scores of grammar rules* are the same as those proposed in [13]. The rule's original score S is replaced with the result of

---

[7] The Prolog operator *"is"* allows evaluating the arithmetic expression at its right hand side.

evaluating expression 27 if the score is *increased*, and with the result of evaluating expression 28 if the score is *decreased*. The constant μ is a leaning parameter which is set to 0.1.

$$maximum(1,\ S + \mu) \tag{27}$$

$$minimum(0,\ S - \mu) \tag{28}$$

If the meaning interpreted by the hearer it is not equal to the meaning the speaker had in mind, the game fails, and speaker and hearer decrease the scores of the rules they used for generating and interpreting the sentence, respectively. This way the rules that have been used without success are inhibited.

If the speaker can generate a sentence for the meaning it has in mind, but the hearer cannot interpret that sentence, the hearer adopts a holistic rule associating the meaning and the sentence used by the speaker. This holistic rule can be simplified and chunked later using the rest of the rules in the hearer's grammar.

In order to simplify the agents's grammars and avoid possible sources of ambiguity a **mechanism for purging rules** that have not been useful in past language games is introduced. Every ten language games the rules which have been used more than thirty times and have scores lower than 0.01 are removed from the agents' grammars.

4 Experiments

We present the results of some experiments in which three agents construct a shared language that allows communicating the formulas of a logical language $L = \{a, b, c, l, r, u\}$ with six propositional constants. The agents build different, but *compatible, compositional, recursive grammars* that allow them to communicate each other the infinite set of meanings that can be represented in L.

First the agents play 600 language games in which they try to communicate propositional constants. Then they play 1200 language games in which they try to communicate propositional constants and logical formulas constructed using unary and binary connectives (i.e., $\neg, \wedge, \vee, \rightarrow$ and $\leftrightarrow$).

Tables 1 and 2 describe the individual lexicons and grammars built by the agents at the end of a particular simulation run. The grammars built by the agents, although different, are compatible enough to allow total communicative success. That is, the agents always generate sentences that are understood by the other agents.

The grammars of all the agents have recursive rules for expressing formulas constructed using unary and binary connectives. The expression C associated with the connective is always placed at the start of a sentence by the induction algorithm. Let 1 and 2 be the expressions associated with the first and second arguments, respectively, of a formula constructed using a binary connective. The order in which 1 and 2 are concatenated determines thus the form of the sentence. We call *C12-constructions* to those rules that construct a sentence concatenating C, 1 and 2 in C12 order, and *C21-constructions* to those rules that concatenate

Table 1. The lexicons of all the agents are identical, i.e., all the agents prefer the same words for referring to the propositional constants of the language L = { a, b, c, l, r, u}

Lexicon for Propositional Constants		
Lexicon a1	**Lexicon a2**	**Lexicon a3**
s(a1,a,1) → e	s(a2,a,1) → e	s(a3,a,1) → e
s(a1,b,1) → uo	s(a2,b,1) → uo	s(a3,b,1) → uo
s(a1,c,1) → bt	s(a2,c,1) → bt	s(a3,c,1) → bt
s(a1,l,1) → u	s(a2,l,1) → u	s(a3,l,1) → u
s(a1,r,1) → ihg	s(a2,r,1) → ihg	s(a3,r,1) → ihg
s(a1,u,1) → y	s(a2,u,1) → y	s(a3,u,1) → y

them in C21 order. All agents prefer C12-constructions (third rules of a1 and a2, and second rule of a3) for expressing conjunctive and disjunctive formulas, and they prefer to C21-constructions (sixth rules of a1 and a2, and fifth rule of a3) for expressing implications and equivalences. Agents a1 and a2 have invented a syntactic category (c3) for unary connectives, because they probably had several words for expressing negation which were eliminated afterwards by the purging mechanism; a3 has a specific rule for formulas constructed using negation, which uses the word "ps" preferred by the others.

All agents have created syntactic categories (c2, c1) for *binary connectives used in C12-constructions* and they prefer the same words for the connectives *and* and *or* (scores 1). They have created syntactic categories for *binary connectives used in C21-constructions* and they prefer the same words for the connectives *if* and *iff* (scores 1). There are no alternative words for any connective. This is probably due to the fact that the purging mechanism has eliminated such words from the lexicons of the agents.

Figure 1 shows some preliminary results about the evolution of the communicative success, averaged over ten simulation runs with different initial random seeds, for a population of three agents[8].

The agents reach a communicative success of 98% in 250 language games and of 100% in 1000 language games. That is, after each agent has played, on average, 200 language games about propositional constants, and 333 language games about propositional constants and formulas constructed using logical connectives.

5   Related Work

Batali [6] studies the emergence of recursive communication systems as the result of a process of negotiation among the members of a population. The alternative explored in this research is that learners simply store all of their analyzed ob-

---

[8] The *communicative success* is the average of successful language games in the last ten language games played by the agents.

Table 2. Grammars constructed by the agents at the end of a simulation run

Grammars for Propositional Logic

Gram a1

s(a1,[X,Y],R) → c3(X,P), s(Y,Q), {R is P*Q*1}
c3(a1,not,1) → ps

s(a1,[X,Y,Z],T) → c2(X,P), s(Y,Q), s(Z,R), {T is P*Q*R*1}
c2(a1,and,1) → oyv
c2(a1,or,1) → gs

s(a1,[X,Y,Z],T) → c1(X,P), s(Z,Q), s(Y,R), {T is P*Q*R*1}
c1(a1,if,1) → ogb
c1(a1,iff,1) → qan

Gram a2

s(a2,[X,Y],R) → c3(X,P), s(Y,Q), {R is P*Q*1}
c3(a2,not,1) → ps

s(a2,[X,Y,Z],T) → c1(X,P), s(Y,Q), s(Z,R), {T is P*Q*R*1}
c1(a2,and,1) → oyv
c1(a2,or,1) → gs

s(a2,[X,Y,Z],T) → c2(X,P), s(Z,Q), s(Y,R), {T is P*Q*R*1}
c2(a2,if,1) → ogb
c2(a2,iff,1) → qan

Gram a3

s(a3,[not,Y],R) → ps, s(Y,Q), {R is Q*1}

s(a3,[X,Y,Z],T) → c1(X,P), s(Y,Q), s(Z,R), {T is P*Q*R*1}
c1(a3,and,1) → oyv
c1(a3,or,1) → gs

s(a3,[X,Y,Z],T) → c2(X,P), s(Z,Q), s(Y,R), {T is P*Q*R*1}
c2(a3,if,1) → ogb
c2(a3,iff,1) → qan

servations as exemplars. No rules or principles are induced from them. Instead exemplars are used directly to convey meanings and to interpret signals.

The agents acquire their exemplars by recording observations of other agents expressing meanings. A learner finds the cheapest phrase with the observed string and meaning that can be created by combining or modifying phrases from its existing set of exemplars, creating new tokens and phrases if necessary.

As an agent continues to record learning observations, its exemplar set accumulates redundant and contradictory elements. In order to choose which of a

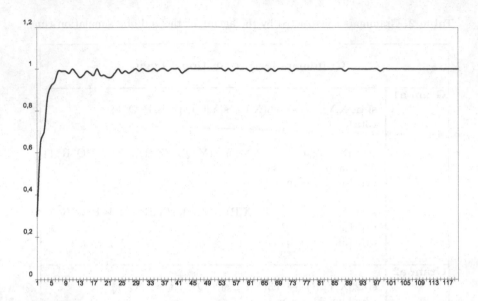

Fig. 1. Evolution of communicative success in experiments involving 3 agents and 1200 language games about propositional constants and formulas of $L = \{a, b, c, r, l, u\}$ constructed using unary and binary connectives (i.e., $\neg, \wedge, \vee, \rightarrow$ or $\leftrightarrow$)

set of alternative exemplars, or modified analyses based on them, will be used in a particular episode the cost of different solution phrases are compared, and a competition process among exemplars based on reinforcement and discouragement is established. An exemplar is reinforced when it is used in the phrase an agent constructs to record a learning observation, and it is discouraged when it is found to be inconsistent with a learning observation. Reinforcement and discouragement implement therefore a competition among groups of exemplars.

In the computational simulations described in [6] ten agents negotiate communication systems that enable them to accurately convey meanings consisting of sets of 2 to 7 atomic formulas (constructed from 22 unary and 10 binary predicates) which involve at most 3 different variables, after each agent has made fewer than 10000 learning observations. Each agent acquires several hundred exemplars, of which a few dozen are singleton tokens identical to those of other agents in the population.

The agents express meanings by combining their singleton tokens into complex phrases using the order of phrases, as well as the presence and position of empty tokens, to indicate configurations of predicate arguments. Empty tokens are also used to signal the boundaries of constituents, the presence of specific argument maps, and details of the structure of the phrases containing them.

Kirby [7] studies the emergence of basic structural properties of language, such as compositionality and recursion, as a result of the influence of learning on the complex dynamical process of language transmission over generations.

This paper describes computational simulations of language transmission over generations consisting of only two agents: an adult speaker and a new learner.

Each generation in a simulation goes through the following steps: 1.- The speaker is given a set of meanings, and produces a set of utterances for expressing them either using its knowledge of language or by some random process of invention. 2.- The learner takes this set of the utterance-meaning pairs and uses it as input for its induction learning algorithm. 3.- Finally a new generation is created where the old speaker is discarded, the learner becomes the new speaker, and a new individual is added to become a new learner. At the start of a simulation run neither the speaker nor the learner have any grammar at all.

The induction algorithm thus proceeds by taking an utterance, incorporating the simplest possible rule that generates that utterance directly, searching then through all pairs of rules in the grammar for possible subsumptions until no further generalisations can be found, and deleting finally any duplicate rules that are left over. The inducer uses *merging* and *chunking* to discover new rules that subsume pairs of rules that have been learnt through incorporation, and *simplification* for generalising some rules using other rules in the grammar.

The meaning space of the second experiment described in [7] consists of formulas constructed using 5 binary predicates, 5 objects and 5 embedding binary predicates. Reflexive expressions are not allowed (i.e., the arguments of each predicate must be different). Each speaker tries to produce 50 degree-0 meanings, then 50 degree-1 meanings, and finally 50 degree-2 meanings. The grammar of generation 115 in one of the simulation runs has syntactic categories for nouns, verbs, and verbs that have a subordinating function. It also has a grammar rule that allows expressing degree-0 sentences using VOS (verb, object, subject) order, and another recursive rule that allows expressing meanings of degree greater than 0. In the ten simulation runs performed the proportion of meanings of degrees 0, 1 and 2 expressed without invention in generation 1000 is 100%.

6   Conclusions

This paper has addressed the problem of the acquisition of the syntax of propositional logic. An approach based on general purpose cognitive capacities such as invention, adoption, parsing, generation and induction has been proposed. Self-organisation principles have been used to show how a shared set of preferred lexical entries and grammatical constructions, i.e., a *language*, can emerge in a population of autonomous agents which do not have any initial linguistic knowledge.

Experiments in which a population of autonomous agents comes up with a language that allows them to communicate about the formulas of a propositional language have been presented. This language although simple has interesting properties found in natural languages, such as compositionality and recursion.

Acknowledgements

The author would like to thank the anonymous reviewers for their valuable comments and suggestions on how to improve the structure of the paper.

References

1. Steels, L.: The origins of syntax in visually grounded robotic agents. Artificial Intelligence **103(1-2)** (1998) 133–156
2. Steels, L.: The emergence of grammar in communicating autonomous robotic agents. In: Proceedings of the European Conference on Artificial Intelligence. IOS Publishing, Amsterdam. (2000)
3. Steels, L.: Constructivist development of grounded construction grammars. In: Proc. Annual Meeting of Association for Computational Linguistics. (2004) 9–16
4. Steels, L., Wellens, P.: How grammar emerges to dampen combinatorial search in parsing. In: Proc. of Third International Symposium on the Emergence and Evolution of Linguistic Communication. (2006)
5. Hurford, J.: Social transmission favors linguistic generalization. In: The Evolutionary Emergence of Language: Social Function and the Origins of Linguistic Form, Cambridge University Press (2000) 324–352
6. Batali, J.: The negotiation and acquisition of recursive grammars as a result of competition among exemplars. In: Linguistic Evolution through Language Acquisition: Formal and Computational Models, Cambridge U.P. (2002) 111–172
7. Kirby, S.: Learning, bottlenecks and the evolution of recursive syntax. In: Linguistic Evolution through Language Acquisition: Formal and Computational Models, Cambridge University Press (2002) 96–109
8. Vogt, P.: The emergence of compositional structures in perceptually grounded language games. Artificial Intelligence **167(1-2)** (2005) 206–242
9. McCarthy, J.: Formalizing Common Sense. Papers by John McCarthy. Ablex. Edited by Vladimir Lifschitz (1990)
10. Sierra-Santibáñez, J.: Grounded models as a basis for intuitive reasoning. In: Proceedings of the Seventeenth International Joint Conference on Artificial Intelligence. (2001) 401–406
11. Sierra-Santibáñez, J.: Grounded models as a basis for intuitive and deductive reasoning: The acquisition of logical categories. In: Proceedings of the European Conference on Artificial Intelligence. (2002) 93–97
12. Sierra-Santibáñez, J.: Grounded models as a basis for intuitive reasoning: the origins of logical categories. In: Papers from AAAI–2001 Fall Symposium on Anchoring Symbols to Sensor Data in Single and Multiple Robot Systems. Technical Report FS-01-01, AAAI Press. (2001) 101–108
13. Steels, L.: The Talking Heads Experiment. Volume 1. Words and Meanings. Special Pre-edition for LABORATORIUM, Antwerpen (1999)
14. Steels, L., Kaplan, F., McIntyre, A., V Looveren, J.: Crucial factors in the origins of word-meaning. In: The Transition to Language, Oxford Univ Press (2002) 252–271
15. Steels, L.: Macro-operators for the emergence of construction grammars. SONY CSL (2004)
16. Steels, L.: The synthetic modeling of language origins. Evolution of Communication **1(1)** (1997) 1–35

Robots That Learn Language: Developmental Approach to Human-Machine Conversations

Naoto Iwahashi[1,2]

[1] National Institute of Information and Communication Technology,
[2] ATR Spoken Language Communication Research Labs
2-2-2 Hikaridai, Seika-cho, Soraku-gun, Kyoto 619-0288 Japan
naoto.iwahashi@atr.jp
http://www.slc.atr.jp/~niwaha/

Abstract. This paper describes a machine learning method that enables robots to learn the capability of linguistic communication from scratch through verbal and nonverbal interaction with users. The method focuses on two major problems that should be pursued to realize natural human-machine conversation: a scalable grounded symbol system and belief sharing. The learning is performed in the process of joint perception and joint action with a user. The method enables the robot to learn beliefs for communication by combining speech, visual, and behavioral reinforcement information in a probabilistic framework. The beliefs learned include speech units like phonemes or syllables, a lexicon, grammar, and pragmatic knowledge, and they are integrated in a system represented by a dynamical graphical model. The method also enables the user and the robot to infer the state of each other's beliefs related to communication. To facilitate such inference, the belief system held by the robot possesses a structure that represents the assumption of shared beliefs and allows for fast and robust adaptation of it through communication with the user. This adaptive behavior of the belief systems is modeled by the structural coupling of the belief systems held by the robot and the user, and it is performed through incremental online optimization in the process of interaction. Experimental results reveal that through a practical, small number of learning episodes with a user, the robot was eventually able to understand even fragmental and ambiguous utterances, act upon them, and generate utterances appropriate for the given situation. This work discusses the importance of properly handling the risk of being misunderstood in order to facilitate mutual understanding and to keep the coupling effective.

1 Introduction

The process of human communication is based on certain beliefs shared by those communicating. Language is one such shared belief, and it is used to convey meaning based on its relevance to other shared beliefs [1]. These shared beliefs are formed through interaction with the environment and other people, and the meaning of utterances is embedded in such shared experiences.

P. Vogt et al. (Eds.): EELC 2006, LNAI 4211, pp. 143–167, 2006.
© Springer-Verlag Berlin Heidelberg 2006

From the perspective of objectivism, if those communicating want to logically convince each other that proposition p is a shared belief, they must prove that the infinitely nested proposition, "They have information that they have information that ... that they have information that p," also holds. However, in reality, all we can do is assume, based on a few clues, that our beliefs are identical to those of the other people we are talking to. In other words, it can never be guaranteed that our beliefs are identical to those of other people. Because shared beliefs defined from the viewpoint of objectivism do not exist, it is more practical to see shared beliefs as a process of interaction between the belief systems held by each person communicating. The processes of generating and understanding utterances rely on the system of beliefs held by each person, and this system changes autonomously and recursively through these two processes. Through utterances, people simultaneously send and receive not only the meanings of their words but also, implicitly, information about each other's system of beliefs. This dynamical process works in a way that makes the belief systems consistent with each other. In this sense, we can say that the belief system of one person couples structurally with the belief systems of those with whom he or she is communicating [2].

Communication by spoken language is one of the most natural methods for human-machine interfaces. The progress made in sensor technologies and in the infrastructure of ubiquitous computing has enabled machines to sense physical environments as well as the behavior of users. In the near future, machines that change their behavior according to the situation in order to support human activities in everyday life will become more and more common, and for this they should feature user-centered intelligent interfaces. One way to obtain such interfaces is through personalization [3], and one of the most essential features of personalized multimodal interfaces is the ability of the machine to share experiences with the user in the physical world. In the future, spoken language interfaces will become increasingly important not only because they enable hands-free interaction but also because of the nature of language, which inherently conveys meaning based on shared experiences as mentioned above. For us to take advantage of such interfaces, language processing methods must make it possible to reflect shared experiences.

However, existing language processing methods, which are characterized by fixed linguistic knowledge, do not satisfy this requirement [4]. In these methods, information is represented and processed by symbols whose meaning has been pre-defined by the machines' developers. In most cases, the meaning of each symbol is defined by its relationship to other symbols, and it is not connected to perception or to the physical world. The precise nature of experiences shared by a user and a machine, however, depends on the situation. Because it is impossible to prepare symbols for all possible situations in advance, machines cannot appropriately express and interpret experiences under dynamically changing situations. As a result, users and machines fail to interact in a way that accurately reflects shared experiences.

To overcome this problem and realize natural linguistic communication between humans and machines, the methods should satisfy the following requirements.

Scalable Grounded Symbol System: The machines themselves must be able to create a symbol system that reflects their experiences in natural ways. Such a symbol system has to include symbols for perceptual categories, abstract concepts, words, and the map between word sequences (or forms) and meanings (or functions). The information of language, perception, and actions should be processed in an integrative fashion. Perceptual categories should be extracted from this information, and the abstract concepts created based on these categories [5]. The created symbols should then be embedded in an adaptively changing belief system, in which the relations among symbols are represented based on experienced events in the real world. The grounding of the meanings of utterances in conversation in the physical world was explored in [6] and [7], but they did not pursue the learning of grounded symbols.

Belief Sharing: In communications, grounded beliefs held by a user and a machine should ideally be as identical or consistent to each other as possible, with the machine and the user coordinating their utterances and actions to form such beliefs. To achieve such coordination, the machines should include a mechanism that enables the user and machine to infer the state of each other's belief system in a natural way. When a participant interprets an utterance based on their assumptions that certain beliefs are shared and is convinced, based on certain clues, that the interpretation is correct, he or she strengthens the confidence that the beliefs are shared. On the other hand, since the sets of beliefs assumed to be shared by participants actually often contain discrepancies, the more beliefs a listener needs to understand an utterance, the greater the risk that the listener misunderstands it. Therefore, to realize appropriate coupling of belief systems, the computational mechanism should produce utterances so as to control the balance between the transmissions of the meanings of utterances and the information on the state of belief systems. Theoretical research [8] and computational modeling [9] focused on the formation of shared beliefs through the transmission of utterance meanings have attempted to represent the formation of shared beliefs as a procedure- and rule-driven process. In contrast, we should focus on the system of beliefs to be used in the process of generating and understanding utterances in a physical environment; moreover, it is important to represent the formation of this system by a mathematical model to achieve robust communication.

Both of these requirements show that the capability of learning is essential in communications. The cognitive activities related to a scalable grounded symbol system and belief sharing can be observed clearly in the process of language acquisition by infants as well as in everyday conversation by adults. To focus on learning capabilities in communication, we have been taking on the challenge of developing a method that enables robots to learn linguistic communication capability from scratch through verbal and nonverbal interaction with users [10,11,12], instead of directly pursuing language processing for everyday conversation.

Language acquisition by machines has been attracting interest in various research fields [13], and several pioneering studies have developed algorithms based on inductive learning by using a set of pairs, where each pair consists of a word sequence and nonlinguistic information about its meaning. In [14,15,16,17,18], visual information, rather than symbolic, was given as nonlinguistic information. Spoken-word acquisition algorithms based on the unsupervised clustering of speech tokens have also been described [19,15,17]. In [20,21], the socially interactive process for the evolution of grounded linguistic knowledge shared by communication agents was examined from the viewpoint of game theory and a complex adaptive system. In [22], a connectionist model for acquiring the semantics of language through the behavioral experiences of a robot was presented, focusing on the compositionality of semantics.

In contrast, the method described in this paper focuses on online learning of a pragmatic capability in the real world through verbal and nonverbal interaction with humans, as well as consideration to the above two requirements. This approach enables a robot to develop the pragmatic capability within a short period of interaction by fast and robust adaptation of its belief system relative to a user. This fast and robust adaptation is a very important feature, since a typical user cannot tolerate extended interaction with a robot that does not possessed communication capability and, moreover, situations in actual everyday conversation continuously change.

The learning method applies information from raw speech and visual observations as well as behavioral reinforcement, which is integrated in a probabilistic framework. A system of beliefs belonging to the robot includes speech units like phonemes or syllables, a lexicon consisting of words whose meanings are grounded in vision and motion, simple grammar, non-linguistic beliefs, the representation of the assumption of shared beliefs, and the representation of the consistency between the belief systems of the user and the robot. This belief system is represented by a dynamical graphical model (e.g. [23]), and expands step-by-step through learning. First, the robot learns the basic linguistic beliefs, which comprise speech units, lexicon, and grammar, based on joint perceptual experiences between the user and the robot [10,12]. Then, the robot learns an entire belief system based on these beliefs online in an interactive way to develop a pragmatic capability [11]. The belief system has a structure that reflects the state of the user's belief system; thus, the learning makes it possible for the user and the robot to infer the state of each other's belief systems. This mechanism works to establish appropriate structural coupling, leading to mutual understanding.

This paper proceeds as follows. Section 2 describes the setting for the robot to learn linguistic communication. The requirements on a scalable grounded symbol system and belief sharing are mainly addressed from Sec. 3 to Sec. 5 and in Sec. 6, respectively. Section 3 explains the method of learning speech units, followed by Sec. 4, which describes the learning method of words referring to

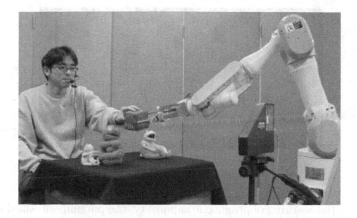

Fig. 1. Interaction between a user and a robot

objects, motions, and abstract concepts. Section 5 relates to the learning method of simple grammar. Section 6 addresses the method for learning pragmatic capability, which enables the structural coupling of belief systems held by a robot and a user. Section 7 discusses the findings and mentions future works.

2   Setting for Learning

2.1   Interaction

The spoken-language acquisition task in this work was set up as follows. A camera unit and a robot arm with a hand were set alongside a table, and a participant and the learning robot saw and moved the objects on the table as shown in Fig. 1. The robot arm had seven degrees of freedom and the hand had one. A touch sensor was attached to the robot's hand. The robot initially did not possess any concepts regarding the specific objects or the ways in which they can be moved, nor did it have any linguistic knowledge.

The interactions for step-by-step learning were carried out as follows. First, in learning speech units, a participant spoke for approximately one minute. Second, in learning words that refer to objects, the participant pointed to an object on the table while speaking a word describing it. A sequence of such learning episodes provides a set of pairs, each of which is comprised of the image of an object and the speech describing it. The objects used included boxes, stuffed and wooden toys, and balls (examples are shown in Fig. 2). In addition, in each of the episodes for learning words referring to motions, the participant moved an object while speaking a word describing the motion. Third, in each of the episodes for learning grammar, the participant moved an object while uttering a sentence describing the action. By the end of this learning, the participant and the robot had shared certain linguistic beliefs consisting of a lexicon and simple grammar, and the robot could understand utterances [1] to some extent.

---

[1] No function words are included in the lexicon.

Fig. 2. Examples of objects used

Finally, in the learning of pragmatic capability, the participant asked the robot to move an object by making an utterance and a gesture, and the robot acted in response. If the robot responded incorrectly, the user slapped the robot's hand. The robot also asked the user to move an object, and the user acted in response. The robot's system of beliefs was formed incrementally, online, through such interaction.

2.2   Speech and Image Signal Processing

A close-talk microphone was used for speech input. The camera unit contained three separate CCDs so that three-dimensional information on each scene could be obtained. The information regarding the position in terms of the depth coordinate was used in the attention-control process.

Speech was detected and segmented based on changes in the short-time power of speech signals, and objects were detected when they were located at a distance of 50-80 cm from the stereo camera unit. All speech and visual sensory output was converted into predetermined features. The speech features used were Mel-frequency cepstral coefficients [24], which are based on short-time spectrum analysis, their delta and acceleration parameters, and the delta of short-time log power. These features (25-dimensional) were calculated in 20-ms intervals with a 30-ms-wide window. The visual features used were position on the table (two-dimensional: horizontal and vertical coordinates), velocity (two-dimensional), L*a*b* components (three dimensions) for the color, complex Fourier coefficients (eight dimensions) of 2D contours for the shape [25], and the area of an object (one dimension) for the size. Trajectory of the object's motion is represented by a time-sequence of its positions.

3   Learning Speech Units

3.1   Difficulty

Speech is a time-continuous one-dimensional signal. The method learns statistical models of the speech units from such a signal without any transcription on phoneme sequence nor any boundaries between phonemes being given. The difficulty of learning speech units is ascribed to the difficulties of speech segmentation and the clustering of speech segments into speech units.

3.2 Method Using Hidden Markov Models

It is possible to cope with the difficulty described above by using Hidden Markov Models (HMMs) and their learning algorithm called the Baum-Welch algorithm [26]. The HMM is a particular form of a graphical model that statistically represents dynamic characteristics of time-series data. It consists of unobservable states, each of which has a probability distribution of observed data, and the probabilities of transitions between them. The Baum-Welch algorithm makes it possible to perform the segmentation, clustering, and learning of HMM parameters simultaneously.

In this method, each speech unit HMM includes three states and allows for left-to-right transitions. Twenty speech unit HMMs were connected to one another to construct a whole speech unit HMM (Fig. 3), in which transitions were allowed from the last states of the speech unit HMMs to their first states. All parameters of this HMM were learned using speech data approximately one minute in length without any phoneme transcriptions. After learning the speech unit HMMs, the individual speech unit HMMs h_1, h_2, h_3, ..., and h_{N_p} were separated from one another by deleting edges between them, and a speech unit HMM set was constructed. The model for each spoken word was represented by connecting these speech unit HMMs.

3.3 Number of Speech Units

In the above method, the number N_p of speech unit models was determined empirically. However, ideally it should be learned from speech data. Such a method has already been presented [10], which learns the number of speech units and the number of words simultaneously from data comprising pairs of an image of an object and a spoken word describing it. The model performs in a batch-like manner using mutual information between the image and speech observations.

4 Learning Words

4.1 Words Referring to Objects

Difficulty. In general, the difficulty of acquiring spoken words and the visual objects they refer to as their meanings can be ascribed to the difficulties in specifying features and extending them.

   Specification: The acoustic features of a spoken word and the visual features of an object to which it refers should be specified using spatiotemporally continuous audio-visual data. For speech, this means that a continuously spoken utterance is first segmented into intervals, after which acoustic features are extracted from one of the segmented intervals. For objects, this means that

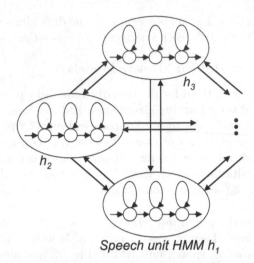

Speech unit HMM h_1

Fig. 3. Structure of HMM for learning speech units

an object is first selected for a given situation, and then the spatial part of the object is segmented; after that, visual features are extracted from the segmented part of the object.

Extension: In order to create categories for a given word and its meaning, it is necessary to determine what other features fall into the category to which the specified features belong. This extension of the features of a word's referent to form the word's meaning has been investigated through psychological experiments [27]. When shown an object and given a word for it, human subjects tend to extend the features of the referent immediately to infer a particular meaning of the word, a cognitive ability called *fast mapping* (e.g. [28]), although such inference is not necessarily correct. For machines, however, the difficulty in acquiring spoken words arises not only from the difficulty in extending the features of referents but also from that in understanding spoken words. This is because the accuracy of speech recognition by machines is currently much lower than that by humans, meaning it is not easy for machines to determine whether two different speech segments belong to the same word category.

Learning Method. The method described here mainly addresses the problem of extension, in which learning is carried out in an interactive way [12]. The user shows a physical object to the robot and at the same time speaks the name of the object or its description. The robot then decides whether the input word is a word in its vocabulary (whether it is a *known* word) or not (whether it is an *unknown* word). If the robot judges that the input word is an unknown word, it enters the word into its vocabulary. If the robot judges that it cannot make an accurate decision, it asks the user a question to confirm whether the input word is part of its vocabulary. For the robot to make a correct decision, it uses not only speech but also visual information about the objects to make an accurate

Fig. 4. A scene in which utterances were made and understood

decision about an unknown word. For example, when the user shows an orange and says the word /ɔrinʒ/, even if the speech recognizer outputs an unknown word /areːʒ/ as the first candidate, the system can modify it to the correct word /ɔrinʒ/ in the lexicon using visual clues. Such a decision is carried out by using a function that represents the confidence that an input pair of image o and speech s belongs to each existing word category w and is adaptively changed online.

Each word or lexical item to be learned includes statistical models, $p(s|w)$ and $p(o|w)$, for the spoken word and an object image category for its meaning. The model for each image category $p(o|w)$ is represented by a Gaussian function in a twelve-dimensional visual feature space (in terms of shape, color and size), and learned based on a Bayesian method (e.g. [29]) every time an object image is given. The Bayesian method makes it possible to determine the area in the feature space that belongs to an image category in a probabilistic way, even if only a single sample is given. Learned words include those that refer to the whole objects, shapes, colors, sizes, and combinations of them. The model for each spoken word $p(s|w)$ was represented by a concatenation of speech unit HMMs; this extends a speech sample to a spoken word category.

4.2 Words Referring to Motions

The concept of motion of moving objects represents the time-varying spatial relation between a trajector and a landmark [30]. In Fig. 4, for instance, if the stuffed toy in the middle and the box at the right are considered landmarks, the movements of the trajector are understood as *move over* and *move onto*, respectively. The robot has to infer the landmark selected in each scene, which is not observed in the learning data. In addition, the coordinates in the space should be determined to appropriately represent the graphical model for each concept of a motion.

In the proposed method [31], the concepts regarding motions are represented by probability density functions of the trajectory u of moved objects. The probability density function $p(u|o_{t,p}, o_{l,p}, w)$ for the trajectory of the motion referred by word w is represented by a HMM given the positions $o_{t,p}, o_{l,p}$ of a trajector and a landmark. The HMMs of the motions are learned while the coordinates and the landmarks are being inferred based on the EM algorithm, in which

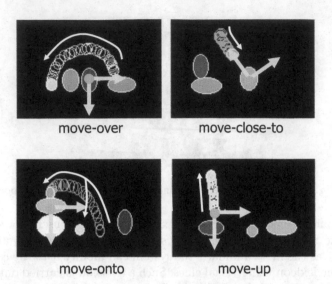

move-over   move-close-to

move-onto   move-up

Fig. 5. Examples of trajectories of objects moved in the learning episodes, and selected landmarks and coordinates

a landmark is taken as a latent variable. Examples of inferred landmarks and coordinates in the learning of some motion concepts are shown in Fig. 5.

The trajectory for the motion referred by a word is generated by maximizing the output probability of the learned HMM, given the positions of a trajector and a landmark. This maximization is carried out by the algorithm described in [32].

A graphical model of the lexicon containing words referring to objects and motions is shown in Fig. 6

4.3   Abstract Meanings

The categories that are learned by the previously mentioned methods are formed directly from perceptual information. However, we have to consider words that refer to concepts whose levels of abstractness are higher and that are not formed directly from perceptual information, such as "tool," "food," and "pet." In a study on the abstract nature of symbols' meanings [33], it was shown that chimpanzees could learn the lexigrams (graphically represented words) that refer to not only individual object categories (e.g. "banana," "apple," "hammer" and "key") but also the functions ("tool" and "food") of the objects. They could also learn the connection between the lexigrams referring to these two kinds of concepts and generalize it appropriately to connect new lexigrams for individual objects to one of the lexigrams for functions.

A method enabling robots to have this capability of chimpanzees was proposed in [34]. In that method, the motions given to objects are taken as their functions. The main problem is the decision regarding whether the meaning of a new input word is for a concept formed directly from perceptual information

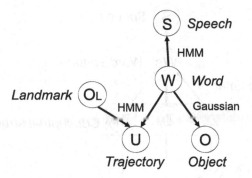

Fig. 6. A graphical model of a lexicon containing words referring to objects and motions

or for a function of objects. Because these two kinds of concepts are allocated to the states of different nodes in the graphical model, the problem becomes the selection of the structures of the graphical model. This selection is performed by the Bayesian principle with the calculation of posterior probabilities using the variational Bayes method [35].

5   Learning Grammar

5.1   Difficulty

In learning grammar using moving images of actions and speech describing them, the robot should detect the correspondence between a semantic structure in the moving image and a syntactic structure in speech. However, such semantic and syntactic structures are not observable. While we can extract an enormous number of structures from a moving image and speech, we ideally select the ones for which the correspondence between them is the most appropriate. The grammar should be statistically learned using such correspondences, and inversely used to extract the correspondence.

5.2   Learning Method

The set comprising triplets of a scene O before an action, the action a, and a sentence utterance s describing the action, $\mathcal{D}_g = \{(s_1, a_1, O_1), (s_2, a_2, O_2), \ldots, (s_{N_g}, a_{N_g}, O_{N_g})\}$, is given in this order as learning data. Scene O_i includes the set of positions $o_{j,p}$ and features $o_{j,f}$ concerning color, size, and shape, $j = 1, \ldots, J_i$, of all objects in the scene. The action a_i is represented by a pair, (t_i, u_i), of trajector object t_i and the trajectory u_i of its movement.

It is assumed that each utterance is generated based on the stochastic grammar G. The grammar G is learned by maximizing the likelihood of the joint probability density function $p(s, a, O; L, G)$, where L denotes a parameter set of the lexicon. This function is represented by a graphical model with an internal structure that includes the parameters of the grammar G and the conceptual structure z that the utterance represents (Fig. 7).

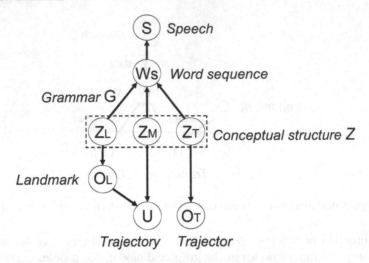

Fig. 7. Graphical model of lexicon and grammar

The conceptual structure used here is expressed with three attributes as the elements in an image schema - [motion], [trajector], and [landmark] - that are initially given to the system, and they are fixed. For instance, when the image is the one shown in Fig. 4 and the corresponding utterance is the sequence of spoken words *"large Kermit brown box move-onto"*, the conceptual structure might be

$$\begin{bmatrix} Z_T \text{ [trajector]} & : large\ Kermit \\ Z_L \text{ [landmark]} & : brown\ box \\ Z_M \text{ [motion]} & : move\text{-}onto \end{bmatrix},$$

where the right-hand column contains the spoken word sub-sequences referring to trajector, landmark, and motion, in a moving image. Let y denote the order of conceptual attributes, which also represents the order of the constituents with the conceptual attributes in an utterance. For instance, in the above utterance example, the order is [trajector]-[landmark]-[motion]. The grammar is represented by the set comprising occurrence probabilities of the possible orders as $G = \{P(y_1), P(y_2), ..., P(y_k)\}$. By assuming $p(z, O\ ; L, G)$ is constant, the joint log-probability density function is written as

$$\log p(s, a, O\ ; L, G)$$

$$= \log \sum_z p(s|z\ ; L, G) p(a|z, O\ ; L, G) p(z, O\ ; L, G)$$

$$\approx \alpha \max_{z,l} \Bigg(\log p(s|z\ ; L, G) \qquad\qquad\qquad\qquad \text{[Speech]}$$

$$+ \log p(u|o_{t,p}, o_{l,p}, W_M\ ; L) \qquad\qquad\qquad \text{[Motion]}$$

$$+ \log p(o_{t,f}|W_T\ ; L) + \log p(o_{l,f}|W_L\ ; L)\Bigg) \quad . \quad \text{[Static Image of Object]}$$

$$(1)$$

where α is a constant value of $p(z, O; L, G)$. Furthermore, t and l are discrete variables across all objects in each moving image, and represent, respectively, a trajector object and a landmark object. In addition, W_M, W_T, and W_L are, respectively, word sequences corresponding to the motion, trajector, and landmark in the conceptual structure z.

The estimate $\tilde{G}_i$ of grammar G given ith learning data is obtained as the maximum values of the posterior probability distribution as

$$\tilde{G}_i = \underset{G}{\mathrm{argmax}}\, p(G \mid \mathcal{D}_g^i ; L) \quad . \tag{2}$$

where $\mathcal{D}_g^i$ denotes learning sample set $\{(s_1, a_1, O_1), (s_2, a_2, O_2), \ldots, (s_i, a_i, O_i)\}$. An utterance asking the robot to move an object is understood using the lexicon L and the grammar G, and one of the objects in the current scene O is accordingly grasped and moved by the robot arm. The algorithm that understands speech s infers the conceptual structure $z = (W_T, W_L, W_M)$ and generates action $\tilde{a} = (\tilde{t}, \tilde{u})$ as

$$\tilde{a} = \underset{a}{\mathrm{argmax}}\, \log p(s, a, O ; L, \tilde{G}) \quad . \tag{3}$$

The robot arm is controlled according to the generated trajectory $\tilde{u}$.

6 Learning Pragmatic Capability Based on Coupling of Belief Systems

6.1 Difficulty

As mentioned in Sec. 1, a pragmatic capability relies on the capability to infer the state of another participant's belief system. The computational mechanism should enable the robot to adapt its assumption of shared beliefs rapidly and robustly through verbal and nonverbal interaction. It also should control the balance between transmissions of the meaning of utterances and the information on the state of belief systems. The following is an example of generating and understanding utterances based on the assumption of shared beliefs. Suppose that in the scene shown in Fig. 4 the object on the left, Kermit, has just been put on the table. If the user in the figure wants to ask the robot to move Kermit onto the box, he may say, *"Kermit box move-onto"*. In this situation, if the user assumes that the robot shares the belief that the object moved in the previous action is likely to be the next target for movement and the belief that the box is likely to be something for the object to be moved onto, he might just say *"move-onto"*. To understand this fragmental utterance, the robot has to possess similar beliefs. If the user knows that the robot has acted as he has asked in response, he would strengthen the confidence that the beliefs he has assumed to be shared are really shared. Inversely, when the robot wants to ask the user to do something, the beliefs that it assumes to be shared are used in the same way. We can see that the former utterance is more effective than the latter in transmitting the meaning of the utterance, while the latter is more effective in transmitting the information on the state of belief systems.

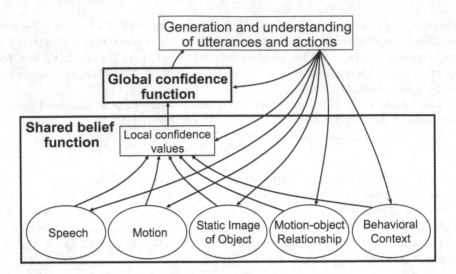

Fig. 8. Belief system of the robot that consists of shared belief and global confidence functions

6.2   Representation of a System of Beliefs

To cope with the above difficulty, a system of beliefs needs to consist of the following two parts:

Shared belief function, which represents the assumption of shared beliefs and is composed of a set of belief modules with values (local confidence) representing the degree of confidence that each belief is shared by the robot and the user.

Global confidence function, which represents the degree of confidence for the shared belief function.

Such a belief system is depicted in Fig. 8. The beliefs we used are those concerning speech, motions, static images of objects, behavioral context, and motion-object relationship. The behavioral context and motion-object relationship are represented as follows.

Motion-object relationship $B_R(o_{t,f}, o_{l,f}, W_M; R)$**:** The motion-object relationship represents the belief that in the motion corresponding to motion word W_M, feature $o_{t,f}$ of object t and feature $o_{l,f}$ of object l are typical for a trajector and a landmark, respectively. This belief is represented by a conditional multivariate Gaussian probability density function, $p(o_{t,f}, o_{l,f} | W_M; R)$, where R is its parameter set.

Effect of behavioral context $B_H(i, q; H)$**:** The effect of behavioral context represents the belief that the current utterance refers to object i, given behavioral context q. Here, q includes information on whether object i was a trajector or a landmark in the previous action and whether the user's current gesture is referring to object i. This belief is represented by a parameter set H.

6.3   Shared Belief Function

The beliefs described above are organized and assigned local confidence values to obtain the shared belief function used in the processes of generating and understanding utterances. This shared belief function Ψ is the extension of $\log p(s, a, O; L, G)$ in Eq. 1. The function outputs the degree of correspondence between utterance s and action a, and it is written as

$$
\Psi(s, u, O, q, L, G, R, H, \Gamma)
$$

$$
= \max_{l,z} \Bigg(\gamma_1 \log p(s|z \; ; \; L, G) \qquad\qquad\qquad\qquad \text{[Speech]}
$$

$$
+ \gamma_2 \log p(u|o_{t,p}, o_{l,p}, W_M \; ; \; L) \qquad\qquad \text{[Motion]}
$$

$$
+ \gamma_2 \Big(\log p(o_{t,f}|W_T \; ; \; L) + \log p(o_{l,f}|W_L \; ; \; L) \Big) \qquad \text{[Static Image of Object]}
$$

$$
+ \gamma_3 \log p(o_{t,f}, o_{l,f}|W_M \; ; \; R) \qquad\qquad \text{[Motion-Object Relationship]}
$$

$$
+ \gamma_4 \Big(B_H(t, q \; ; \; H) + B_H(l, q \; ; \; H) \Big) \Bigg) \quad . \qquad \text{[Behavioral Context]}
$$

$$
\tag{4}
$$

where $\Gamma = \{\gamma_1, \ldots, \gamma_4\}$ is a set of local confidence parameters for beliefs corresponding to the speech, motion, static images of objects, motion-object relationship, and behavioral context. Given O, q, L, G, R, H, and Γ, the corresponding action, $\tilde{a} = (\tilde{t}, \tilde{u})$, understood to be the meaning of utterance s, is determined by maximizing the shared belief function as

$$
\tilde{a} = \arg \max_a \Psi(s, a, O, q, L, G, R, H, \Gamma) \quad . \tag{5}
$$

6.4   Global Confidence Function

The global confidence function f outputs an estimate of the probability that the robot's utterance s will be correctly understood by the user, and it is written as

$$
f(d) = \frac{1}{\pi} \arctan \left(\frac{d - \lambda_1}{\lambda_2} \right) + 0.5 \quad , \tag{6}
$$

where λ_1 and λ_2 are the parameters of this function. Input d of this function is a margin in the value of the output of the shared belief function between an action that the robot asks a user to do and other actions in the process of generating an utterance. Margin d in generating utterance s to refer to action a in scene O under behavioral context q is defined as

$$
d(s, a, O, q, L, G, R, H, \Gamma)
$$
$$
= \Psi(s, a, O, q, L, G, R, H, \Gamma) - \max_{A \neq a} \Psi(s, A, O, q, L, G, R, H, \Gamma) \quad . \tag{7}
$$

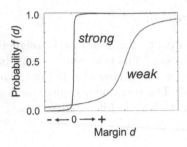

Fig. 9. Examples of the shapes of global confidence functions

The examples of the shapes of global confidence functions are shown in Fig. 9. Clearly, a large margin increases the probability of the robot being understood correctly by the user. If there is a high probability of the robot's utterances being understood correctly even when the margin is small, we can say that the robot's beliefs are consistent with those of the user. The example of a shape of such a global confidence function is indicated by "strong". In contrast, the example of a shape in the case when a large margin is necessary to get a high probability is indicated by "weak". When the robot asks for action a in scene O under behavioral context q, the robot generates utterance $\tilde{s}$ so as to bring the value of the output of f as close as possible to the value of parameter ξ, which represents the target probability of the robot's utterance being understood correctly. This utterance can be represented as

$$\tilde{s} = \arg\min_s \Big(f(d(s, a, O, q, L, G, R, H, \Gamma)) - \xi \Big) \quad . \tag{8}$$

The robot can increase its chance of being understood correctly by using more words. On the other hand, if the robot can predict correct understanding with a sufficiently high probability, it can manage with a fragmental utterance using a small number of words.

6.5   Learning Methods

The shared belief function and the global confidence function are learned separately in the processes of utterance understanding and utterance generation.

The decision function is learned incrementally, online, through a sequence of episodes, each of which comprises the following steps.

1. Through an utterance and a gesture, the user asks the robot to move an object.
2. The robot acts on its understanding of the utterance.
3. If the robot acts correctly, the process is terminated. Otherwise, the user slaps its hand.
4. The robot acts in a different way.
5. If the robot acts incorrectly, the user slaps its hand. The process is terminated.

The robot adapts the values of parameter set R for the belief about the motion-object relationship, parameter set H for the belief about the effect of the behavioral context, and local confidence parameter set Γ. Lexicon L and grammar G were learned beforehand as described in the previous sections, and they were fixed. When the robot acts correctly in the first or second trials, it learns R by applying the Bayesian learning method using the information of features of trajector and landmark objects $o_{t,f}, o_{l,f}$ and motion word W_M in the utterances. In addition, when the robot acts correctly in the second trial, the robot associates utterance s, correct action a, incorrect action A done in the first trial, scene O, and behavioral context q with one another and makes these associations a learning sample. When the ith sample $(s_i, a_i, A_i, O_i, q_i)$ is obtained based on this process of association, H_i and Γ_i are adapted to approximately minimize the probability of misunderstanding as

$$(\tilde{H}_i, \tilde{\Gamma}_i) = \arg \min_{H, \Gamma} \sum_{j=i-K}^{i} w_{i-j}\, g\big(\Psi\,(s_j, a_j, O_j, q_j, L, G, R_i, H, \Gamma)$$
$$- \Psi\,(s_j, A_j, O_j, q_j, L, G, R_i, H, \Gamma)\big), \quad (9)$$

where $g(x)$ is $-x$ if $x < 0$ and 0 otherwise, and K and w_{i-j} represent the number of latest samples used in the learning process and the weights for each sample, respectively.

The global confidence function f is learned incrementally, online, through a sequence of episodes that consist of the following steps.

1. The robot generates an utterance to ask the user to move an object.
2. The user acts according to his or her understanding of the robot's utterance.
3. The robot determines whether the user's action is correct.

In each episode, the robot generates an utterance that brings the value of the output of global confidence function f as close to ξ as possible. After each episode, the value of margin d in the utterance generation process is associated with information about whether the utterance was understood correctly, and this sample of associations is used for learning. The learning is done online incrementally so as to approximate the probability that an utterance will be understood correctly by minimizing the weighted sum of squared errors in the most recent episodes. After the ith episode, parameters λ_1 and λ_2 are adapted as

$$[\lambda_{1,i}, \lambda_{2,i}] \leftarrow (1 - \delta)[\lambda_{1,i-1}, \lambda_{2,i-1}] + \delta[\tilde{\lambda}_{1,i}, \tilde{\lambda}_{2,i}], \quad (10)$$

where

$$(\tilde{\lambda}_{1,i}, \tilde{\lambda}_{2,i}) = \arg \min_{\lambda_1, \lambda_2} \sum_{j=i-K}^{i} w_{i-j}(f(d_j\,; \lambda_1, \lambda_2) - e_j)^2, \quad (11)$$

where e_i is 1 if the user's understanding is correct and 0 if it is not, and δ is the value that determines the learning speed.

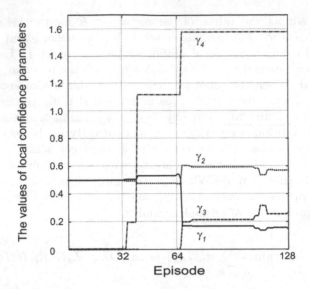

Fig. 10. Changes in the values of local confidence parameters

6.6 Experimental Results

Utterance understanding by the robot. Sequence $\mathcal{D}_d$ of quadruplets (s_i, a_i, O_i, q_i), $i = 1, \ldots, N_d$, comprising the user's utterance s_i, scene O_i, behavioral context q_i, and action a_i that the user wants to ask the robot to perform, was used for the interaction. At the beginning of the sequence, the sentences were relatively complete (e.g., "*green kermit red box move-onto*"). Then the lengths of the sentences were gradually reduced (e.g., "*move-onto*") to become fragmental so that the meanings of the sentences were ambiguous. At the beginning of the learning course, the local confidence values γ_1 and γ_2 for speech, static images of objects, and motions were set to 0.5, while γ_3 and γ_4 were set to 0.

R could be estimated with high accuracy during the episodes in which relatively complete utterances were given and understood correctly. In addition, H and Γ could be effectively estimated based on the estimation of R during the episodes in which fragmental utterances were given. Figure 10 shows changes in the values of γ_1, γ_2, γ_3, and γ_4. The values did not change during the first thirty-two episodes because the sentences were relatively complete and the actions in the first trials were all correct. Then, we can see that the value γ_1 for speech decreased adaptively according to the ambiguity of a given sentence, whereas the values γ_2, γ_3 and γ_4 for static images of objects, motions, the motion-object relationship, and behavioral context increased. This means that nonlinguistic information was gradually being used more than linguistic information.

Figure 11 (a) shows the decision error (misunderstanding) rates obtained during the course of the interaction, along with the error rates obtained for the same learning data by keeping the values of the parameters of the shared belief function fixed to their initial values. In contrast, when fragmental utterances

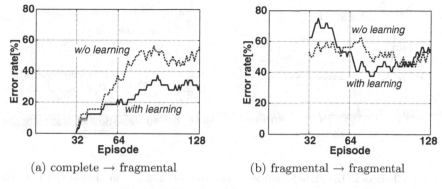

(a) complete → fragmental   (b) fragmental → fragmental

Fig. 11. Change in decision error rate

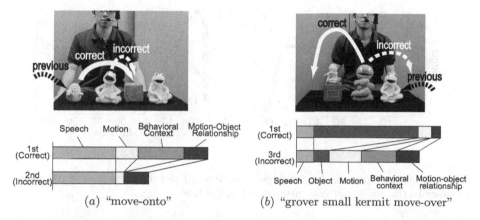

(a) "move-onto"   (b) "grover small kermit move-over"

Fig. 12. Examples of actions generated as a result of correct understanding and the weighted ouput log-probabilities from the beliefs, along with the second and third action candidates, that led to incorrect actions

were provided all over the sequence of interaction, the learning was not effective (Fig. 11 (b)) because the robot misunderstood the utterances too often.

Examples of actions generated as a result of correct understanding are shown together with the output log-probabilities from the weighted beliefs in Figs. 12 (a) and (b), along with the second and third action candidates, which led to incorrect actions. It is clear that each nonlinguistic belief was used appropriately in understanding the utterances according to their relevance to the situations. Beliefs about the effect of behavioral context were more effective in Fig. 12 (a), while in Fig. 12 (b), beliefs about the concepts for the static images of objects were more effective than other nonlinguistic beliefs in leading to the correct understanding.

Utterance generation by the robot. A sequence of triplets (a, O, q) consisting of scene O, behavioral context q, and action a that the robot needed to ask the user to perform was given beforehand for the interaction. In each episode,

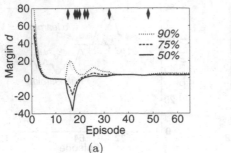
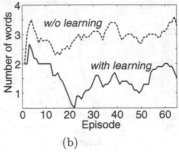

(a)   (b)

Fig. 13. Changes in the global confidence function (a) and the number of words needed to describe the objects in each utterance (b), $\xi = 0.75$

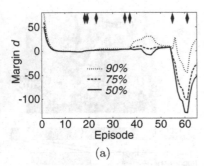
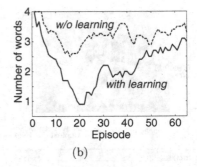

(a)   (b)

Fig. 14. Changes in the global confidence function (a) and the number of words needed to describe the objects in each utterance (b), $\xi = 0.95$

the robot generated an utterance so as to make the global confidence function as close to 0.75 as possible. Even when the target value was fixed at 0.75, we found that the obtained values were distributed widely around it. The initial shape of the global confidence function was set so as to make $f^{-1}(0.9) = 161$, $f^{-1}(0.75) = 120$, and $f^{-1}(0.5) = 100$, meaning that a large margin was necessary for an utterance to be understood correctly. In other words, the shape of f in this case represents weak confidence. Note that when all of the values are close to 0, the slope in the middle of f is steep, and the robot makes the decision that a small margin is sufficient for its utterances to be understood correctly. The shape of f in this case represents strong confidence.

The changes in $f(d)$ are shown in Fig. 13 (a), where three lines have been drawn for $f^{-1}(0.9)$, $f^{-1}(0.75)$, and $f^{-1}(0.5)$ to make the shape of f easily recognizable. The episodes in which the utterances were misunderstood are depicted in the upper part of the graph by the black lozenges. Figure 13 (b) displays the changes in the moving average of the number of words used to describe the objects in each utterance, along with the changes obtained in the case when f was not learned, which are shown for comparison. After the learning began, the slope in the middle of f rapidly became steep, and the number of words decreased.

The function became temporarily unstable with $f^{-1}(0.5) < 0$ at around the 15th episode. The number of words then became too small, which sometimes led to misunderstanding. We might say that the robot was overconfident in this period. Finally, the slope became steep again at around the 35th episode.

We conducted another experiment in which the value of parameter ξ was set at 0.95. Figure 14 shows the result of this experiment. It is clear that after approximately the 40th episode the change in f became very unstable, and the number of words became large. We found that f became highly unstable when the utterances with a large margin, d, were not understood correctly.

7 Discussion

Sharing the risk of being misunderstood. The experiments in learning a pragmatic capability illustrate the importance of sharing the risk of not being understood correctly between the user and the robot. In the learning period for utterance understanding by the robot, the values of the local confidence parameters changed significantly when the robot acted incorrectly in the first trial and correctly in the second trial. To facilitate the learning, the user had to gradually increase the ambiguity of utterances according to the robot's developing ability to understand them and had to take the risk of not being understood correctly. In the robot's learning period for utterance generation, it adjusted its utterances to the user while learning the global confidence function. When the target understanding rate ξ was set to 0.95, the global confidence function became very unstable in cases where the robot's expectations of being understood correctly at a high probability were not met. This instability could be prevented by using a lower value of ξ, which means that the robot would have to take a greater risk to be understood correctly.

Accordingly, in human-machine interaction, both users and the robots must face the risk of not being understood correctly and thus adjust their actions to accommodate such risk in order to effectively couple their belief systems. Although the importance of controlling the risk of error in learning has generally been seen as an exploration-exploitation trade-off in the field of reinforcement learning by machines (e.g. [36]), we argue here that the mutual accommodation of the risk of error by those communicating is an important basis for the formation of mutual understanding.

Partiality of information and fast adaptation of function. An utterance includes only partial information that is relevant to what a speaker wants to convey to a listener. The method interpreted such an utterance by using the belief system under a given situation, and this enabled the robot and the user to adapt to each other rapidly.

In the field of autonomous robotics, the validity of the architecture in which sub-systems are allocated in parallel has been shown [37]. This architecture can flexibly cope with two problems faced by systems interacting with the physical world: the partiality of information and real-time processing [38]. On the other hand, statistical inference using partial information has been studied intensively, particularly in the research on Bayesian networks [39], in which parallel connection of sub-systems is not necessarily important.

The shared belief function Ψ is a kind of Bayesian network in which a small number of weighting values Γ are added to some nodes, and it has an architecture with belief modules allocated in parallel as shown in Eq.4. Due to this structure of the belief system, the method could successfully cope with the partiality of information and enable rapid and robust adaptation of the function by changing weighting values.

Initial setting. *No free lunch theory* [40] shows that when no prior knowledge on a problem exists, it is not possible to assume that one learning algorithm is superior to another. That is, there is no learning method that is efficient for all possible tasks. This suggests that we should pay attention to domain specificity as well as versatility.

In the methods described here, the initial setting for the learning was decided by taking into account the generality and efficiency of language learning. The semantic attributes – [motion], [trajector], and [landmark] – were given beforehand because they would be general and essential in linguistic and other cognitive processes. With this setting, however, the constructions the method could learn were limited to those like transitive and ditransitive ones. Overcoming this limitation is a future work.

Integrated learning. In the method, speech units, lexicon, grammar, and pragmatic capability were learned step-by-step separately. These learning processes, however, should be carried out simultaneously. In developmental psychology, it has been shown that a pragmatic capability facilitates the process of learning other linguistic knowledge, such as the specification of referents in word learning [41]. The computational mechanism for such cognitive bootstrapping should be pursued.

Prerequisites for conversation. Language learning can be regarded as a kind of role reversal imitation [42]. To coordinate roles in a joint action among participants, they should read the intentions of the others. It is known that in the very early stage of development infants become able to understand the intentional actions of others [43] and even to understand that others might have beliefs different from the ones held by themselves [44].

The method described here enabled the robot to understand the user's utterances, act, and make utterances to ask the user to act. The roles in this speak-and-act task, however, were given to the robot and the user beforehand, and they knew it. For the robot to learn the conversational (speak-and-speak) capability, the robot should find its role in a joint action by itself and coordinate it with the user.

Psychological investigation. The experimental results showed that the robot could learn the system of beliefs that the robot had assumed the user had. Because the user and the robot came to understand fragmental and ambiguous utterances, they must have shared similar beliefs and must have been aware of that. It would be interesting to investigate through psychological experiments the dynamics of belief sharing between users and robots.

8 Conclusion

A developmental approach to language processing for grounded conversations was presented. It can cope with two major requirements that existing language processing methods cannot satisfy: a scalable grounded symbol system and belief sharing. The proposed method enabled a robot to learn a pragmatic capability online in a short period of verbal and nonverbal interaction with a user by rapid and robust adaptation of its grounded belief system.

Acknowledgements. I would like to thank Komei Sugiura and an anonymous reviewer for comments on earlier drafts of this manuscript. This work was supported by a research grant from the National Institute of Informatics.

References

1. Sperber, D., Wilson, D.: Relevance (2nd Edition). Blackwell (1995)
2. Maturana, H.R.: Biology of language – the epistemology of reality. In Miller, G.A., Lenneberg, E., eds.: Psychology and Biology of Language and Thought – Essay in Honor of Eric Lenneberg. (1978) 27–64
3. Negroponte, N.: Being Digital. Alfred A. Knopf Inc. (1995)
4. Allen, J., Byron, D., Dzikovska, M., Ferguson, G., Galescu, L., Stent, A.: Toward conversational human-computer interaction. AI Magazine (2001)
5. Johnson, M.: The Body in the Mind - The Bodily Basis of Meaning, Imagination, and Reason. University of Chicago Press (1987)
6. Winograd, T.: Understanding Natural Language. Academic Press New York (1972)
7. Shapiro, C.S., Ismail, O., Santore, J.F.: Our dinner with Cassie. In: AAAI 2000 Spring Symposium on Natural Dialogues with Practical Robotic Devices. (2000) 57–61
8. Clark, H.: Using Language. Cambridge University Press (1996)
9. Traum, D.R.: A computational theory of grounding in natural language conversation. Doctoral dissertation, University of Rochester (1994)
10. Iwahashi, N.: Language acquisition through a human-robot interface by combining speech, visual, and behavioral information. Information Sciences **156** (2003)
11. Iwahashi, N.: A method of coupling of belief systems through human-robot language interaction. In: IEEE Workshop on Robot and Human Interactive Communication. (2003)
12. Iwahashi, N.: Active and unsupervised learning of spoken words through a multimodal interface. In: IEEE Workshop on Robot and Human Interactive Communication. (2004)
13. Brent, M.R.: Advances in the computational study of language acquisition. Cognition (61) (1996) 1–61
14. Dyer, M.G., Nenov, V.I.: Learning language via perceptual/motor experiences. In: Proc. of Annual Conf. of the Congnitive Science Society. (1993) 400–405

15. Nakagawa, S., Masukata, M.: An acquisition system of concept and grammar based on combining with visual and auditory information. Trans. Information Society of Japan 10(4) (1995) 129–137
16. Regier, T.: The Human Semantic Potential. MIT Press (1997)
17. Roy, D.: Integration of speech and vision using mutual information. In: Proc. Int. Conf. on Acoustics, Speech and Signal Processing. (2000) 2369–2372
18. Steels, L., Kaplan, K.: Aibo's first words. the social learning of language and meaning. Evolution of Communication 4(1) (2001) 3–32
19. Gorin, A., Levinson, S., Sanker, A.: An experiment in spoken language acquisition. IEEE Trans. on Speech and Audio Processing 2(1) (1994) 224–240
20. Steels, L., Vogt, P.: Grounding adaptive language games in robotic agents. In: Proc. of the Fourth European Conf. on Artificial Life. (1997)
21. Steels, L.: Evolving grounded communication for robots. Trends in Cognitive Science 7(7) (2003) 308–312
22. Sugita, Y., Tani, J.: Learning semantic combinatoriality from the interaction between linguistic and behavioral processes. Adaptive Behavior (13(1)) 33–52
23. Jordan, M.I., Sejnowski, T.J., eds.: Graphical Models - Foundations of Neural Computation. The MIT Press (2001)
24. Davis, S., Mermelstein, P.: Comparison of parametric representations for monosyllabic word recognition in continuously spoken sentences. IEEE Transactions on Acoustics, Speech and Signal Processing 28(4) (1980) 357–366
25. Persoon, E., Fu, K.S.: Shape discrimination using Fourier descriptors. IEEE Trans Systems, Man, and Cybernetics 7(3) (1977) 170–179
26. Baum, L.E., Petrie, T., Soules, G., Weiss, N.: A maximization technique occurring in the statistical analysis of probabilistic functions of Markov chains. Annals of Mathematical Statistics 41(1) (1970) 164–171
27. Bloom, P.: How children learn the meanings of words. MIT Press (2000)
28. Imai, M., Gentner, D.: A crosslinguistic study of early word meaning – universal ontology and linguistic influence. Cognition 62 (1997) 169–200
29. DeGroot, M.H.: Optimal Statistical Decisions. McGraw-Hill (1970)
30. Langacker, R.: Foundation of cognitive grammar. Stanford University Press, CA (1991)
31. Haoka, T., Iwahashi, N.: Learning of the reference-point-dependent concepts on movement for language acquisition. Tech. Rep. of the Institute of Electronics, Information and Communication Engineers PRMU2000-105 (2000)
32. Tokuda, K., Kobayashi, T., Imai, S.: Speech parameter generation from HMM using dynamic features. In: Proc. Int. Conf. on Acoustics, Speech and Signal Processing. (1995) 660–663
33. Savage-Rumgaugh, E.: Ape Language – From Conditional Response to Symbol. Columbia Univ. Press (1986)
34. Iwahashi, N., Satoh, K., Asoh, H.: Learning abstract concepts and words from perception based on Bayesian model selection. Tech. Rep. of the Institute of Electronics, Information and Communication Engineers PRMU-2005-234 (2006)
35. Attias, H.: Inferring parameters and structure of latent variable models by variational Bayes. In: Int. Conf. on Uncertainty in Artificial Intelligence. (1999) 21–30
36. Dayan, P., Sejnowski, T.J.: Exploration bonuses and dual conrol. Machine Learning 25 (1996) 5–22
37. Brooks, R.: A robust layered control system for a mobile robot. IEEE Journal of Robotics and Automation (1) (1986) 14–23
38. Matsubara, H., Hashida, K.: Partiality of information and unsolvability of the frame problem. Japanese Society for Artificial Intelligence 4(6) (1989) 695–703

39. Pearl, J.: Probabilistic reasoning in intellignet systems: Networks of Plausible Inference. Morgan Kaufmann (1988)
40. Wolpert, D.H.: The relationship between PAC, the statistical physics framework, the Bayesian framework, and the VC framework. In Wolpert, D.H., ed.: The mathematics of Generalization, Addison-Wesley, Reading, MA (1995)
41. Tomasello, M.: The pragmatics of word learning. Cognitive Studies 4(1) (1997) 59–74
42. Carpenter, M., Tomasello, M., Striano, T.: Role reversal imitation and language in typically developing infants and children with autism. INFANCY 8(3) (2005) 253–278
43. Behne, T., Carpenter, M., Call, J., Tomasello, M.: Unwilling versus unable – infants' understanding of intentional action. Developmental Psychology 41(2) (2005) 328–337
44. Onishi, K.H., Baillargeon, R.: Do 15-month-old infants understand false beliefs? Science 308 (2005) 225–258

Simulating Meaning Negotiation Using Observational Language Games*

Tiina Lindh-Knuutila, Timo Honkela, and Krista Lagus

Adaptive Informatics Research Centre
Helsinki University of Technology
P.O. Box 5400, FIN-02015 TKK, Finland
firstname.lastname@tkk.fi

Abstract. In this article, we study the emergence of associations between words and concepts using the self-organizing map. In particular, we explore the meaning negotiations among communicating agents. The self-organizing map is used as a model of an agent's conceptual memory. The concepts are not explicitly given but they are learned by the agent in an unsupervised manner. Concepts are viewed as areas formed in a self-organizing map based on unsupervised learning. The language acquisition process is modeled in a population of simulated agents by using a series of language games, specifically observational games. The results of the simulation experiments verify that the agents learn to communicate successfully and a shared lexicon emerges.

1 Introduction

The acquisition of concepts can be viewed as the process of grounding them in language use. How do concepts form, to begin with, when no language exists in the environment? The relationship between cognitive and linguistic development can be pinpointed to the question: how do conceptual emergence and the formation of names for the concepts connect? An associated important question is how an agreement on the use of words is reached in a community of agents. This process of converging towards a shared use of words is called meaning negotiation.

We study the emergence of associations between concepts and words with help of a computer simulation and consider the hypothesis that concepts are modeled as areas in some conceptual space (see [1]). Furthermore, we utilize the self-organizing map [2,3] as a model for an agent's conceptual memory [4]. The feasibility of this conceptual memory model is then studied using multi-agent language games, in which agents learn to associate words to meanings in a communicative setting. Prior to learning word-meaning-associations, a conceptual representation is also learned individually by each agent based on sensory data.

1.1 Concept Formation

To be able to model conceptual representations in a cognitive framework, we are using the conceptual spaces theory [1]. According to the theory, concepts can be modeled

---

* This work was supported by the Academy of Finland through *Adaptive Informatics Research Centre* that is a part of the Finnish Centre of Excellence Programme.

P. Vogt et al. (Eds.): EELC 2006, LNAI 4211, pp. 168–179, 2006.

as geometrical areas in a multidimensional conceptual space rather than as symbols or connections among neurons. Gärdenfors proposes that certain neural network or statistical methods, e.g. multi-dimensional scaling or self-organizing maps can be used as a basis for a domain in a conceptual space [1]. It is assumed that concepts are not innate but learned in interaction with the world (consider e.g. [5]).

The self-organizing map (SOM) [3] is a neural network model developed originally in the early 1980s [2]. The SOM model is widely known and the details are not presented here. More information can be found in [3].

We use the self-organizing map as an implementation of a conceptual memory. A domain of a conceptual space of an agent is represented by a self-organizing map trained with observation data. Color data, the RGB values of color pictures, are used for training of the map. Following Gärdenfors' vocabulary, there are then three *quality dimensions* in this *domain* of the conceptual space: R(ed), G(reen) and B(lue). The individual self-organizing maps are trained with the color data prior to the language acquisition. After the initial training of the SOM, the map is not changed. This corresponds to a situation in which a child initializes its feature representations based on natural visual data. When an object (color vector) is perceived during the simulation, it is mapped to the trained SOM by finding a unit whose distance to the perceived input is the smallest. This map node is the best-matching unit (BMU) [3]. In our experiments, a cognitive agent does not have any initial ordering or access to the inputs and thus the initialization of the self-organizing map is random. The objects that the agents see belong to eight different categories: What the agents perceive are slightly different instances of these categories. This differs from previous approaches, e.g. [6], where the meanings are presented simply as integers.

The meaning of a word is taken to be a node or a group of (neighboring) nodes in a self-organizing map. Thus, the word is not directly associated with 'something in the world', the referent, which in our case is the perceived data vector but to a representation: The representation of the data vector is the best-matching unit (BMU) in the map.

The association between a word and a concept is implemented by assigning a word to a certain node in a conceptual map. The mapping between words and conceptual map nodes is many-to-many. A node may have several words associated with it and a word may be associated with several nodes. We make a hypothesis that a general agreement among the agents on the word use emerges during the simulation.

1.2 Language Games

To model the language acquisition process, we are using simulated language games based originally on the notion of Wittgenstein [7]: Every occasion of language use is a language game. In a language game there is a dialogue between two agents, a speaker and a hearer, within a particular contextual setting. It offers a possibility to study the cultural evolution process of language in subsequent language games instead of subsequent agent generations.

There are several types of simulated language games that have been tested within this framework. Here, we briefly present three of them, the observational game, the guessing game and the selfish game. So far, we have implemented only the observational game in which both agents know in advance the topic of the game. The learning is associative: The hearer agent learns the name the speaker uses for that topic.

In the guessing game, both agents are presented a small number of objects. The hearer must then guess which object is the one the speaker refers to with the word it uttered. In the end of the game, the speaker gives some corrective feedback to the hearer telling whether the guess was right or not. In the selfish game introduced by Vogt [8] and Smith [9], the agents do not receive any feedback of the success of their communication. Thus, the learner must infer the meanings of words from their co-occurrences in different contexts or situations. The game is called 'selfish' as in some way the speaker does not care whether the message was correctly understood.

1.3 Related Work

In the domain of concept acquisition modeling, Schyns [10] demonstrated how simple concepts could be learned with a modular neural network model. The model has two modules, one for categorizing the input in an unsupervised manner and another module for learning the names in a supervised mode.

Cangelosi and Parisi [11] as well as Grim et al. [12] use feedforward multilayer neural networks whereas we use self-organizing maps [2,3]. Oudeyer [13] models the self-organization of combinatoriality and phonotactics in vocalization systems with a neural network model that is close to the self-organizing map, without any dimensionality reduction. The self-organizing map is based on an unsupervised learning principle which makes it possible to learn efficiently statistical characteristics of input even when no interpretation or classification for the input is given. In a related work [14], the self-organizing maps are used to model the semantic representations of action verb meanings and their clustering, depending on the body part they are related to. Raitio et al. [15] consider the similarity of representations that emerge in unsupervised, self-organization process of neural lattices when exposed to color spectrum stimuli. Self-organizing maps are trained with color spectrum input, using various vectorial encodings for representation of the input. Furthermore, Raitio et al. use the SOM for a heteroassociative mapping to associate color spectrum with color names.

The language game models discussed here were introduced by Steels [16] to study how a coherent lexicon may emerge by means of cultural interactions, individual adaptation and self-organization. The games have been simulated, e.g., in [9], [16], [17] and [18], or implemented in a population of physical robots, e.g., in [8] and [19].

Our work on the multi-agent learning borrows much from the research on the observational games by Vogt [6,17,8]. Our specific contribution is a detailed model for how perception-to-concept mapping can take place. In [6], there is no categorization at all. In [17], there is a spatial conceptual space which would allow variation around the prototype, but only prototypical colors are used in the simulated world. In our work, we are using the self-organizing map as a spatial conceptual representation, and the colors the agents can perceive contain variation around the prototypes. This means that the mapping between perceptions and concepts is many-to-one: the agents are performing categorization as well.

Learning concepts and language simultaneously is considered in [17]. In our work the conceptual information is learned prior to learning the word-meaning-associations.

This choice does not reflect a position according which language does not influence the formation of conceptual structures. In these experiments, our aim was to consider a situation in which there is originally little or no categorical information available. Simultaneous and continuous learning of conceptual structures and word-meaning-associations would be possible, for instance, by using the self-refreshing self-organizing map [20].

In [17], the compositionality of language is mainly studied using the iterated learning model (ILM) [21] that contains subsequent generations of adult and child agents. The adults are mainly the teachers and the children are the learners of the emerging language. Neither the ILM or the compositionality of language is considered here.

2   Methodology

We implemented the observational game model to study our hypotheses of conceptual modeling and grounding concepts in the language use. In an observational game both agents know in advance the topic of the game. In Vogt's and Steels' robotic experiments this was accomplished by pointing, and later in simulations by using other extra-linguistic information. Our solution is that the agents are able to perceive only one object at the time and this is the topic of the language game. These objects and their properties used in our simulations are presented in more detail later.

Each agent has a conceptual memory based on a SOM and a lexicon. The lexicon contains all words that are in the agent's vocabulary, and information on which nodes of the SOM they are associated to. It also contains a counter value for the word-node pair describing how successfully a word has been used to express a meaning previously. The minimum value of the counter is zero and the maximum value we have used is twenty.

2.1   Algorithm of the Observational Game

Each language game in the simulation proceeds in the following way.

1. Two agents are chosen randomly from the population of agents. One is arbitrarily assigned the role of the speaker, the other the hearer.
2. The topic of the language game is chosen randomly from the set of topics and shown to both agents.
3. Both the speaker and the hearer search for a node in their own conceptual map that best matches the topic (the BMU).
4. The speaker searches for the word that could match the topic. The search is performed in a neighborhood of the best-matching unit (BMU) defined by R, which is an integer, $R \geq 1$. The process of the word search is described later in more detail. If no possible word is found, a new word is invented and associated to the BMU. This word is communicated to the hearer.
5. The hearer searches for a set of possible words that could denote the topic. The search is performed in a similar way as in the case of speaker, but instead of one best word, all the words that are found are returned. If the word the speaker has uttered belongs to this set, the language game is considered a success, otherwise the game fails.

6. In case of a successful game, both the speaker and the hearer increase their counter for the word by one. If the uttered word was not among the labels of the BMU, it is then added to it. The maximum value of the counter is set to 20.
7. If the game fails, the speaker decreases by one the counter of the uttered word. The minimum value allowed for the counter is zero. If the speaker's BMU node did not contain any label but the word was instead found from the neighborhood, the word is not added to the BMU node of the speaker. The hearer labels its BMU with the spoken utterance in any case.

2.2   Utterances

In the simulation framework, each word is a discrete symbol. A word is a string of characters generated from a simple artificial language and it is uttered when needed. If there does not exist a word that could be used to denote the topic of the conversation, a novel word is generated from the language.

In our experiments, a limited artificial language is used. In this language, there are words that contain either four or six characters. The alphabet contains vowels $V = (a, e, i)$ and consonants $C = (b, c, d, f, g, h)$. In total, the alphabet consists of nine letters. Each word of this language begins with a consonant which is then followed by a vowel. The pattern is repeated either once or twice, so all the words are either of the form 'CVCV' or 'CVCVCV'.

In many previous simulations, e.g., [11], the set of words that could be used was small and fixed. In these simulations the set of words is finite but open: new words can enter to the simulation, whereas the number of topics of the language games is fixed.

2.3   Word Search Process Using the SOM

When an agent is shown the topic, i.e. the vector containing the features of the topic, it finds a prototype vector from its conceptual memory that best matches the given input vector. This prototype vector is called the best-matching unit (BMU). The prototype vectors can be assigned labels, the words. The search algorithm searches for words used to label the BMU and nearby nodes that are within the radius R in the neighborhood of the BMU. This means that if there already exists a word associated to a similar enough concept (i.e. there is a word in the neighborhood R of the node), this word can be used to name the new object even if the BMU itself was not associated with any word. As the neighborhood is considered, later in the simulation there are often several possible words the speaker could use. The uttered word is the one that had been used most successfully earlier in the neighborhood of the BMU, defined by the counter values associated to each word-node pair. In case of multiple words with the same count, one of them is selected randomly. If the set of words is empty, a new word is generated and uttered.

The hearer searches for the possible words in a similar way to the point of finding a set of words. The only difference is that there is no need to select the best word but the set of possible words is compared to the word uttered by the speaker. In general, the competing word-meaning pairs are considered to be either synonymous or polysemous, both being features of natural languages as well. Here synonymy is considered as a relative term: words or phrases may have similar meaning to some degree.

3   Experiments

The purpose of our experiments was two-fold: The first goal of the experiments was to verify the hypothesis that the agents are able to develop an emergent and shared lexicon by engaging in the language games, while using the conceptual memory model based on the self-organizing map. Secondly, we were studying the association between the map nodes and the utterances created by agents and how the areas that are named with the same word are formed. To test how the varying parameters affect the overall learning results, experiments were conducted with different population sizes and varying the search radius.

In all experiments, ten simulations were run with different random seeds for 5000 language games. There were three measures used to evaluate the outcome of the simulations. The communication success was calculated after every language game. The coherence and specificity measures were calculated after every 250 games, and the size of the lexicon was calculated in the end of the simulation. The coherence measure indicates whether a certain word is utilized coherently among the agents to denote a certain meaning in the community. Specificity is a measure that decreases if two meanings are referred to with the same word. These measures are explained later in more detail.

3.1   Color Data and Language Game Topics

The agents' conceptual maps were trained with three-dimensional color data vectors. Components of the vector were R(ed), G(reen) and B(lue) values of a pixel in a color picture. The color data consisted of ten pictures — one for each agent. The size of these pictures was 100×100 pixels. Thus, for each agent, the size of the training set was 10000 samples, the total number of pixels in the training picture.

The color pictures were created by drawing filled ellipses and rectangles in color onto a white background. As a starting point, we were using the RGB values of eight different 'prototypical' colors: black, blue, green, cyan, red, magenta, yellow and white. To get less spiky distributions for each color, uniformly distributed noise was added independently to each of the three color channels (RGB) of the picture. The level of noise was set to 20% of the total color range.

In the experiments, a hexagonal map topology was used. The size of the used map was 16×12 map nodes. The maps were initialized randomly. All the maps were trained in a batch training mode. [3]

A set of 400 additional color pictures were utilized as language game topics. They were generated in similar manner as the training data, but were not part of the training set. For the purpose of limiting computational workload, the size of a picture used as a topic was limited to 20×20 pixels. The topic was chosen randomly from this group for each game.

3.2   Evaluation Measures

To evaluate the agent learning, we utilized four measures: communication success, coherence, specificity and lexicon size.

In a successful language game, the word the speaker used to denote a given topic was found among the words that also the hearer associated with the topic. Communication success is a longer-term outcome of the language games. It is defined in a similar way as in [6,8,18] as the average number of correctly played games in the past 100 games or less if no 100 games had been played yet. It is calculated after every language game.

Coherence is a population measure, which measures whether a certain word is utilized coherently among the agents to denote a certain meaning in the community. It is the rate in which agents would produce a certain word to express a particular meaning. The coherence measure calculation used in this work is taken from [18]. For each topic, a fraction of agents that has the same word as a preferred word is calculated and the maximum fraction is taken. This is then averaged over all topics. If an agent does not have a word to express a certain meaning, the coherence is set to zero.

Specificity measure developed by De Jong was used: "Specificity indicates to what degree the words an agent uses determine the referent that is the subject of communication" [18]. Specificity decreases if two meanings are referred to with the same word. Thus it also describes the degree of polysemy in the lexicon: the higher the specificity, the less polysemy there is. Here, the specificity based on preferred words [18] is used.

For each agent, A_i, the specificity, $spec(A_i)$, is calculated using the following formula:

$$spec(A_i) = \frac{n_s^2 - \sum_{k=1}^{n_s} f_k}{n_s^2 - n_s}, \tag{1}$$

where n_s is the number of referents, and f_k is frequency of the word related to the concept that describes how many referents the word is associated to. The specificity of the population, $spec$, is then defined as the average specificity of the agents:

$$spec = \frac{\sum_{i=1}^{n_a} spec(A_i)}{n_a}, \tag{2}$$

where $spec(A_i)$ is the specificity of an agent and n_a is the number of agents. Additionally, if there is no word to denote a certain referent (or topic), it means that the referent cannot be separated from other referents.

In the end of each simulation run, the average size of lexicon was also calculated. In the lexicons, there were also words having a zero counter value, which means that they were not used successfully at all in the course of the simulation. This means that an agent had come up with a new word but this word had not been used successfully and another one had been preferred since. To better show the difference in lexicon sizes, the average size of the lexicon was calculated both before and after the removal of the non-used words. The average lexicon size was calculated as a mean of individual agent lexicon sizes.

4   Results

In all our experiments, the results were averaged over 10 simulation runs. All simulations were run for the population sizes of 2, 4, 6, 8 and 10 agents. The results with varying population size are presented in Fig. 1. The communication success (Fig. 1 a) climbs quickly close to the maximum value of 1.0. The communication success level 1.0 indicates that each of the previous 100 language games ended successfully. The

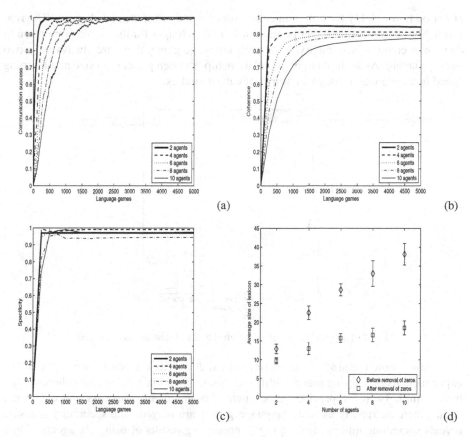

Fig. 1. Communication success (a), coherence (b), specificity (c) and the lexicon size (d) for varying population size, when $R = 2$ and the map size is 16×12

larger the population is, the longer it takes to reach the maximum level, but even in the case of 10 agents the level of 0.9 is reached after approximately 1250 games.

The coherence level (Fig. 1 b) increases also quite rapidly. In the case of population size of 10 agents, the coherence level reaches 0.86, whereas with smaller population sizes it is 0.9 or higher. Thus, as simulation advances, the agents begin to use more and more the same word to denote the same referent, thus forming a shared vocabulary. As pointed out earlier, the coherence does not say anything whether the agents are using the same word to denote *each* referent. The specificity (Fig. 1 c), rises over 0.9 already after 250 games with each population size. Thus, there seems to be little polysemy in this case: The agents are using a separate word for each prototypical color.

The average size of the lexicon (Fig. 1 d) stays between 10 and 17, rising only a little as a function of the population size. The whiskers describe the amount of standard deviation in the average values. The size of the lexicon, all words included, is a function of the population size.

The results seem promising: They clearly show that the agents can develop a shared lexicon to denote the objects they perceive. The size of the population seems only to affect on how quickly the communication success and coherence levels grow. The reason behind this is that in larger populations, it takes longer for the whole population to develop a common vocabulary, as in each language game, there are always only two agents playing. As such, though, the relationship between population size and learning speed is known well through a number of earlier studies.

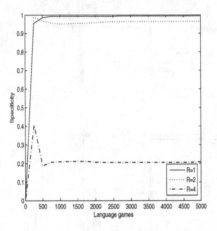

Fig. 2. The specificity values when the search radius was changed

To study how the size of the search radius, R affects the results we repeated the experiment using varying search radii. The communication success and coherence behaved similarly to the previous experiment. Communication success and coherence values increase rapidly as more language games are played. The specificity measure reveals something interesting (see Fig. 2 presenting results of using six agents). With the smaller radii, the specificity rises again over 0.95 after only 500 language games. But when using the largest radius, $R = 4$, the specificity first rises to the level of 0.4 and then drops to the level of 0.3 as the simulation advances: This indicates that in the beginning of the simulation there is some variation in the names for the language game topics. As the simulation advances only few names are gaining popularity: In the end the agents use only a couple of names to denote all the topics.

Examples of conceptual maps from simulations with six agents are shown in Fig. 3. They show the conceptual space of one agent after the simulation run. The self-organizing map is labeled with the words that have been used during the simulation. The figure on the left shows a case where $R = 1$ and in the figure on the right, $R = 4$. A thorough visual interpretation of these figures may be hard since the language is made up by the agents themselves and in the each simulation run, the self-organizing maps look different due to random initialization. Thus, they are shown for general interest only. In the map on the right, there is one dominant word, 'bihi' that is used to label almost everything. In the figure on the left-hand side, there are different words that seem to be dominant in different areas. By only inspecting the visualization of the map, it is impossible to say which words are used the most.

The low specificity value does not affect the communication success at all. The agents just have one or two common words to denote everything. The large search

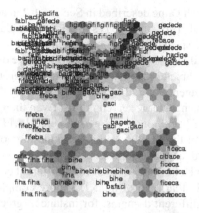 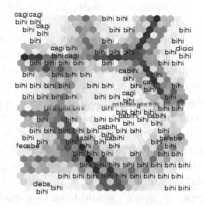

Fig. 3. Two example conceptual maps from simulations with six agents. On the left, a small search radius, $R = 1$, was used. On the right, $R = 4$. The shades of gray denote distances in the original space: The larger the distance, the darker the color. One can see that there are eight clusters on each map which corresponds to the number of prototypical colors used in the input.

radius makes it possible to use a word already in the lexicon for observed topics, even if the best-matching unit related to that word is very far from the new observation. This is caused by the nature of the observational game: There is no need to make distinctions between observations and thus nothing is inhibiting this behavior, as communication success stays high, which was also noticed by Vogt (e.g., [6]).

5 Conclusions and Discussion

In this article, some aspects of language acquisition and conceptual modeling have been considered. In the field of conceptual modeling, the conceptual spaces theory by Gär-denfors [1] has been adopted. The theory provides a medium between the symbolic level of words and the sensory level of 'raw' sensations. The notion of distance provides a possibility to make graded conceptual system: The more prototypical instances of a concept can be seen as more central than the less prototypical instances of the category.

We have described how simulated agents map the perceptions to their conceptual map and associate utterances to these maps. The topological ordering of the maps gives rise, for instance, to a rather natural way for finding names for previously un-named topics. As a model for shared vocabulary acquisition, different types of language games were discussed in this article. A computer simulation to model one of them, the observational game, was implemented based on the work presented in [6], [8] and [16].

The results of the experiments show clearly that when using the observational game model and the SOM-based conceptual maps (1) the agents learned to communicate suc-cessfully on the topics of the games, and (2) a shared lexicon was developed during the simulations. According our definition of successful communication, the agents are also able to communicate successfully and develop a shared lexicon based on adaptation.

Implementing the guessing game and the selfish game described in Section 1.2 in addition to the observational game, would be useful. The language is somehow redundant in the observational game framework: Both the speaker and the hearer know for sure what the topic of the game is and there is no need to have distinct words to separate different objects. One could study if the need to be able to identify the topic from a group of objects is a pressure enough to prevent the agents of calling all referents with the same word as demonstrated in our experiment using a large search radius. Even though comparisons between the different games have been conducted earlier (e.g., [6,17]), we find it important to determine how the use of the SOM-based conceptual memory influences the results in the case of the other two language games.

In future research, the use multiple maps can be be studied, each for a different conceptual domain (consider, for instance, [14]). In that kind of model, a more complex concept say 'apple', would have properties in different domains, for instance, 'green' (or 'yellow', or 'red') in the color domain, 'round(ish)' in the shape domain, and 'sweet' in the taste domain. Gärdenfors [1] argues that the properties that are relevant in the case of a particular concept depend on the context. The context-dependency would then cause some properties to be more salient in that context. It is possible that these saliencies could be modeled with some kinds of weights. Possibly, the research could be expanded further to somewhat complex concepts: to those with properties extending to different domains of conceptual spaces.

References

1. Gärdenfors, P.: Conceptual spaces: The Geometry of Thought. MIT Press (2000)
2. Kohonen, T.: Self-organized formation of topologically correct feature maps. Biological Cybernetics **43** (1982) 59–69
3. Kohonen, T.: Self-Organizing Maps. Springer Series in Information Sciences. Springer (2001)
4. Honkela, T.: Neural nets that discuss: a general model of communication based on self-organizing maps. In Gielen, S., Kappen, B., eds.: Proceedings of ICANN'93, International Conference on Artificial Neural Networks, Amsterdam, the Netherlands, Springer-Verlag, London (1993) 408–411
5. Steels, L.: Perceptually grounded meaning creation. In Tokoro, M., ed.: ICMAS96, AAAI Press (1996)
6. Vogt, P., Coumans, H.: Investigating social interaction strategies for bootstrapping lexicon development. Journal of Artificial Societies and Social Simulation **6**(1) (2003)
7. Wittgenstein, L.: Philosophical Investigations. The Macmillan Company (1963)
8. Vogt, P.: Lexicon Grounding in Mobile Robots. PhD thesis, Vrije Universiteit Brussel (2000)
9. Smith, A.D.M.: Establishing communication systems without explicit meaning transmission. In Kelemen, J., Sosik, P., eds.: Proceedings of the 6th European Conference on Artificial Life, ECAL 2001, Berlin, Heidelberg, Springer-Verlag (2001)
10. Schyns, P.: A modular neural network model of concept acquisition. Cognitive Science **15** (1991) 461–508
11. Cangelosi, A., Parisi, D.: The emergence of a 'language' in a population of evolving neural networks. Connection Science **10**(2) (1998) 83–97
12. Grim, P., Kokalis, T., Tafti, A., Kilb, N.: Evolution of communication with a spatialized genetic algorithm. Evolution of Communication **3**(2) (1999)

13. Oudeyer, P.Y.: The self-organization of combinatoriality and phonotactics in vocalization systems. Connection Science **17**(3-4) (2005) 325–341
14. Wermter, S., Elshaw, M.: Learning robot actions based on self-organising language memory. Neural Networks **16** (2003) 691–699
15. Raitio, J., Vigário, R., Särelä, J., Honkela, T.: Assessing similarity of emergent representations based on unsupervised learning. In: Proc. of International Joint Conference on Neural Networks (IJCNN 2004), Budapest, Hungary (2004) 597–602
16. Steels, L.: Emergent adaptive lexicons. In Maes, P., ed.: SAB96, Cambridge, MA, MIT Press (1996)
17. Vogt, P.: The emergence of compositional structures in perceptually grounded language games. Artificial Intelligence **167**(1-2) (2005) 206–242
18. De Jong, E.: Autonomous Formation of Concepts and Communication. PhD thesis, Vrije Universiteit Brussel (2000)
19. Steels, L., Vogt, P.: Grounding adaptive language games in robotic agents. In Husbands, C., Harvey, I., eds.: Proceedings of the Fourth European conference on Artificial Life, Camridge, MA and London, MIT Press (1997)
20. Pöllä, M., Lindh-Knuutila, T., Honkela, T.: Self-refreshing SOM as a semantic memory model. In: Proceedings of AKRR'05, International and Interdisciplinary Conference on Adaptive Knowledge Representation and Reasoning, Espoo, Finland (2005) 171–174
21. Kirby, S.: Spontaneous evolution of linguistic structure: an iterated learning model of the emergence of regularity and irregularity. IEEE Transactions on Evolutionary Computation **5**(2) (2001) 102–110

Symbol Grounding Through Cumulative Learning

Samarth Swarup[1], Kiran Lakkaraju[1], Sylvian R. Ray[1], and Les Gasser[1,2]

[1] Dept. of Computer Science,
[2] Graduate School of Library and Information Science,
University of Illinois at Urbana-Champaign,
Urbana, IL 61801, USA
{swarup, klakkara, s-ray1, gasser}@uiuc.edu

Abstract. We suggest that the primary motivation for an agent to construct a symbol-meaning mapping is to solve a task. The meaning space of an agent should be derived from the tasks that it faces during the course of its lifetime. We outline a process in which agents learn to solve multiple tasks and extract a store of "cumulative knowledge" that helps them to solve each new task more quickly and accurately. This cumulative knowledge then forms the ontology or meaning space of the agent. We suggest that by grounding symbols to this extracted cumulative knowledge agents can gain a further performance benefit because they can guide each others' learning process. In this version of the symbol grounding problem meanings cannot be directly communicated because they are internal to the agents, and they will be different for each agent. Also, the meanings may not correspond directly to objects in the environment. The communication process can also allow a symbol meaning mapping that is dynamic. We posit that these properties make this version of the symbol grounding problem realistic and natural. Finally, we discuss how symbols could be grounded to cumulative knowledge via a situation where a teacher selects tasks for a student to perform.

1 Introduction

Where do meanings come from? This is one of the most important questions underlying the study of cognition, language, and artificial intelligence. In the field of artificial intelligence, the intellectual history of this problem traces back to the earliest speculations on the nature of intelligence [1]. Alan Turing, in the conclusion to his classic article which introduced the Turing test, suggested that there might be at least two routes to building intelligent machines: attempting very abstract activities like playing chess, or outfitting a computer with sensory devices and then attempting to teach it natural language [2]. In subsequent years the purely symbolic approach gained dominance, partly due to the comparative ease of building purely symbolic systems, and partly due to the influence of the

---

[1] It should be pointed out that this question has a much longer history in philosophy. See, e.g., [1] for a review.

P. Vogt et al. (Eds.): EELC 2006, LNAI 4211, pp. 180–191, 2006.
© Springer-Verlag Berlin Heidelberg 2006

Physical Symbol System Hypothesis of Newell and Simon [3], which says that a set of symbols, combined with appropriate rules for their manipulation (essentially, a *formal system*), is sufficient for general intelligent action. The implicit assumption underlying this view is that intelligent behavior from a machine does not require that the machine "understand" things in the same way as we do.

In response, Searle argued, using his famous Chinese Room Argument, that there is a distinction between intelligent *behavior* and true intelligence [4]. A person could undertake the Turing test in a language unknown to him (say, Mandarin), if he possessed an appropriate program. This program would be a set of rules for manipulating symbols in Mandarin, which he would use to transform questions into answers, and thereby pass the Turing test (if the rules are good enough). Since the person does not know Mandarin, the symbols have no *meaning* for him, though it would appear so to the observer. Intuitively, it seems, a machine using this program would not be *truly* intelligent.

In an attempt to bridge this gap between a symbolic system and a truly intelligent system, Harnad formulated the *symbol grounding* problem. In his words, the problem is thus, "How can the semantic interpretation of a formal symbol system be made intrinsic to the system, rather than just parasitic on the meanings in our heads?" [5]. Though this problem arose in the context of the limitations of purely symbolic systems in cognitive modeling, it was realized to be of fundamental importance in the study of language evolution and the design of artificial languages. Symbol grounding, in this context, concerns the problem of relating the conceptualizations underlying a linguistic utterance to the external world through an agent's sensori-motor apparatus [6].

Harnad suggested that the symbol grounding problem could be solved by building a hybrid symbolic-nonsymbolic system in which symbolic representations are grounded bottom-up in non-symbolic representations which are either *iconic* or *categorical*. Iconic representations correspond directly to objects and events, and categorical representations are based on generalizations from iconic representations (i.e. concepts such as "animal", which do not have direct real-world analogs). This highlights one very important aspect of the symbol-grounding problem: it is concerned with ontology construction. However it ignores another, equally important, aspect: a symbol is a convention between two (or more) agents. Thus it makes no sense for a single agent to try to ground symbols. Further, ontology construction and the construction of a corresponding symbolic system (i.e. lexicon acquisition) are inter-dependent. A new symbol might be created for a new ontological category. Conversely, a new ontological category may be created in response to the use of a symbol by another agent.

This interdependence between symbols and meanings has been understood and incorporated in subsequent work on lexicon acquisition and symbol grounding, most clearly in the well-known series of Talking Heads experiments. See [7] for a review of these and other experiments based on language games. The main issue we have with these experiments is that they consider the development of a shared lexicon to be the *primary* task in which the agents are engaged. Thus, in these experiments, meanings are created primarily through the process of the language game. The argument of this paper, however, is that meanings should be derived from the tasks that a cognitive agent is faced with in the course of its lifetime. Otherwise they will have no relevance to the agent. In other words, the agent will have the means but not the need to communicate. In what follows, we outline a method for combining the processes of solving multiple problems, and developing a grounded symbolic communication system to aid problem-solving.

We first discuss the process of ontology construction, and how an ontology might be extracted from the process of learning to solve multiple related problems. We call this process *cumulative learning*, because the knowledge extracted from the tasks accumulates over time. Since each agent extracts its own cumulative knowledge, these meanings are entirely internal to the agent. We then discuss how it might be possible to ground symbols to this cumulative knowledge, followed by a discussion of some of the consequences of this process. In the concluding section, we discuss some of the advantages and limitations of our approach, and possible future work.

2   Ontology Construction

An ontology determines the domain of discourse, i.e. what a language talks about. From the point of view of an agent, these are the entities that are relevant to the problems or tasks with which it is confronted. The ontology of an agent in a mushroom world, e.g., might contain types of mushrooms, features (such as color, size, and shape) by which these might be distinguished, etc. It might also contain more abstract concepts, like "edible", "poisonous", etc. [8]. Some of these ontological entities might be pre-specified, the result of processes like biological evolution or engineering design. Other entities would be discovered by the agent as it learns to perform the task of distinguishing edible from poisonous mushrooms. This is a primary task for the agent, and each agent could try to solve this task in isolation. However, they clearly stand to gain by developing a language to communicate about these concepts:

- an agent, Alice, who is proficient in distinguishing edible mushrooms from inedible ones, might communicate to another agent, Bob, whether a particular mushroom is edible,
- Alice might be able to teach Bob to distinguish edible mushrooms from poisonous ones himself, assuming he has the same ontology,
- Alice might be able to help Bob acquire the necessary ontological categories for distinguishing edible mushrooms from poisonous ones.

The point is that the ontology emerges from the primary task, though its acquisition might be facilitated by the secondary task of language acquisition. Thus the meanings in a lexicon must have some functional significance for the agent. This is an aspect of language evolution that is missing from most previous work on symbol grounding, with some exceptions [8,9].

Over its lifetime, an agent is expected to encounter many tasks, which might be related to each other. Ideally, the agent should not just learn to solve each task, but should also *learn how to learn*. In other words, if the tasks are related, the agent should be able to improve its learning performance, exhibiting quicker and more robust learning on each new task. This is a subject of much research in the machine learning community and is known variously as transfer learning, multi-task learning, lifelong learning, etc. Generally the improvement in learning performance is achieved by using some learnt information, such as invariants, priors, etc., to bias the learning of new tasks. Our suggestion here is that this learnt information, which we call *cumulative knowledge*, could form the ontology of the agent. We discuss this in more detail below.

3   Cumulative Learning

We use the term cumulative learning to refer to the case where an agent explicitly accumulates a store of knowledge that is extracted from solving multiple tasks and is useful for solving new tasks. The key issue in cumulative learning is that of recognizing, and exploiting, similarities between tasks. That human language is efficacious in this process is suggested by studies of analogical thinking in problem solving [10]. In fact, it has been argued that analogy-making is the core of cognition [11].

A cumulative learning system consists of two parts: a learning mechanism and a knowledge extraction mechanism. These two mechanisms could conceivably use two different representations: effectively a task-dependent, and a task-independent representation, e.g. the learning mechanism could be a recurrent neural network, and knowledge could be extracted in the form of finite state automata [12]. People have also attempted to combine feed-forward neural networks with symbolic rules [13]. However, the drawback to these approaches is that there is always the possibility of translation noise. A recurrent neural network, e.g., is capable of embedding some context-free and context-sensitive grammars [14], and therefore attempting to represent the learnt recurrent net as a finite-state automaton might create errors.

Other approaches attempt to directly transfer parts of the learned neural network, such as the first layer of weights. The idea is that these might represent features that are useful for multiple tasks [15,16]. The limitation of this approach is that knowledge transfer is only possible within-domain, because if the neural networks do not have the same dimension, it is not possible to reuse the weights.

To get around these two problems, we have presented a cumulative learning method that uses graph-structured representations [17]. Learning is done with a genetic algorithm, and knowledge is extracted by mining frequent subgraphs. The idea is that these frequent subgraphs can be used as primitives by the genetic algorithm in the construction of candidate solutions for new tasks, thereby learning faster. Since these networks do not have fixed dimension, we avoid the inflexibility of neural networks. We tested this idea on a set of Boolean function domains. The domains are parameterized by their dimension, n, and the tasks are parameterized by the number of adjacent 1's, k, that must be present in the input for a positive example. For example, a task might consist of inputs of

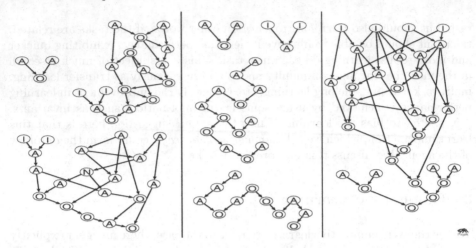

Fig. 1. The left box shows networks learned on the first three tasks (4inputs-2adj-ones, 8inputs-2adj-ones, and 8inputs-3adj-ones). The middle box shows 4 of the 18 subnetworks, extracted by the graph-mining algorithm CloseGraph [18], which appear in at least two of the networks on the left. These would constitute the "meanings" for symbolic communication. The right box shows the network learned for the 12inputs-2adj-ones task, in which some of the subnetworks are seen to appear several times.

dimension four, where an input is classified as positive if two adjacent 1s appear in the input vector. We name this task 4inputs-2adj-ones.

Initially, the agents have a very small set of primitives, consisting of just single nodes that compute the AND, OR, and NOT functions. During the cumulative learning process, they extract many more primitives which are small networks that can be combined together to solve many tasks. This is illustrated in figure 1. The left box in the figure shows the networks learnt on the first three tasks: 4inputs-2adj-ones, 8inputs-2adj-ones, and 8inputs-3adj-ones. AND nodes are labeled A, OR nodes are labeled O, NOT nodes are labeled N, and nodes labeled I are "input" nodes which copy their input unchanged to their output. A and O nodes are assumed to take two inputs, and N and I nodes are assumed to take one input. All arrows in the figure point downward. If a node has fewer inputs shown than it is assumed to require, the remaining inputs are to be supplied externally (i.e. from the input vector).

The middle box in the figure shows some of the sub-networks extracted by the CloseGraph algorithm [18]. These sub-networks are used by the genetic algorithm as primitives when learning to solve the next task: 12inputs-2adj-ones. The right box shows the network learned for this task. Some of the sub-networks are seen to appear in this new network, either whole or in part (where they have been incorporated and then further mutated).

Though this is a very artificial set of tasks, the same kind of representation and cumulative learning method could be used in a more realistic setting, such as motion planning with robots. The idea of primitives carries over easily to this domain, and "behavior networks" (see fig. 2) have been used to represent motion plans [19].

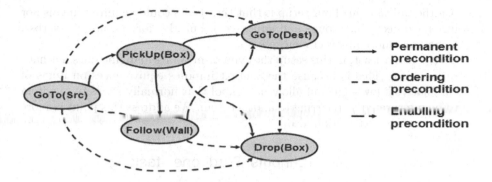

Fig. 2. An example behavior network. Reproduced from [19].

Figure 3 shows a typical comparison of learning curves with and without transfer of knowledge from previously learnt similar tasks. Knowledge transfer results in both faster learning and reduced variance in error (i.e. more robust learning). If another agent, who already knows how to solve the given problem, is able to tell the agent which primitives to use to solve the task, learning would converge even faster.

A natural follow-up to the idea of cumulative learning, therefore, is that the extracted cumulative knowledge might constitute the ontology or meaning space of the agent. To use a somewhat provocative term, an agent *understands* a new task in terms of its cumulative knowledge. The challenge, then, is to develop a symbol system which maps onto the agents' cumulative knowledge and enables communication that helps in learning. We posit that this is a very natural and realistic version of the symbol grounding problem for the following reasons:

- In this setup, meanings are internal to the agents and are not (indeed cannot be) directly communicated. Direct meaning communication is a problem with a lot of the previous work on symbol grounding, as various researchers have begun to point out [20], and work around [21,22].
- Different agents may (and probably will) have somewhat different sets of internal meanings, depending on the sets of problems they have encountered. This is both a problem to be surmounted, and a realistic feature of our setup. We address this further in the next section. Previous work on language evolution has often assumed that all the agents have the same fixed set of meanings. There have been a few notable exceptions, such as [20,23].
- Meanings may not necessarily correspond to objects in the environment. The common example is, what is the meaning of the symbol "chair"? It seems that "chair" corresponds to some prototypical chair which only exists in our minds, and not necessarily in the environment. In the same way, the extracted cumulative knowledge may not necessarily correspond to objects in the environment, though if the same objects are encountered sufficiently often, they might be represented in the cumulative knowledge.

- Another advantage of our setup is that the agents could acquire symbols not just for objects (i.e. nouns and adjectives), but also for actions (i.e. verbs), or perhaps more abstract concepts.
- Last, but not least, in this setup the symbol-meaning mapping does not have to be static. This is because the context imposes equivalences on items of cumulative knowledge and allows a symbol that normally refers to one item to be interpreted as referring to another item. We address this point in more detail in the next section also.

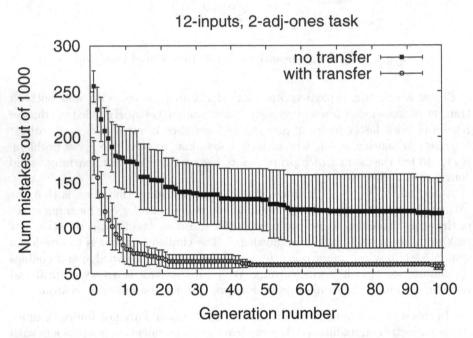

Fig. 3. A typical comparison of learning performance with and without transfer of knowledge. Transfer of knowledge from similar tasks results in faster and more robust learning.

4   Learning to Ground Symbols to Cumulative Knowledge

We now address the question: what might be a learning procedure that leads to the development of a communication system based on cumulative knowledge?

The underlying goal is to create a language that is useful in learning new tasks. Thus the development of the communication system should be guided by learning performance. Suppose Alice knows how to solve a task, i.e. she knows which of *her* internal primitives she can compose to create a solution to a particular task. If she could communicate this information to Bob (and assuming he has the same internal primitives), Bob could learn to solve that particular task essentially in one step.

There are at least two major hurdles to grounding symbols to cumulative knowledge. The first is that cumulative knowledge is entirely internal to the agent. There is nothing the agents can point to, nor can we use the cross-situational learning strategy of [20,22]. The second problem is deeper: since meanings depend on the tasks that have been encountered by the agent and the solutions that the agent has discovered, there is a danger that the meanings may be too different to allow successful communication. In other words, we need some mechanism to keep the ontologies aligned.

To surmount these two problems, we suggest a parent-child (or teacher-student) scenario. This is not an unrealistic assumption, and has been made before, e.g. in the Iterated Learning Model [24]. The parent selects tasks for the child to perform. This gives the parent some measure of control over the ontology that the child is likely to develop. Let us suppose, for simplicity, that the agents are learning Boolean functions. The parent selects a task for the child by creating a training set of labeled examples, which the child must now learn to classify. The child initially has a small set of primitives. Let us assume that the child knows how to compute the AND, OR, and NOT functions. The parent and child, however, do not have a shared symbol system corresponding to these primitives. The parent can easily establish a set of symbols for these functions by selecting extremely simple tasks for the child to perform. For example, if the first task is to perform the AND operation on two inputs, the parent presents the child with the training set: $\{\{(0, 0), 0\}, \{(0, 1), 0\}, \{(1, 0), 0\}, \{(1, 1), 1\}\}$, and the symbol AND. The symbol is meant to indicate which primitive the child should use to solve the task. The child does not know to which of its primitives the symbol AND corresponds, but attempting to solve the task quickly tells it that there is only one primitive which works. It is, of course, possible that the child happens to generate a more complicated network that computes the AND function, so we might need to assume an in-built bias towards smaller networks in the learning algorithm (similar to Ockham's razor).

In a similar way, the parent and child could develop symbols for the OR and NOT functions also. This small shared lexicon provides a foothold for the development of a more complex ontology and a corresponding symbol system. As the parent selects more complex tasks for the child to perform, they will need to develop a convention for communicating about combinations of primitives. This could be something simple, such as generating a sentence by ordering primitives by the number of times they are used in the task, e.g. "AND OR" would indicate that the AND function is to be used more than the OR function in the new task.

As the child learns more complex tasks, its ontology will grow (by mining frequent subgraphs). The parent will not know exactly what the subgraphs that the child has discovered are, but by judicious selection of tasks, it should be possible to guide the emergence of the child's ontology, and to maintain a shared lexicon.

4.1   The Importance of Starting Small

Note that it is very important to *start small*. The parent and child could not develop a shared lexicon if the initial tasks don't serve to bootstrap the communication system. This is rather reminiscent of Elman's work on learning and development with neural networks [25]. He has talked about a rather interesting phenomenon about the learning of natural language: that it is much easier to train neural networks to process natural language sentences if we use a developmental paradigm where initially the networks are severely restricted with respect to their working memory. This essentially focuses the attention of the network on precisely those linguistic structures which help it to subsequently learn the more complex structures (see also [26]). Our symbol grounding procedure suggests that ontology alignment might be a reason why natural languages exhibit this surprising property.

There is a deeper reason for starting small as well. The process of cumulative learning itself benefits greatly from starting small. In other words, even if an isolated agent were learning to solve multiple related problems, it would benefit from starting with small problems. The reason is that for any given problem there are multiple networks that will perform well on it. Not all of them are good from the point of view of knowledge transfer however. One of the problems in cumulative learning, then, is how to find the networks which have subgraphs that can be reused for solving other problems? One solution is to start with small problems, which have very few easy to find solutions. Once the agent starts building up its cumulative knowledge, there is reinforcing effect. Using the cumulative knowledge to find solutions to new problems ensures that more cumulative knowledge will be found. This is a kind of *cumulative advantage* [27].

4.2   Dynamic Symbol Grounding

In real life, symbol grounding has a dynamic or contextual aspect to it. Heidegger refers to this as the "as-ness" of language [28]. In other words, language enables us to see the world (or the context) in a new way. Suppose Alice says to Bob, "I need a hammer." Bob, seeing no hammers around, hands her a rock. This is clearly a successful case of communication, even though the word "hammer" was grounded to a rock by Bob. In fact, Alice's request enabled Bob to see his surroundings in a different way (to see rocks as hammers). This is the "as-ness" that Heidegger is talking about. Our setup also permits dynamic symbol grounding. The task imposes equivalences on the items of cumulative knowledge. This is easy to see with the Boolean function domain. An training set which does not include all possible examples means that there are several Boolean functions which would classify the examples correctly. Further, more complex scenarios might contain situations where not every item in the cumulative knowledge of the agent can be applied, e.g. in fig. 2, some of the preconditions might not be satisfied. The parent might not know which of the child's primitives are inapplicable in a given context, since the primitives of the parent and child will not be identical. Therefore it is easy to imagine situations where the parent suggests using a primitive which the child cannot apply. In such a situation, the child will be forced to interpret the symbol differently, and will apply a perhaps contextually equivalent primitive. The interpretation process can be put in probabilistic terms: the task imposes a prior distribution on which items of cumulative knowledge can be applied, and the child computes a posterior distribution by combining this prior with the suggestion supplied by the parent (which corresponds to a conditional).

5   Conclusion

We have presented our speculations on how a symbolic communication system could be grounded in cumulative knowledge. The advantages of this particular method of meaning construction are several:

- The agents are engaged in multiple tasks over a lifetime, and communication helps in improving performance on these tasks.
- All the agents are not assumed to have the same fixed set of meanings.
- Meanings are internal to the agents, and there is no need for direct meaning communication.
- Symbols and meanings arise in an interdependent manner.
- Symbols can be interpreted in context, i.e. symbol grounding is done dynamically.

There are, however, some limitations to this account as well. One of the main problems is that of ontological structure. Cumulative knowledge, as described here, consists of a set of frequent subgraphs that are useful for multiple tasks. It has no further structure. Ontologies are generally assumed to be hierarchically organized. In this sense, the use of cumulative knowledge as the meaning space of the agent is somewhat unrealistic. On the other hand, it is not clear what could be gained by attempting to give the cumulative knowledge some structural organization. It could be done, however. E.g. if a particular item of cumulative knowledge is a subgraph of another, that implies a `PartOf` relation between them.

Another potential challenge is that of preventing divergence in the meaning space of the agents. The constructive approach we have suggested seems promising in that regard, but it would be sensitive to the "curriculum" chosen by the parent. This bears further investigation. It might also help in answering the question, when does language not evolve?

It might also be argued that not all meanings are cumulative knowledge. We often have names for very specific things, such as "Eiffel tower". This suggests that our account of lexicon development should be combined with other accounts in order to develop a more complete communication system.

Despite these limitations, we believe that there are important connections between cumulative learning and language evolution, and our purpose here is to identify some of these and bring them to the attention of our audience. We believe this can be an area of much fruitful research.

References

1. Sowa, J.F.: Signs, processes, and language games. Available Online: http://www.jfsowa.com/pubs/signproc.htm (1999)
2. Turing, A.M.: Computing machinery and intelligence. Mind **49** (1950) 433–460

3. Newell, A., Simon, H.: Computer science as empirical inquiry: Symbols and search. Communications of the ACM **19** (1976) 113–126
4. Searle, J.: Minds, brains, and programs. Behavioral and Brain Sciences **3** (1980) 417–457
5. Harnad, S.: The symbol grounding problem. Physica D **42** (1990) 335–346
6. Steels, L.: The evolution of communication systems by adaptive agents. In Alonso, E., D.K., Kazakov, D., eds.: Adaptive Agents and Multi-Agent Systems: Adaptation and Multi-Agent Learning. LNAI 2636, Springer Verlag, Berlin (2003) 125–140
7. Vogt, P.: Language evolution and robotics: Issues in symbol grounding and language acquisition. In: Artificial Cognition Systems. Idea Group (2006)
8. Cangelosi, A., Harnad, S.: The adaptive value of symbolic theft over sensorimotor toil: Grounding language in perceptual categories. Evolution of Communication **4**(1) (2000) 117–142
9. Vogt, P.: Anchoring symbols to sensorimotor control. In: Proceedings of the 14th Belgian/Netherlands Artificial Intelligence Conference, BNAIC'02. (2002)
10. Dunbar, K., Blanchette, I.: The inVivo/inVitro approach to cognition: The case of analogy. Trends in Cognitive Sciences **5** (2001) 334–339
11. Hofstadter, D.R.: Analogy as the Core of Cognition. In: The Analogical Mind: Perspectives from Cognitive Science. The MIT Press (2001) 499–538
12. Omlin, C.W., Giles, C.L.: Extraction of rules from discrete-time recurrent neural networks. Neural Networks **9**(1) (1996) 41–52
13. Shavlik, J.: Combining symbolic and neural learning. Machine Learning **14**(3) (1994) 321–331
14. Bodén, M., Wiles, J.: Context-free and context-sensitive dynamics in recurrent neural networks. Connection Science **12**(3,4) (2001) 197–210
15. Thrun, S., Mitchell, T.: Lifelong robot learning. Robotics and Autonomous Systems **15** (1995) 25–46
16. Caruana, R.: Multitask learning. Machine Learning **28** (1997) 41–75
17. Swarup, S., Ray, S.R.: Cross domain knowledge transfer using structured representations. In: Proceedings of the Twenty-First National Conference on Artificial Intelligence (AAAI), Boston, MA, USA (2006)
18. Yan, X., Han, J.: CloseGraph: Mining closed frequent graph patterns. In: Proceedings of the 9th ACM SIGKDD conference on Knowledge-Discovery and Data Mining (KDD 2003). (2003)
19. Nicolescu, M.N., Matarić, M.J.: Task Learning Through Imitation and Human-Robot Interaction. In: Models and Mechanisms of Imitation and Social Learning in Robots, Humans and Animals: Behavioural, Social and Communicative Dimensions. (2005)
20. Smith, A.D.M.: Mutual Exclusivity: Communicative Success Despite Conceptual Divergence. In: Language Origins: Perspectives on Evolution. Oxford University Press (2005) 372–388
21. Smith, A.D.M.: Stable communication through dynamic language. In: Proceedings of the 2nd International Symposium on the Emergence and Evolution of Linguistic Communication. (2005) 135–142
22. Beule, J.D., Vylder, B.D., Belpaeme, T.: A cross-situational learning algorithm for damping homonymy in the guessing game. In Rocha, L.M., Bedau, M., Floreano, D., Goldstone, R., Vespignani, A., Yaeger, L., eds.: Proceedings of the Xth Conference on Artificial Life, Cambridge, MA, USA, The MIT Press (2006)
23. Steels, L., Vogt, P.: Grounding adaptive language games in robotic agents. In Husbands, C., Harvey, I., eds.: Proceedings of the Fourth European Conference on Artificial Life, Cambridge and London, MIT Press (1997)

24. Smith, K., Kirby, S., Brighton, H.: Iterated learning: A framework for the emergence of language. Artificial Life **9**(4) (2003) 371–386
25. Elman, J.L.: Learning and development in neural networks: The importance of starting small. Cognition **48** (1993) 71–99
26. Clark, A., Thornton, C.: Trading spaces: Computation, representation and the limits of uninformed learning. Behavioral and Brain Sciences **20**(1) (1997) 57–67
27. de Solla Price, D.: A general theory of bibliometric and other cumulative advantage processes. Journal of the American Society for Information Science **27** (1976) 292–306
28. Heidegger, M.: On the Way to Language. Harper, San Francisco (1982)

The Human Speechome Project

Deb Roy[1], Rupal Patel[2], Philip DeCamp[1], Rony Kubat[1], Michael Fleischman[1], Brandon Roy[1], Nikolaos Mavridis[1], Stefanie Tellex[1], Alexia Salata[1], Jethran Guinness[1], Michael Levit[1], and Peter Gorniak[1]

[1] Cognitive Machines Group, MIT Media Laboratory
[2] Communication Analysis and Design Laboratory, Northeastern University
dkroy@media.mit.edu

Abstract. The Human Speechome Project is an effort to observe and computationally model the longitudinal course of language development for a single child at an unprecedented scale. We are collecting audio and video recordings for the first three years of one child's life, in its near entirety, as it unfolds in the child's home. A network of ceiling-mounted video cameras and microphones are generating approximately 300 giga-bytes of observational data each day from the home. One of the worlds largest single-volume disk arrays is under construction to house approximately 400,000 hours of audio and video recordings that will accumulate over the three year study. To analyze the massive data set, we are developing new data mining technologies to help human analysts rapidly annotate and transcribe recordings using semi-automatic methods, and to detect and visualize salient patterns of behavior and interaction. To make sense of large-scale patterns that span across months or even years of observations, we are developing computational models of language acquisition that are able to learn from the childs experiential record. By creating and evaluating machine learning systems that step into the shoes of the child and sequentially process long stretches of perceptual experience, we will investigate possible language learning strategies used by children with an emphasis on early word learning.

1 The Need for Better Observational Data

To date, the primary means of studying language acquisition has been through observational recordings made in laboratory settings or made at periodic intervals in children's homes. While laboratory studies provide many useful insights, it has often been argued that the ideal way to observe early child development is in the home where the routines and context of everyday life are minimally disturbed.

Unfortunately, the quality and quantity of home observation data available is surprisingly poor. Observations made in homes are sparse (typically 1-2 hours per week), and often introduce strong observer effects due to the physical presence of researchers in the home. The fine-grained effects of experience on language acquisition are poorly understood in large part due to this lack of dense longitudinal data [1].

P. Vogt et al. (Eds.): EELC 2006, LNAI 4211, pp. 192–196, 2006.

In general, many hypotheses regarding the fine-grained interactions between what a child observes and what the child learns to say cannot be investigated due to a lack of data. How are a child's first words related to the order and frequency of words that the child heard? How does the specific context (who was present, where was the language used, what was the child doing at the time, etc.) affect acquisition dynamics? What specific sequence of grammatical constructions did a child hear that led her to revise her internal model of verb inflection? These questions are impossible to answer without far denser data recordings than those currently available.

2 Pilot Study

The Human Speechome Project (HSP) attempts to address these shortcomings by creating the most comprehensive record of a single child's development to date, coupled with novel data mining and modeling tools to make sense of the resulting massive corpus. The recent surge in availability of digital sensing and recording technologies enables ultra-dense observation: the capacity to record virtually *everything* a child sees and hears in his/her home, 24 hours per day for several years of continuous observation. We have designed an ultra-dense observational system based on a digital network of video cameras, microphones, and data capture hardware. The system has been carefully designed to respect infant and caregiver privacy and to avoid participant involvement in the recording process in order to minimize observer effects.

The recording system has been deployed and at the time of this writing (June 2006), the data capture phase is ten months into operation. Two of the authors (DR, RP) and their first-born child (male, now six months of age, raised with English as the primary language) are the participants. Their home has been instrumented with video cameras and microphones.

Our ultimate goal is to build computational models of language acquisition that can "step into the shoes" of a child and learn directly from the child's experience. The design and implementation details of any computational model will of course differ dramatically from the mental architecture and processes of a child. Yet, the success of a model in learning from the same input as a child provides evidence that the child may employ similar learning strategies.

3 Ultra-Dense Observation for Three Years

Eleven omni-directional mega-pixel resolution color digital video cameras have been embedded in the ceilings of each room of the participants' house (kitchen, dining room, living room, playroom, entrance, exercise room, three bedrooms, hallway, and bathroom). Video is recorded continuously from all cameras since the child may be in any of the 11 locations at any given time. In post processing, only the relevant video channel will be analyzed for modeling purposes. Video is captured at 14 images per second whenever motion is detected, and one image per second in the absence of motion. The result is continuous and complete full-motion video coverage of all activity throughout the house.

Boundary layer microphones (BLM) are used to record the home's acoustic environment. These microphones use the extended surface in which they are embedded as sound pickup surfaces. BLMs produce high quality speech recordings in which background noise is greatly attenuated. We have embedded 14 microphones throughout the ceilings of the house placed for optimal coverage of speech in all rooms. Audio is sampled from all 14 channels at greater than CD-quality (16-bit, 48KHz). When there is no competing noise source, even whispered speech is clearly captured.

Concealed wires deliver power and control signals to the cameras and microphones, and transmit analog audio and networked digital video data to a cluster of 10 computers and audio samplers located in the basement of the house. The computers perform real-time video compression and generate time-stamped digital audio and video files on a local 5-terabyte disk array. With video compression, approximately 300 gigabytes of raw data are accumulated each day. A petabyte (i.e., 1 million gigabyte) disk array is under construction at MIT to house the complete three-year data set and derivative metadata. Data is transferred periodically from the house to MIT using tape storage.

Audio and video recordings can be controlled by the participants in the house using miniature wall-mounted touch displays. Cameras are clustered into eight visual zones (cameras that view overlapping physical spaces are grouped into zones). Eight touch displays are installed next to light switches around the house, each enabling on/off control over video recording in each zone by touching the camera icon. Audio recording can also be turned on and off by touching the microphone icon. To provide physical feedback on the status of video recording, motorized shutters rotate to conceal cameras when they are not recording. The "oops" button at the bottom of the display (marked with an exclamation mark) opens a dialog box that allows the user to specify any number of minutes of audio and/or video to retroactively and permanently delete from the disk array.

4   Data Management

The network of cameras and microphones are generating an immense flow of data: an average of 300 gigabytes of data per day representing about 132 hours of motion-compressed video per day (12 hours x 11 cameras) and 182 hours of audio (13 hours x 14 microphones). In just the first six months we have collected approximately 24,000 hours of video and 33,000 hours of audio. At this rate, the data set is projected to grow to 142,000 hours of video and 196,000 hours of audio by the end of the three year period. Clearly, new data mining tools must be designed to aid in analysis of such an extensive corpus.

We are developing a multichannel data visualization and and annotation system that will enable human analysts to quickly navigate, search, transcribe salient regions of data. Our long term plan is to adapt and apply computer vision techniques to the video corpus in order to detect, identify, and track people and salient objects. Since the visual environment is cluttered and undergoes constant lighting changes (from direct sunlight to dimmed lamps), automatic methods are inherently unreliable. Thus, similar to our approach with speech transcription, we plan to design semi-automatic tools with which humans can efficiently perform error correction on automatically generated meta-data. The combination of automatic motion tracking with human-generated identity labels will yield complete spatiotemporal trajectories of each person over the entire three year observation period. The relative locations, orientations, and movements of people provide a basis for analyzing the social dynamics of caregiver-child interactions.

5   Modeling *In Vivo* Word Learning

In previous related work, we developed a model of early word learning called CELL (Cross-Channel Early Lexical Learning) which learned to segment and associate spoken words with acquired visual shape categories based on untranscribed speech and video input [2]. CELL was evaluated on speech recordings of six mothers as they played with their pre-verbal infants using toys. This model demonstrated that a single mechanism could be used to resolve three problems of word learning: spoken unit discovery, visual category formation, and cross-situational mappings from speech units to visual categories. The model operated under cognitively plausible constraints on working memory, and provided a means for analyzing regularities in infant-directed observational recordings.

Three simplifications made in CELL may be contrasted with our new modeling effort using the HSP corpus. First, CELL was evaluated on a relatively small set of observations. Caregiver-infant pairs were only observed for two one-hour play sessions, held about a week apart. The data was thus a snapshot in time and could not be used to study developmental trajectories. Second, observations were conducted in an infant lab leading to behaviors that may not be representative of natural caregiver-infant interactions in the home. It is unclear whether CELL's learning strategy would work with a more realistic distribution of input. Third, visual input was oversimplified and social context was ignored. The only context available to CELL was video of single objects placed against controlled backdrops. As a consequence, the model of conceptual grounding in CELL was limited to visual categories of shapes and colors underlying words such as *ball* and *red*. It could not learn verbs (since it did not model actions), nor could it learn social terms such as *hi* and *thank you*.

The HSP corpus overcomes the limitations inherent in collecting small corpora within laboratory settings as was done with CELL. To move beyond the simple speech-to-image semantics of CELL, we will apply new semantic representations including sensory-motor grounded "semiotic schemas" [3] and "perceived affordances" [4,5]. In the latter, stochastic grammars are used to model the hierarchical and ambiguous nature of intentional actions. In [5], sequences of observed movements are parsed by behavior grammars yielding lattices of inferred higher level intentions. Verb and noun learning is modeled as acquiring cross-situational mappings from constituents of utterances to constituents of intention lattices. We plan to use a similar approach with the HSP data, but with a semi-automatic procedure for learning behavior grammars from video data. Words related to routines (baths, meals, etc.) and names of locations (crib, highchair, etc.) might be modeled on this basis.

6   Conclusions

The Human Speechome Project provides a natural, contextually rich, longitudinal corpus that serves as a basis for studying language acquisition. An embedded sensor network and data capture system have been designed, implemented, and deployed to gather an ultra-dense corpus of a child's audio-visual experiences from birth to age three. We have described preliminary stages of data mining and modeling tools that have been developed to make sense of 400,000 hours of observations. These efforts make significant progress towards the ultimate goal of modeling and evaluating computationally precise learning strategies that children may use to acquire language.

References

1. Tomasello, M., Stahl, D.: Sampling children's spontaneous speech: How much is enough? Journal of Child Language **31** (2004) 101–121.
2. Roy, D., Pentland, A.: Learning words from sights and sounds: A computational model. Cognitive Science **26(1)** (2002) 113–146.
3. Roy, D.: Semiotic schemas: A framework for grounding language in action and perception. Artificial Intelligence **167(1-2)** (2005) 170–205.
4. Gorniak, P.: The Affordance-Based Concept. PhD thesis, Massachusetts Institute of Technology (2005).
5. Fleischman, M., Roy, D.: Why are verbs harder to learn than nouns? Initial insights from a computational model of situated word learning. In: Proceedings of the 27th Annual Meeting of the Cognitive Science Society (2005)
6. Deb Roy, Rupal Patel, Philip DeCamp, Rony Kubat, Michael Fleischman, Brandon Roy, Nikolaos Mavridis, Stefanie Tellex, Alexia Salata, Jethran Guinness, Michael Levit, Peter Gorniak. (2006). The Human Speechome Project. Proceedings of the 28th Annual Cognitive Science Conference.

Unify and Merge in
Fluid Construction Grammar

Luc Steels[1,2] and Joachim De Beule[2]

[1] SONY Computer Science Laboratory - Paris
[2] Vrije Universiteit Brussel, Artificial Intelligence Laboratory
Pleinlaan 2, B-1050 Brussel

Abstract. Research into the evolution of grammar requires that we
employ formalisms and processing mechanisms that are powerful enough
to handle features found in human natural languages. But the formalism needs to have some additional properties compared to those used
in other linguistics research that are specifically relevant for handling
the emergence and progressive co-ordination of grammars in a population of agents. This document introduces Fluid Construction Grammar,
a formalism with associated parsing, production, and learning processes
designed for language evolution research. The present paper focuses on
a formal definition of the unification and merging algorithms used in
Fluid Construction Grammar. The complexity and soundness of the algorithms and their relation to unification in logic programming and other
unification-based grammar formalisms are discussed.

1 Introduction

Computational research into the origins of language and meaning is flourishing.
There is a growing set of experiments showing how certain aspects of human
natural languages emerge in a population of agents endowed with specific cognitive components such as a bi-directional associative memory or an articulatory
and auditory apparatus. (See overviews and representative samples of current
work in [3], [4], [18], [28]). Most of the solid results so far have been reached for
the emergence of lexicons and perceptually grounded categories. Although there
have been a number of experiments on the role of syntax and grammar (see e.g.
[12] [26], [1], [25]), there are as yet only very few demonstrations where non-
trivial grammars arise in grounded situated interactions between robotic agents.
Part of the reason is of course that the problem of grammar emergence is much
more encompassing than that of lexicons and many fundamental questions remain unanswered. In addition, the world models of agents and the nature of their
interactions needs to be much more complex than in lexical experiments. But
another reason, we believe, has to do with the nature of the computational apparatus that is required to do serious systematic experiments. Whereas lexicon
emergence can be studied with relatively standard neural networks, grammar
requires much more powerful symbolic processing which falls outside the scope

P. Vogt et al. (Eds.): EELC 2006, LNAI 4211, pp. 197–223, 2006.

of connectionist modeling today. Our group has therefore been working for many years on a formalism that would be adequate for handling phenomena typically found in natural language grammars, but that would at the same time support highly flexible parsing and production (even of ungrammatical sentences or partially unconventionalised meanings) and invention and learning operators that could lead to the emergence, propagation, and further evolution of grammar, all this in a multi-agent setting. Our formalism has been called Fluid Construction Grammar, as it is in line with the approaches advocated in usage-based cognitive approaches to language in general and construction grammar in particular, and because it is designed to support highly flexible language processing in which conventions are not static and fixed but fluid and emergent. At this point the FCG system is ready for use by others. An implementation on a LISP substrate has been released for free download through http://arti.vub.ac.be/FCG/. This site also contains very specific examples on how to do experiments in language evolution with FCG. The goal of the present paper is to define some core aspects of FCG more precisely, building further on earlier reports [8], [29]. The application of FCG to various issues in the emergence of grammar is discussed in some other papers (see [27], [7], [24]). Fluid Construction Grammar (FCG) uses as much as possible existing widely accepted notions in theoretical and computational linguistics, specifically feature structures for the representation of syntactic and semantic information during parsing and production, and abstract templates or rules for the representation of lexical and grammatical usage patterns, as in [19] or [2]. Contemporary linguistic theories propose general operators for building up syntactic and semantic structures, such as Merge in Chomsky's Minimalist Grammar [5] or Unify in Jackendoff's framework [14]. Unification based grammars [19,15,2] are similarly based on a unification operator, and more generally many generic inference systems, particularly within the logic programming framework, use some form of unification [22]. There is also some research on finding the neural coordinates of unify and merge in language processing [13]. Unfortunately there are quite substantial differences between the use of the terms unify and merge in all these different frameworks and one of the goals of this paper is to clarify in detail the unify and merge operators that form the core of FCG. For this, we build further on the comparative analysis done by Sierra-Sàntibañez [21] who reformulated FCG in PROLOG. The remainder of the paper has five parts. The next section defines first the requirements for grammar formalisms needed to do experiments in the emergence of nontrivial grammars and the basic ideas behind the Fluid Construction Grammar approach. Then there is a section with some preliminary definitions and background notions. The remainder of the paper focuses on a formal definition of the unify and merge operations in FCG. Section 4 defines the unification in general, and particularly the FCG extensions to standard unification, section 5 then applies this to FCG feature structures. Section 6 defines merging in general, and section 7 applies it to FCG feature structures. Section 7 contains a worked out example.

2   Fluid Construction Grammars

It is obvious that there are many possible formalisms could be (and have been) invented for capturing aspects of language, depending on the nature of the linguistic theory and the types of processing one wants to study. For example, generative (derivational) grammar is adequate for studying ways to generate the set of all possible sentences of a language but it is not well suited for parsing or production, while a constituent structure grammar is adequate for studying syntactic structure but not helpful for investigating how case frames intervene between the mapping from meaning to form, etc. Fluid Construction Grammar takes a strong stance with respect to current linguistic theorising and attempts in addition to satisfy specific requirements which arise when one wants to do experiments in the emergence of grammar in grounded situated interactions.

2.1   Linguistic Assumptions

The linguistic perspective of FCG is in the general line of cognitive grammar [17] and more specifically construction grammar [11]. This means the following: 1. *FCG is usage-based*: The inventories available to speakers and hearers consist of templates which can be highly specialised, perhaps only pertaining to a single case, or much more abstract, covering a wide range of usage events. There is no sharp distinction therefore between idiomatic and general rules. New sentences are constructed or parsed by assembling the templates using the unify and merge operators defined later in this paper. 2. *The grammar and lexicon consist of symbolic units*: A symbolic unit associates aspects of meaning with aspects of form. The templates of FCG are all symbolic units in this sense. They feature a semantic pole and a syntactic pole. Templates are always bi-directional, and so are usable both for production *and* for parsing. This makes FCG unique not only with respect to derivational formalisms (like generative grammar or HPSG) but also with respect to other construction grammar formalisms which tend to be uni-directional (such as Embodied Construction Grammar). 3. *There is a continuum between grammar and the lexicon*. Not only can templates be at different levels of abstraction, but there is also no formal distinction in the structure or the processing of lexical and grammatical entries. In the case of lexical entries, the syntactic pole concerns mostly a lexical stem and the semantic pole tends to be equal to some concrete predicate-argument structure. In the case of grammatical constructions, the syntactic pole contains various syntactic categories constraining the sentence, and the semantic pole is based on semantic categories, but otherwise there is no formal difference between the two types of templates. 4. *Schematisation occurs through variables and categorisation.* A template has the same form as an association between a semantic structure and a syntactic structure, in other words both poles of a template are feature structures. However, templates are more abstract (or schematic) in three ways: Some parts of the semantic or syntactic structure are left out, variables are used instead of units and values, and syntactic or semantic categories are introduced to constrain the possible values of the semantic and syntactic pole. These categories are often established by syntactic or semantic categorisation rules. In some experiments the categories have been defined using a memory-based approach with typical examples and prototypes but this is not yet embedded in the current software release of FCG[1]. 5. *Syntagmatic and Paradigmatic Compositionality*: To produce or parse a sentence, templates can be combined (several templates all matching with different parts of the meaning in production or with parts of the sentence in parsing are simply applied together) or integrated (using hierarchical templates that combine partial structures into larger wholes, possibly after a modification of the syntactic or semantic aspects of the component units). Apart from this syntagmatic composition, there is also the possibility that several templates are overlayed and each contribute additional constraints to the final sentence. This is paradigmatic compositionality. Both forms of compositionality are completely supported with the unify and merge operators defined later in the paper. Of particular importance is that the FCG unify and merge operators handle linking (resolving equalities introduced by separate lexical items) by unifying variables in merge. This topic is discussed more extensively in [29].

2.2 Additional Requirements

In addition to these characteristics, which we take to be general features of cognitive grammars and construction grammars, there are some additional requirements for a formalism if it is to be adequate for modeling emergent natural language-like grammars. 1. *All inventory entries have scores*: We assume that speakers and hearers create new templates which are often competing with each other. Not all templates are widely accepted (entrenched) in the population and there is a negotiation process. To enable this capability we associate with every item in the lexico-grammar a score that reflects the degree of entrenchment of that item. It is based on feedback from success or failure in the language games in which the item has been used. We know from our other experiments in lexicon emergence that an appropriate lateral inhibition dynamics is the most adequate way for driving a population to a sufficiently co-ordinated repertoire to have success in communication and the same dynamics is part of FCG. 2. *The set of syntactic and semantic categories is open*. Often linguistic formalisms posit specific sets of semantic categories (for example semantic roles like agent, patient, etc.) or syntactic categories (such as parts of speech, syntactic features, and others). Because we are interested in how all these categories arise, we make the formalism completely open in this respect. Constraints on feature values are expressed as propositions or predicate- argument clauses so that the set of categories can be expanded at any time. In our experiments there are typically hundreds or even thousands of new categories built. This openness of categories is in line with the Radical Construction Grammar approach which argues that linguistic categories are not universal and subject to evolution [6]. 3. *The multi-agent perspective*: In traditional Chomskyan linguistics only the grammar or lexicon of an 'idealised speaker or hearer' is considered. In contrast, when we

---

[1] version 0.9; for information about FCG software releases see
http://arti.vub.ac.be/FCG.

want to study how grammar arises in a population we need to take a multi-agent perspective, where every agent possibly has a different inventory. We need to understand in particular how agents co-ordinate their inventories to be successful in communication. This raises a large number of computational issues (for example linguistic knowledge is always local to an agent) as well as issues in how to track and measure 'the grammar' in the population. Although all these issues are dealt with in the current FCG design and implementation, the remainder of this paper focuses only on the core of the system, namely the unify and merge operators.

3   Preliminaries

This section starts the more formal discussion and assumes some familiarity with FCG (e.g. from [27], [29], [8] or the FCG website http://arti.vub.ac.be/FCG). We will adopt the standard terminology of logic, which is unfortunately different from the terminology often used in other unification-based approaches to natural language. In logic, the term 'unification' does not involve the merging of two structures or a change to a structure, so unification is a kind of 'matching' in which it is tested whether a source structure matches a target or pattern structure, but no new resulting structure is constructed.

Example 1. Consider the following syntactic FCG unit (FCG units will be defined formally later on):

    (John-unit (form ((string John-unit "John"))))

And the following template unit which could be part of the right-pole of a morphological FCG template:

    (?john-unit (form ((string ?john-unit "John"))))

Symbols starting with a question mark, like ?john-unit, are variables. The unification of the template unit with the syntactic unit results in the binding [?john-unit/John-unit]. In contrast, the template unit would not unify with unit below because they do not 'match' (the string value "walks" differs from "John"):

    (walks-unit (form ((string walks-unit "walks"))))

In contrast with simpler forms of matching (as used in many production rule systems), variables can be present both in the source and in the target. This is the meaning of 'unify' as used in the rest of the paper. Because we also want a way to extend or build up structure based on templates, we have an additional operator called 'merge' which takes a source structure and a target structure and combines them into a new structure.

Example 2. Consider again the John-unit from the previous example:

    (John-unit (form ((string John-unit "John"))))

and now also the template unit shown below, which could be the *left*-pole of the morphological template from the previous example:

```
(?john-unit (syn-cat ((lex-cat Proper-Noun))))
```

Given the binding [?john-unit/John-unit], this template unit merges with the John-unit resulting in the following new unit:

```
(John-unit (form ((string John-unit "John")))
           (syn-cat ((lex-cat Proper-Noun))))
```

We now introduce some definitions which are common in logic (see e.g. [22,10]) and which will allow us to formally define the notion of structures, templates, unification and merging. The atomic elements of our formalism are called **Symbols**. For example the template-unit in example 1 contains the symbols ?john-unit, form, string and "John". Symbols starting with a question mark are **variables**, like ?john-unit. $\mathcal{A}$ denotes the set of all symbols, $\mathcal{V} \subset \mathcal{A}$ the set of all variables. Symbols that are not variables are **constants**. A **simple expression** is defined as a symbol or a list of one or more simple expressions. More complex expressions can be created with operators which take zero or more argument expressions to produce a new expression. More formally, let $(.|.)$ be the list-creator operator (similar to CONS in LISP [30]) and let $()$ be an operator of arity 0 (similar to NIL in LISP).

Definition 1. *Let $\mathcal{E}_s$ denote the set of* **simple expressions***:*

- *All elements of $\mathcal{A}$ as well as $()$ are elements of $\mathcal{E}_s$.*
- *If $e_1 \in \mathcal{E}_s$ and $e_2 \in \mathcal{E}_s$ and if e_2 is not in $\mathcal{A}$ then $(e_1|e_2) \in \mathcal{E}_s$.*

Hence, all symbols and the syntactic and template units in examples 1 and 2 are simple expressions. In addition to simple expressions, we will consider later non-simple expressions which feature special operators and will be called general FCG-expressions or simply expressions. Let us denote the set of variables in an expression e by **vars(e)**. Often an expression of the form $(e_1|(e_2|...(e_k|())...))$ is represented as $(e_1 e_2...e_k)$ and is called a **list of length k**. The operator $()$ is called a list of length 0. A **binding** $[?x/X]$ specifies the value X (a simple expression) of a variable $?x$. If X is itself a variable then such a binding is called an **equality**. A set of bindings $B = \{[?x_1/X_1], ..., [?x_n/X_n]\}$ defines a function $\sigma_B : \mathcal{E}_f \rightarrow \mathcal{E}_s$ such that $\sigma_B(e) = e$ except for the set of variables $?x_1$ to $?x_n$ in B. This set is called the **domain** of σ_B and denoted dom(σ_B). For $?x_i \in$ dom(σ_B) it holds that $\sigma_B(?x_i) = X_i$, $1 \leq i \leq n$. The set $\{X_1, ..., X_n\}$ is called the **range** of σ_B and denoted ran(σ_B). Such a function σ_B is called a **substitution** and the set of bindings B is sometimes called the **graph** of σ_B and is written simply as $[?x_1/X_1, ..., ?x_n/X_n]$. Often a substitution σ_B is represented by its graph B. The empty substitution (the identity function) is denoted by ϵ. Furthermore define *fail* to be a special symbol which will be used to specify the failure to find a substitution. The extension of a substitution to the domain $\mathcal{E}_s$ can be defined using structural induction. If σ_B is the substitution constructed from the set of bindings B then the application of σ_B to an expression e is written either as $\sigma_B(e)$ or as $[e]_B$.

Example 3. The binding B =[?john-unit/John-unit] from example 1 defines
a substitution σ_B that leaves all expressions unchanged except for the variable
?john-unit, which is mapped onto the constant John-unit. Hence:
    σ_B(?john-unit)=John-unit
and
    σ_B(((?john-unit (form ((string ?john-unit "John"))))))
        $= \sigma_B$(((John-unit (form ((string John-unit "John"))))))
        $=$ ((John-unit (form ((string John-unit "John"))))))
The domain of σ_B is {?john-unit} and its range is {John-unit}.

Definition 2. *Two simple expressions x and y are said to be* **equal** *(written as*
$x = y$*) if and only if either:*

1. *x and y are both the same atom*
2. *both $x = (x_1...x_n)$ and $y = (y_1...y_m)$ are lists of the same length ($m = n$)
   and for every $i = 1..n : x_i = y_i$.*

Substitutions can be ordered according to the pre-order $\preceq_{\mathcal{V}}$ which is defined as
follows: If σ_1 and σ_2 are two substitutions then $\sigma_1 \preceq_{\mathcal{V}} \sigma_2$ if and only if there
exists a substitution λ such that $\sigma_1(v) = (\sigma_2 \circ \lambda)(v) = \sigma_2(\lambda(v))$ for each $v \in \mathcal{V}$.
When clear from the context, $\sigma_1 \preceq_{\mathcal{V}} \sigma_2$ is written as $\sigma_1 \preceq \sigma_2$. If $\sigma_1 \preceq_{\mathcal{V}} \sigma_2$ and
$\sigma_2 \preceq_{\mathcal{V}} \sigma_1$ then we say that $\sigma_1 =_{\mathcal{V}} \sigma_2$.

Definition 3. *Two simple expressions e_1 and e_2 are said to* **unify** *if and only if
there exists a substitution σ such that $\sigma(e_1) = \sigma(e_2)$. In this case the substitution
σ is called a* **unifier** *of the two expressions and the set of all unifiers of e_1 and
e_2 is written as $U(e_1, e_2)$.*

Example 4. From example 3 it can be seen that the expressions
    ((?john-unit (form ((string ?john-unit "John"))))))
and
    ((John-unit (form ((string John-unit "John"))))))
indeed unify with unifier σ_B; B =[?john-unit/John-unit].

It is easy to see that the set of unifiers of two unifiable expressions e_1 and e_2 is
infinite (if $\mathcal{V}$ is infinite.) Indeed, a unifier can always be extended with an additional binding for a variable that is not an element of either $vars(e_1)$ or $vars(e_2)$.
In order to exclude these unifiers we only assume unifiers that satisfy the **protectiveness** condition. A unifier σ of two expressions e_1 and e_2 satisfies this condition if and only if $dom(\sigma) \subseteq vars(e_1) \cup vars(e_2)$ and $dom(\sigma) \cap vars(ran(\sigma)) = \emptyset$

Example 5. Both
    B =[?john-unit/John-unit]
and
    B' =[?john-unit/John-unit,?walks-unit/Walks-unit]
define unifiers of
    e_1 =((?john-unit (form ((string ?john-unit "John"))))))

and
$$e_2 = ((\text{John-unit} (\text{form} ((\text{string John-unit "John"})))))).$$
However, only B satisfies the protectiveness condition. Indeed:
$$dom(\sigma_{B'}) = \{?\text{john-unit}, ?\text{walks-unit}\}$$
$$\not\subseteq vars(e_1) \cup vars(e_2) = \{?\text{john-unit}\}$$

A **complete set** of unifiers $c(e_1, e_2)$ is a subset of $U(e_1, e_2)$ that satisfies the additional condition that for any unifier σ of e_1 and e_2 there exists a $\theta \in c(e_1, e_2)$ such that $\theta \preceq \sigma$. The **set of most general unifiers** $\mu(e_1, e_2)$ is a complete set of unifiers that additionally satisfies the **minimality condition**: for any pair $\mu_1, \mu_2 \in \mu(e_1, e_2)$, if $\mu_1 \preceq \mu_2$ then $\mu_1 = \mu_2$. It is well known that if two simple expressions x and y unify, then there always is only one most general unifier (see e.g. [22]). In example 5 the bindings B define the unique most general unifier of e_1 and e_2. Let $f_\mu(x, y, \epsilon)$ be a function that computes the most general unifier of two simple expressions x and y if one exists and returns *fail* otherwise:

$$f_\mu(x, y, \epsilon) = \begin{cases} \mu(x, y) & \text{if } x \text{ and } y \text{ unify} \\ fail & \text{otherwise} \end{cases}$$

We will now define $f_\mu(x, y, B)$, with B a non-empty substitution, which will allow us to show how $f_\mu(x, y, \epsilon)$ can be computed. For this we need the notion of valid extension. Let B be a set of bindings and let $X \in \mathcal{E}_s$ be a simple expression. If it exists, then the valid extension $\Xi(B, [?x/X])$ of B with $[?x/X]$ is a substitution that has $?x$ in its domain: $?x \in dom(\sigma_{\Xi(B,[?x/X])})$. For example, if $X \in \mathcal{C}$ and $?x \notin dom(\sigma_B)$, that is if X is a constant and $?x$ is not yet bound in B, then B is simply extended to include the binding $[?x/X]$:

$$X \in \mathcal{C} \text{ and } ?x \notin dom(\sigma_B): \quad \Xi(B, [?x/X]) \equiv B \cup [?x/X]$$

However, if B already specifies a value for $?x$ then this might conflict with the new value X for $?x$ as specified by $[?x/X]$. The following two definitions takes care of this (and of other possible conflicts). Note that both definitions depend on each other, but in such a way that both functions are always computable.

Definition 4. *The* **valid extension** $\Xi(B, b)$ *of a set of bindings* $B = [?x_1/X_1, ..., ?x_n/X_n]$ *with a binding* $b = [?x/X]$ *(with* $X, X_i \in \mathcal{E}_s$*) is defined as follows:*

$$\Xi(B, b) = \begin{cases} f_\mu(X, X_i, B) & \text{if } ?x =?x_i \text{ for some } i \in \{1, ..., n\} \\ f_\mu(?x, X_j, B) & \text{if } X =?x_j \text{ for some } j \in \{1, ..., n\} \\ fail & \text{if } ?x \text{ occurs anywhere in } X \text{ or in } \sigma_B(X) \\ B \cup [?x/X] & \text{otherwise.} \end{cases}$$

Definition 5. *Let* $x, y \in \mathcal{E}_s$ *and* B *be a set of bindings or* fail*. Then*

$$f_\mu(x, y, B) = \begin{cases} fail & \text{if } B = fail \\ B & \text{if } x = y \\ \Xi(x, y, B) & \text{if } x \in \mathcal{V} \\ \Xi(y, x, B) & \text{if } y \in \mathcal{V} \\ f_\mu(x_r, y_r, f_\mu(x_1, y_1, B)) & \text{if } x = (x_1 | x_r) \text{ and } y = (y_1 | y_r) \\ fail & \text{otherwise} \end{cases}$$

With these definition the standard unification function $f_\mu(x, y, \epsilon)$ on simple expression x and y is also defined. As will be shown in the next section, FCG unification $f_{FCG}(x, y, \{\epsilon\}) = f_\mu(x, y, \epsilon)$ if both x and y are simple expressions.

4   Unifying

General FCG expressions are more extensive than simple expressions because they may include special operators such as the includes-operator '==' which specifies which elements should be included in a feature's value, or the J-operator which plays a key role in defining hierarchy.[2] Each of these operators has a dedicated function for defining how unification should be carried out.

Example 6. Consider the following source syntactic unit

```
(walks-unit (form ((stem walks-unit "walk")
                   (affix walks-unit "-s"))))
```

Now assume we want to build a template unit that is capable of 'recognizing' all present tense forms of the verb "to walk", independent of person (i.e. indendent of the affix "-s"). As a first attempt we could write:

```
(?walk-unit (form ((stem ?walk-unit "walk"))))
```

Unfortunately, this template unit does not unify with (or 'recognize') the source unit because it does not contain the affix part. The FCG solution to this is to use the includes special operator, written as ==, in the template unit as follows:

```
(?walk-unit (form (== (stem ?walk-unit "walk"))))
```

An includes list (like the (== (stem ?walk-unit "walk") part above) unifies with all lists that *at least* contain the specified elements, but more elements may be present in the source. As a result the above modified template unit does unify with (or 'recognizes') the source unit as was desired.

We will now formalize this. Let $\mathcal{O}$ be the set of special operator symbols. It includes for example the symbol '=='.

Definition 6. *Let $\mathcal{E}$ denote the set of all* FCG **expressions**. *Then:*

1. *All elements of $\mathcal{A}$ and $\mathcal{O}$ as well as () are elements of $\mathcal{E}$.*
2. *if $e_1 \in \mathcal{E}$ and $e_2 \in \mathcal{E}$ and if e_2 is not in $\mathcal{A} \cup \mathcal{O}$ then $(e_1|e_2) \in \mathcal{E}$.*

In words, the set of all FCG expressions consists of all (nested) lists of which the leaf elements may be symbols but also special operators. The modified template unit in example 6 is thus an FCG expression. It is however not a simple expression because it contains the includes special operator. In the following we will refer to an FCG expression simply as an expression. To extend the notion of unification to the set of all expressions we must specify how special operators are handled.

---

[2] The J-operator is treated in a separate paper [8].

Therefore, for every operator o in $\mathcal{O}$ and for all expressions $e_1 = (o|e_1')$ and e_2 and sets of bindings $\mathcal{B}$ a designated unification function $f_o(e_1, e_2, \mathcal{B})$ must be defined returning a set of unifiers for e_1 and e_2. FCG unification can then be defined as follows:

Definition 7. FCG **unification** $f_{\mathrm{FCG}}(x, y, \mathcal{B})$ *of two expressions* x *and* y, *with* $\mathcal{B}$ *a set of sets of bindings or fail is defined as follows:*

1. $f_{\mathrm{FCG}}(x, y, fail) = fail$
2. *if* $x = (o|x')$ *with* $o \in \mathcal{O}$ *then* $f_{\mathrm{FCG}}(x, y, \mathcal{B}) = f_o(x, y, \mathcal{B})$
3. *else if* $y = (o|y')$ *with* $o \in \mathcal{O}$ *then* $f_{\mathrm{FCG}}(x, y, \mathcal{B}) = f_o(y, x, \mathcal{B})$
4. *else if* $x = (x_1|x_r)$ *and* $y = (y_1|y_r)$ *then*
   $f_{\mathrm{FCG}}(x, y, \mathcal{B}) = f_{\mathrm{FCG}}(x_r, y_r, f_{\mathrm{FCG}}(x_1, y_1, \mathcal{B}))$
5. *else* $f_{\mathrm{FCG}}(x, y, \mathcal{B}) = \{B'|B' = f_\mu(x, y, B); B' \neq fail; B \in \mathcal{B}\}$

It is easy to see that if x and y are simple expressions (i.e. do not contain special operators) then $f_{\mathrm{FCG}}(x, y, \{\epsilon\}) = \{f_\mu(x, y, \epsilon)\}$. In this sense FCG-unification is equivalent to standard unification in the space of simple expressions. For general FCG-expressions the properties of f_{FCG} will depend on the properties of the dedicated unification functions f_o. We now define some of these special operators so that FCG unification of FCG feature structures can be defined. The list of special operators can in principle be extended by defining the relevant unification functions.

4.1   The Includes Operator ==

Let us first define the notion of containment.

Definition 8. *An expression* x_i *is* **contained** *in a list if and only if it* FCG-*unifies with an element in this list.*

A list starting with the **includes operator** (== $x_1...x_n$) unifies with any source list that at least contains the elements x_1 to x_n. The order in which the elements occur in the source list is irrelevant, however every x_i should unify with a *different* element in the source as in the following examples:

Example 7

$$f_{==}((==\ a\ a\ b), (a\ b), \{\epsilon\}) = fail$$
$$f_{==}((==\ a\ a\ b), (a\ a\ b), \{\epsilon\}) = \{\epsilon\}$$
$$f_{==}((==\ a\ a\ b), (b\ a\ a), \{\epsilon\}) = \{\epsilon\}$$
$$f_{==}((==\ a\ ?x), (a\ b\ c), \{\epsilon\}) = \{[?x/b], [?x/c]\} \tag{1}$$

This is formalized as follows:

Definition 9. *Let* $p_n((e_1...e_m))$ *with* $n \leq m$ *be the set of expressions* $(e_{i_1}...e_{i_n})$ *for every variation* $(i_1, ..., i_n)$ *of* n *elements out of* $(1, ..., m)$.[3] *Then*

$$f_{==}((==\ x_1...x_n), (a_1...a_m), \mathcal{B})$$
$$\equiv \{B|B = f_{\mathrm{FCG}}((x_1...x_n), a, \mathcal{B}); B \neq fail; a \in p_n((a_1...a_m))\}$$

---

[3] We intend here the set-theoretic notion of variation, i.e. all subsets of n elements from $(1, ..., m)$ where the order of the elements matters.

Example 8. Consider again the last example in (1). We have to consider all variations of two elements out of $(a\ b\ c)$, i.e. $(a\ b)$, $(b\ a)$, $(a\ c)$, $(c\ a)$, $(b\ c)$ and $(c\ b)$. Unifying these with $(a\ ?x)$ results in $\{[?x/b]\}$, *fail*, $\{[?x/c]\}$, *fail*, *fail* and *fail* respectively. Keeping only the successful ones indeed leads to $\{[?x/b], [?x/c]\}$.

4.2   Special Cases of $f_{==}$

First of all, the unification of two include-lists $x = (==\ x_1...x_n)$ and $y = (==\ y_1...y_m)$ is not well defined. One possibility is to state that two such lists always unify. However, it is not clear what the resulting set of bindings should be. For simplicity we define $f_{FCG}((o_1|x),(o_2|y),\mathcal{B})$ with $o_1, o_2 \in \mathcal{O}$ to *always be equal to fail*. Second, the unification of a pattern $(x_1...x_k == y_1...y_l)$ with a source $(z_1...z_m)$, $m \geq k+l$, is well defined. More formally, the pattern should be written as

$$(x_1...x_k == y_1...y_l) \equiv (x_1|(...|(x_k|(== |(y_1|(...|(y_l|())...).$$

The f_{FCG} function will progressively unify the elements x_1 to x_k with the first k elements in the source. At this point f_{FCG} is recursively applied to the pattern $(== |(y_1|(...|(y_l|())...)$, which can be re-written as $(== y_1...y_l)$, and the source $(z_{k+1}...z_m)$. Third, operators are treated as ordinary symbols if they are not the first element of a list:

$$f_{==}((== \ a\ ?x),(a\ == \ b),\{\epsilon\}) = \{[?x/ ==], [?x/b]\}$$

4.3   Minimality, Completeness and Complexity of $f_{==}$

Theorem 1 (Completeness of $f_{==}$). *The function* $f_{==}((== \ |X), Y, \{\epsilon\})$ *computes a complete set* $c((== \ |X), Y)$ *of unifiers.*

Proof. From the definition of $f_{==}$ it follows that, if a substitution τ is a unifier of $(== \ |X) = (== \ x_1...x_n)$ and $Y = (y_1...y_m)$, then it must be that $\tau(X)$ is a variation of n elements from Y. Let $\sigma \in f_{==}((== \ |X), Y, \{\epsilon\})$ be the substitution that computes this variation, so that $\sigma(X) = \tau(X)$. If X and Y do not contain any special operators then, from the completeness of F_{FCG} for simple expressions, it follows that $\sigma \preceq \tau$ and thus that $f_{==}(X, Y, \{\epsilon\})$ computes a complete set of unifiers. If some element x_i (y_i) of X (Y) is of the form $(== \ |z)$, with z not containing a special operator, then the same argument can be used recursively. Continuing in this way, it follows that $f_{==}$ computes a complete set of unifiers. □

Theorem 2 (Non-minimality of $f_{==}$). *The function* $f_{==}((== \ |X), Y, \{\epsilon\})$ *does not necessarily compute the most general set of unifiers* $\mu((== \ |X), Y)$.

Proof. It suffices to show that $f_{==}$ does not satisfy the minimality condition. Consider the unification of $(== \ ?x\ ?y)$ with $(?x\ ?y)$ which results in $\{\epsilon, [?x/?y]\}$. This is different from the minimal set of unifiers which consists of the empty substitution ϵ only (this example was taken from [21].) □

Theorem 3 (Complexity of $f_{==}$). $f_{==}((== x_1...x_n), (y_1...y_{m \geq n}))$ *is of exponential complexity in* n.

Proof. Basically, the exponential complexity arises from the need to calculate the variations. Indeed, when $x_i \neq y_j$ for all possible combinations of i and j then $f_{==}((== x_1...x_n), (y_1...y_m))$ is equivalent with the subset unification of $\{x_i\}$ and $\{y_j\}$. General subset unification is exponential and the subset-unifiability problem is NP-complete [16,9].   □

The implementation of $f_{==}((== x_1...x_n), (y_1...y_{m \geq n})$ can be made more efficient by calculating in advance the set of candidate expressions $C_i = \{y_j | y_j$ unifies with $x_i\}$ and by only considering combinations of n distinct elements out of each C_i. However the inherent exponential complexity cannot be improved upon in general. In the following we introduce two additional special operators which are defined as special cases of the includes operator. This ensures that the completeness of f_{FCG} is maintained. However they can be computed more efficiently. The need for introducing these operators will become more clear in sections 5 and 7.

4.4 The Permutation Operator $==_p$

The permutation operator is like the includes operator except that the source should contain *exactly* the elements specified in the pattern. Thus we have:

Definition 10

$$
f_{==_p}((==_p x_1...x_n), (a_1...a_m), \mathcal{B})
$$
$$
\equiv \begin{cases} f_{==}((== x_1...x_n), (a_1...a_m), \mathcal{B}) & \text{if } n = m, \\ \text{fail} & \text{otherwise.} \end{cases} \tag{2}
$$

4.5 The Includes-Uniquely Operator $==_1$

The function of this operator will become more important in merging (see later.) However its behavior in unification must be specified because FCG-templates may contain this operator.

Definition 11. *Let* $s = (y_1...y_m)$. *Then* $f_{==_1}((==_1 x_1...x_n), s)$ *is the set* $\{B\} \subset f_{==}((== x_1...x_n), s)$ *of substitutions B that satisfy the following conditions*

1. *No two symbols* $\sigma_B(y_i)$ *and* $\sigma_B(y_j)$ *of* $\sigma_B((y_1...y_n))$ *with* $i \neq j$ *are allowed to unify:* $f_{\text{FCG}}(y_i, y_j, \{B\}) = \text{fail}$ *and*
2. *if* $\sigma_B(y_i) = \sigma_B((y_{i1}|y_{i2}))$ *and* $\sigma_B(y_j) = \sigma_B((y_{j1}|y_{j2}))$ *are two non-atomic elements of* $\sigma_B((y_1...y_n))$ *with* $i \neq j$ *then their first elements are not allowed to unify:* $f_{\text{FCG}}(y_{i1}, y_{j1}, \{B\}) = \text{fail}$

The above definition ensures that every element in $\sigma_B((y_1...y_n)), B \in \mathcal{B}$ is distinct. It also implies that no element $\sigma_B(y_i)$ can be a variable or start with a variable if $n \geq 1$.

Example 9

$$f_{==_1}((==_1 ?x_1\ a), (?y_1\ (?y_2)\ b)) = \{[?y_1/a, ?x_1/(?y_2)], [?y_1/a, ?x_1/b]\}$$
$$f_{==_1}((==_1 ?x_1\ a), (?y_1\ ?y_2\ b)) = fail$$
$$f_{==_1}((==_1 ?x_1), (?y_1\ b)) = fail. \tag{3}$$

In contract with the last of these examples, consider that.

Example 10

$$f_{==}((== ?x_1), (?y_1\ b)) = \{[?x_1/b], [?x_1/?y_1]\}. \tag{4}$$

Note that some includes-uniquely patterns cannot be satisfied (e.g. $(==_1 a\ a)$.)

5   Unifying Feature Structures

We are now ready to define the matching of two FCG structures. We begin by defining FCG feature structures which are more constrained than general FCG expressions. They are also more constrained than feature structures in other unification grammars [19], in the sense that they are not hierarchical. Hierarchy is represented instead by using the name of a unit as the definition of the syn-subunits or sem-subunits slots. This has many advantages, including that a unit can be the subunit of more than one other unit. It also simplifies computation enormously.

5.1   Feature Structures in FCG

A syntactic or semantic structure in FCG consists of a set of units which each consist of a unique name and a set of feature-value pairs. A unit typically corresponds to a lexical item or to constituents like noun phrases or relative clauses. The name can be used to identify or refer to a unit and unit-names can be bound to variables. Feature-values cannot themselves be feature structures. Instead, we always introduce separate units with their own names and associate feature-value pairs with this new unit.

Example 11. The following expression could be a syntactic structure in FCG. The structure contains three units named `sentence-unit`, `subject-unit` and `predicate-unit`. The `sentence-unit` has two features named `syn-subunits` and `syn-cat`, with respective values the lists `(subject-unit predicate-unit)` and `(SV-sentence)`.

```
((sentence-unit (syn-subunits (subject-unit predicate-unit))
                (syn-cat (SV-sentence)))
 (subject-unit (syn-cat (proper-noun (number singular)))
               (form John))
 (predicate-unit (syn-cat (verb (number singular)))
                 (form walks))).
```

Without separate units or unit names (as in other formalisms) this would look
like:

```
(sentence-unit
  (syn-subunits
    ((syn-cat (proper-noun)
              (number singular))
     (form John))
    ((syn-cat (verb)
              (number singular))
     (form walks)))).
```

A template's pole has the same form as a feature structures but typically contains
variables as well as special operators (like '==').

Example 12. The following expression could be the syntactic pole of a template.
Note how agreement in number between subject and verb is handled through
the variable ?number which will be bound to a specific number value.

```
((?sentence-unit
  (syn-cat (SV-sentence))
  (syn-subunits (?subject-unit ?predicate-unit))
  (form (== (precedes ?subject-unit ?predicate-unit))))
 (?subject-unit
  (syn-cat (== proper-noun (number ?number))))
 (?predicate-unit
  (syn-cat (== verb (number ?number))))).
```

The features that may occur are restricted to a limited set of symbols: {sem-
subunits, referent, meaning, sem-cat} for semantic structures and {syn-subunits,
utterance, form, syn-cat} for syntactic structures. The syntactic or semantic
categories are completely open-ended, and so the example categories used here
(like number, proper-noun, etc.) are just intended as illustration. Syntactic and
semantic structures always come in pairs, and units in a syntactic structure are
paired with those in the semantic structure through common unit names. More
formally, we have the following:

Definition 12. *A* **feature-value pair** *is an expression of the form* $(e_n\ e_v)$.
The expression e_n *is called the feature name and* e_v *is the feature value. A* **unit**
is any expression of the form $(e_n\ f_1...f_k)$ *with the expression* e_n *the unit's name*
and $f_i, i = 1...k$ *its features. Unit names are usually but not necessarily symbols.*
Finally a **unit structure** *(or feature structure) is any expression of the form*
$(u_1...u_l)$ *with all of the* u_i *units.*

Thus, a unit structure can be represented by an expression of the form

$$((u_1\ (f_{11}\ v_{11})...(f_{1n_1}\ v_{1n_1}))$$

$$...$$

$$(u_m\ (f_{m1}\ v_{m1})...(f_{mn_m}\ v_{mn_m}))). \tag{5}$$

Here is another (simplistic) example of a syntactic structure for the utterance "red ball":

```
((np-unit (syn-subunits (adjective-unit noun-unit)))
 (adjective-unit (syn-cat (adjective))
                 (form ((stem adjective-unit "red"))))
 (noun-unit (syn-cat (noun))
            (form ((stem noun-unit "ball"))))),
```

which may be associated with the following semantic structure:

```
((np-unit (sem-subunits (adjective-unit noun-unit)))
 (adjective-unit (meaning ((color obj-1 red))))
 (noun-unit (referent obj-1)
            (meaning ((sphere obj-1)(used-for obj-1 play)
                      (mentioned-in-discourse obj-1))))).
```

The names of the units allow cross-referencing between the two structures. Unification in FCG determines the applicability of templates. An example of an FCG template that should be triggered by the above semantic structure is shown below (the template's left (semantic) and right (syntactic) poles are separated by a double-arrow):[4]

```
((?unit (referent ?obj)
        (meaning (== (sphere ?obj) (used-for ?obj play)))))
<-->
((?unit (form (== (stem ?unit "ball")))))
```

However, it can be seen that the left pole of this template does *not* unify with the semantic structure above: only (part of) the noun-unit is specified by the pole but specifications for the other units are missing. Therefore no substitution can make the source structure equal to the pole or vice versa. If however the pole is changed to:

```
(==1 (?unit (referent ?obj)
            (meaning (== (sphere ?obj)(used-for ?obj play))))),
```

then this indeed unifies with the source structure to yield the bindings

```
[?obj/obj-1,?unit/noun-unit].
```

5.2   The Unification of Feature Structures

Definition 13. *The function* **unify-structures(P,S,B)** *takes a pattern structure P, a source structure S and a set of bindings B and can be computed as follows. If P is as represented in (5) then the pattern is first transformed to the pattern P':*

---

[4] These examples have all been simplified for didactic reasons.

$$(==_1(u_1 ==_1 (f_{11} \ v'_{11})...(f_{1n_1} \ v'_{1n_1}))$$

$$...$$

$$(u_m ==_1 (f_{m1} \ v'_{m1})...(f_{mn_m} \ v'_{mn_m})))), \qquad (6)$$

in which the new feature values v'_{ij} are determined as follows: Every non-atomic feature value $v_{ij} = (v_1|v_2)$ in the pattern for which v_1 is not a special operator is replaced by $v'_{ij} = (==_p |v_{ij})$. Atomic feature values remain unchanged: $v'_{ij} = v_{ij}$ if v_{ij} is atomic. Unify-structures(P,S,B) is then defined as $f_{FCG}(P', S, \{B\})$.

6   Merging

Informally, merging a source expression s and a pattern expression p means changing the source expression such that it unifies with the pattern expression. Merging two general fcg-expressions is undefined in this paper, we only consider the case where at least the source is a simple expression (i.e. does not contain special operators.) We first examine the case where also the pattern is a simple expression.

6.1   Merging of Simple Expressions

Definition 14. Let $g(p, s, B)$ denote the merge function that computes a set of tuples $(s', \mathcal{B}')$ of new source patterns s' and bindings sets $\mathcal{B}'$ such that $f_{FCG}(p, s', \{B\}) = \mathcal{B}'$. $g(p, s, B)$ on simple expressions p and s is defined as follows:

1. If $\mathcal{B} = f_{FCG}(p, s, \{B\}) \neq$ fail then $g(p, s, B) = (s, \mathcal{B})$.
2. Else if $p = (p_1|p_2)$ and $s = (s_1|s_2)$ then let $G'_1 = g(p_1, s_1, B)$.
   (a) If $G'_1 \neq \emptyset$ then

$$g(p, s, B) = \bigcup_{(s'_1, B_1) \in G'_1} \left(\bigcup_{g'_2 \in g(p_2, s_2, B_1)} \left(\bigcup_{(s'_2, \mathcal{B}') \in g'_2} \{((s'_1|s'_2), \mathcal{B}')\} \right) \right)$$

   (b) Else, if length$(p) >$ length(s) then let $G'_2 = g(p_2, s, B)$ and let

$$S'_1 = \bigcup_{(s'_2, \mathcal{B}') \in G'_2} \left(\bigcup_{B' \in \mathcal{B}'} \{\sigma_{B'}(p_1)\} \right).$$

   Then

$$g(p, s, B) = \bigcup_{s'_1 \in S'_1} \left(\bigcup_{(s'_2, \mathcal{B}') \in G'_2} \{((s'_1|s'_2), \mathcal{B}')\} \right)$$

3. Else if $p = (p_1|p_2)$ and $s = ()$ then $g(p, s, B) = \{(\sigma_B(p), \{B\})\}$
4. Else $g(p, s, B) = \emptyset$

Let us clarify these steps. The first step is obvious and ensures that no unnecessary modifications are done: the merging of a pattern and a source that unify is equivalent to leaving the source unchanged and unifying them. The second step consists of two possibilities. If the first element of the pattern merges with the first element of the source (case (a)) then the result is further completely determined by the results $g_2' = (s_2', \mathcal{B}')$ of merging the remaining elements of the source and the pattern. Otherwise (case (b), the first elements do not merge), if the pattern is longer then the source we can consider extending the source with the first element of the pattern. The result is then further completely determined by the result G_2' of merging the remaining elements of the pattern with the entire source. And because this might involve a set of bindings which could potentially lead to different expressions for the first element of the pattern p_1, the combinations of such distinct expressions and bindings need to be computed.

Theorem 4 (Termination of $g(p, s, B)$). *The definition above can be viewed as an algorithm to compute the value of $g(p, s, B)$. It is obvious that this algorithm will always terminate when called on a pattern of finite length: although it is called recursively in steps 2(a) and (b), it is always called on a pattern of smaller length. This can only continue until the pattern is of length 0 (i.e. is equal to ()) in which case the algorithm always returns from steps 1 or 4.* □

Example 13. Let a and b be constants. Then:

$$g(a, a, \{\epsilon\}) = \{(a, \{\epsilon\})\}$$
$$g((a\ b), (a), \{\epsilon\}) = \{((a\ b), \{\epsilon\})\}$$
$$g((a\ b), (b), \{\epsilon\}) = \{((a\ b), \{\epsilon\})\}$$
$$g((a\ ?y), (a), \{\epsilon\}) = \{((a?y), \{\epsilon\})\}$$
$$g((?x\ b), (a), \{\epsilon\}) = \{((a\ b), \{[?x/a]\})\}$$
$$g((?x\ ?y), (a), \{\epsilon\}) = \{((a\ ?y), \{[?x/a]\})\}. \tag{7}$$

Example 14. The merging of

```
(?unit (form ?form)
       (syn-cat ((lex-cat Verb))))
```

and

```
(Unit (form ((stem Unit "walk"))))
```

gives the expanded unit

```
(Unit (form ((stem Unit "walk")))
      (syn-cat ((lex-cat Verb))))
```

and bindings

```
[?unit/Unit, ?form/((stem ?unit "walk"))].
```

6.2 Merging a General Pattern

We now turn to the case where the pattern p can be any FCG-expression. As with unification, the merge function g is extended with specialized merge functions whenever the pattern is of the form $p = (o...)$ with $o \in \mathcal{O}$.

The includes operator. Let us first look at the case where $p = (== e_1...e_n)$. The main differences with the simple case is that now neither the order nor the number of elements in the source matters:

Example 15

$$g_{==}((== b\ a), (a\ b), \{\epsilon\}) = \{((a\ b), \{\epsilon\})\}$$
$$g_{==}((== b\ a), (a), \{\epsilon\}) = \{((a\ b), \{\epsilon\})\} \tag{8}$$

Example 16. (Compare with example 14.) The merging of

    (?unit == (syn-cat ((lex-cat Verb))))

and

    (Unit (form ((stem Unit "walk"))))

gives the expanded unit

    (Unit (form ((stem Unit "walk")))
          (syn-cat ((lex-cat Verb))))

and bindings

    [?unit/Unit].

The algorithm presented above can be used to compute the merge of an includes list with only a minimal amount of changes. Let $p = (== |(p_1|p_2))$. First, in step 2, instead of trying to merge p_1 only to the first element of the source, all source elements must be considered. Every source element that merges with p_1 now leads to a case similar to 2(a). The computation of the union of the results for these cases is somewhat more complicated and requires some additional bookkeeping. If no source element merges with the first pattern element then this leads to a case similar to 2(b). G'_2 is now computed as

$$G'_2 = g((== |p_2), s, B)$$

i.e. the includes operator must be propagated. Merging an includes list also always terminates for the same reasons as why the merging of simple expressions terminates.

The permutation operator. Merging a permutation pattern $p = (==_p e_1...e_n)$ is similar to simple merging except that the order of elements in the source is arbitrary. As in the case of the includes operator, this requires that in step 2 all elements in the source are considered instead of only the first. A more easy but possibly less efficient implementation would be to merge the pattern as if it is an includes pattern and only keep those results that are of the same length as the original pattern (without the permutation operator.)

The includes uniquely operator. The includes uniquely operator can be used to block merging. Consider for example the patterns

$p_1 =$ ((?unit (form (== (string ?unit "car"))
                (syn-cat (== (number singular))))))

and

$p_2 =$ ((?unit (form (==$_1$ (string ?unit "car"))
                (syn-cat (==$_1$ (number singular))))))

and the source

$s =$ ((unit (form ((string unit "cars")))
           (syn-cat ((number plural))))).

The source represents (part of) a syntactic structure. The patterns represent template-poles that are tried to merge with the source to obtain a new syntactic structure. In this case both patterns are intended to fail because a unit cannot be both singular (as specified by the patterns) and plural (as specified in the source.) However, merging p_1 and s results in

$g(p_1, s, \epsilon) =$ {(((unit (form ((string unit "car")
                              (string unit "cars")))
                     (syn-cat ((number singular)
                              (number plural))))), {[?unit/unit]})}

whereas p_2 and s do not merge: the merging is blocked by the includes uniquely operator. An includes uniquely pattern can be merged with a source by first treating the pattern as a normal includes pattern and then filtering the result on the conditions of section 4.5. This can be made more efficient by checking whether it is allowed to add a new element to the source in step 2(b) of the merging algorithm.

7   Merging Feature Structures

As with unification, the merging of a pattern feature structure P with a source structure S will be defined as merging a transformed pattern P' with the source. The transformation consists of adding special operators to the pattern. However, the set of special operators defined so far does not suffice. Consider the merging of the pattern:

((?unit (sem-cat (== (agent ?e ?a) (human ?a)))))),

with the following source:

((unit (sem-cat ((agent e a) (motion-event e)))))).

The intended result with bindings [?e/e, ?a/a] is clearly:

((unit (sem-cat ((agent e a) (motion-event e) (human a))))))).

This solution requires that the first includes element is unified with the first source element and that the **human** part is added. However, the first includes element also merges with the second source element by adding **agent** to it, leading to the solution:

```
((unit (sem-cat ((agent e a) (agent motion-event e)
                 (human e))))),
```

with bindings $[?e/\text{motion-event}, ?a/e]$. In this particular case the spurious solution can be ruled out by changing the includes operator $==$ to an includes uniquely operator $==_1$. However, this is not always possible, and some more general mechanism is needed that allows to specify that feature values like (**motion-event e**) may not be modified during merging. Therefore, for every special operator $o \in \mathcal{O}$ a non-destructive version $o!$ is defined which behaves the same in unification (i.e. $f_o = f_{o!}$) but which differs in merging such that the modification of candidate source elements for an element of a non-destructive pattern is prohibited. In terms of the merge algorithm g in section 6.1 this means that the recursive call to g in step 2 to determine G_1' is replaced by a call to f_{FCG} and that steps 2(b) and step 3 are not allowed because they modify the source. By using non-destructive special operators the modification of already present feature value elements can be prohibited. However, there is another problem. Consider the merging of the pattern

```
(==1 (unit1 ==1 (F1 V1))
     (unit2 ==1 (F2 V2))),
```

with the source

```
((unit1)
 (unit2)))
```

One expected result is

```
((unit1 (F1 V1))
 (unit2 (F2 V2))).
```

However, the following is also a valid merge:

```
((unit1 unit2 (F1 V1))
 (unit2 unit1 (F2 V2))).
```

Prohibiting this solution requires the introduction of a final special operator $==_{1l}$ which is equivalent to the includes uniquely operator except that it only allows its elements to be lists.

Definition 15. *The function* **expand-structure(P,S,B)** *which takes a pattern structure P, a source structure S and a set of bindings B is defined as follows. If P is as represented in (5) then the pattern is first transformed to the pattern P':*

$$(==_{1l} (u_1 ==_{1l} (f_{11} v_{11}')...(f_{1n_1} v_{1n_1}'))$$

$$...$$

$$(u_m ==_{1l} (f_{m1} v_{m1}')...(f_{mn_m} v_{mn_m}'))), \qquad (9)$$

with the new feature values determined as follows: Every non-atomic feature value $v_{ij} = (v_1|v_2)$ in the pattern for which v_1 is not a special operator is replaced by $v'_{ij} = (==!_p|v_{ij})$. If v_1 is a special operator then it is replaced by its non-destructive version. Atomic feature values are left unchanged: $v'_{ij} = v_{ij}$ if v_{ij} is atomic. Expand-structures(P,S,B) is then equal to $g(P', S, \{B\})$.

8 Examples

The examples presented in this section are simplified to focus on the unification and merging aspects of FCG-template application and do not take the J-operator into account.

8.1 Example of Syntactic Categorisation in Parsing

Assume the following syntactic structure, which could be built based on the utterance "Mary walks":

```
Syn=((sentence-unit (syn-subunits (Mary-unit walks-unit)))
        (Mary-unit (form ((string Mary-unit "Mary"))))
        (walks-unit (form ((string walks-unit "walks")))))
```

The structure contains three units: one for both words ('strings') in the sentence, and one to keep these together in a sentence unit. The initial corresponding semantic structure might look like:

```
Sem=((sentence-unit (sem-subunits (Mary-unit walks-unit)))
        (Mary-unit)
        (walks-unit))
```

It does not yet contain any meanings because we are in the beginning of the parsing process before application of the lexical templates. As explained elsewhere, the first type of template that is applied during parsing in FCG is concerned with morpho-syntactic transformations and syntactic and semantic categorisations. In parsing, this phase is comparable to more traditional part-of-speech tagging. However, in FCG these templates can be applied both during production and in parsing and the set of form-constraints and syntactic categories (like parts of speech) is open-ended. The following template categorises the string "walks" as the third-person singular form of the verb-stem "walk":

```
((?unit (form (== (stem ?unit "walk")))
          (syn-cat (==1 (number singular)
                        (person third)))))
<-->
((?unit (form (== (string ?unit "walks")))))
```

While producing, the same rule would be applied to establish the third-person singular form "walks" for the stem "walk". To test the applicability of the above template while parsing, the right pole must be unified with the syntactic structure. As explained earlier, this requires first the transformation of the pole to the pattern R' (see equation 6):

```
R'=(==1 (?unit ==1 (form (== (string ?unit "walks"))))),
```

followed by the unification of this new pattern with the syntactic structure:

$$\mathcal{B} = f_{\text{FCG}}(R', Syn, \{\epsilon\}) = \{[\textit{?unit}/\text{walks-unit}]\}$$

Because this yields a valid set of bindings, the template's left pole can be applied to compute a new, extended syntactic structure Syn' (syntactic categorisation rules always work only on syntactic structures). This requires that the template's left pole is merged with the syntactic structure. Therefore, it is first transformed to the pattern L' (see equation 9):

```
L'= (==11 (?unit ==11 (form (==! (stem ?unit "walk") ))
                       (syn-cat (==1! (number singular)
                                      (person third))))),
```

which then is merged with the syntactic structure: $g(L', Syn, \mathcal{B}) = \{(Syn', \mathcal{B})\}$, yielding:

```
Syn'=((sentence-unit (syn-subunits (Mary-unit walks-unit)))
      (Mary-unit (form ((string Mary-unit "Mary"))))
      (walks-unit (form ((string walks-unit "walks")
                         (stem walks-unit "walk")))
                  (syn-cat ((number singular)
                            (person third))))).
```

8.2   Example of Lexicon Lookup in Parsing

Here is next a lexical template associating a predicate-argument structure with the stem "walk":

```
((?unit (referent ?event)
        (meaning (== (walk ?event) (walker ?event ?person)))))
<-->
((?unit (form (== (stem ?unit "walk")))))
```

In parsing, this template is triggered by a successful unification of its right pole with the syntactic structure. Therefore, the pole is first transformed to the pattern R'':

```
R''=(==1 (?unit ==1 (form (== (stem ?unit "walk"))))).
```

It is easy to see that R'' indeed unifies with the syntactic structure Syn' from the previous example with unifier B'=[?unit/walks-unit]. Given successful unification, the left pole can be merged with the semantic structure, yielding the new semantic structure Sem', with $g(L'', Sem, \{B'\}) = \{(Sem', \{B'\})\}$,

```
L''=(==11 (?unit ==11 (meaning (==! (walk ?event)
                                    (walker ?event ?person)))))
```

and thus

```
Sem'=((sentence-unit (sem-subunits (Mary-unit walks-unit)))
      (Mary-unit)
      (walks-unit (referent ?event)
                  (meaning ((walk ?event)
                            (walker ?event ?person))))).
```

8.3   Example of Construction Application in Production

Assume that conceptualization, lexicalisation and categorisation resulted in the following semantic and syntactic structures:

```
Sem=((sentence-unit (sem-subunits (Mary-unit walk-unit)))
     (Mary-unit (referent person-1)
                (meaning ((Mary person-1))))
     (walk-unit (referent ev-1)
                (meaning (walk ev-1)
                         (walker ev-1 person-1))
                (sem-cat (motion-event ev-1)
                         (agent ev-1 person-1))))
```

and

```
Syn=((sentence-unit (syn-subunits (Mary-unit walk-unit)))
     (Mary-unit (form ((stem Mary-unit "Mary")))
                (syn-cat ((person third)
                          (number singular))))
     (walk-unit (form ((strem walk-unit "walk"))))).
```

The above syntactic structure specifies that there are two lexical items involved (the stems "Mary" and "walk"), reflecting the fact that the meaning to express involves some person **person-1** (Mary) and some walk event **ev-1**. However it is not yet specified that it is Mary who fulfills the role of walker (agent) in the walk event. The following simple SV-construction template can be used for this and uses word order and agreement as would be the case in English:

```
((?SV-unit (sem-subunits (?subject-unit ?predicate-unit)))
 (?subject-unit (referent ?s))
 (?predicate-unit (referent ?p)
                  (sem-cat (==1 (agent ?p ?s)))))
<-->
((?SV-unit (syn-subunits (?subject-unit ?predicate-unit))
           (form (== (precedes ?subject-unit ?predicate-unit))))
 (?subject-unit (syn-cat (==1 NP
                              (number ?n)
                              (person ?p))))
 (?predicate-unit (syn-cat (==1 verb
                               (number ?n)
                               (person ?p)))))).
```

Many other syntactic constraints can easily be incorporated into this kind of template. The above template's left pole unifies with the semantic structure **Sem** with unifier

```
B=[?SV-unit/sentence-unit, ?subject-unit/Mary-unit,
    ?predicate-unit/walk-unit, ?s/person-1, ?p/event-1].
```

Thus, a new syntactic structure **Syn'** can be computed by merging the template's right pole with the structure Syn: $g(R', Syn, \{B\}) = \{(Syn', \{B'\})\}$, with

```
R'=(==11
    (?SV-unit ==11
                (syn-subunits (==p! ?subject-unit ?predicate-unit))
                (form (==! (precedes ?subject-unit ?predicate-unit))))
    (?subject-unit
                ==11
                (syn-cat (==1! NP
                            (number ?n)
                            (person ?p))))
    (?predicate-unit
                ==11
                (syn-cat (==1! verb
                            (number ?n)
                            (person ?p))))),
```

```
B'=[?SV-unit/sentence-unit, ?subject-unit/Mary-unit,
    ?predicate-unit/walk-unit, ?s/person-1, ?p/event-1,
    ?n/singular, ?p/third]
```

and

```
Syn'=((sentence-unit
            (syn-subunits (Mary-unit walk-unit))
            (form ((precedes Mary-unit walk-unit))))
        (Mary-unit (form ((stem Mary-unit "Mary")))
                    (syn-cat (NP
                                (person third)
                                (number singular))))
        (walk-unit (form ((strem walk-unit "walk")))
                    (syn-cat (verb
                                (person third)
                                (number singular)))))
```

9   Conclusion

Experiments in the emergence of grammatical languages require powerful formalisms that support the kind of features that are typically found in human natural languages. Linguists have been making various proposals about the nature of these formalisms. Even though a clear consensus is lacking, most formalisms today use a kind of feature structure representation for syntactic and semantic information and templates with variables and syntactic and semantic categories. There are also several proposals on how templates are to be assembled, centering around concepts like match, unify, merge, etc. although the proposals are often too vague to be operationalised computationally. We argued that computer simulations of the emergence of grammar have some additional technically very challenging requirements: the set of linguistic categories must be open-ended, templates can have various degrees of entrenchment, and inventories and processing must be distributable in a multi-agent population with potentially very diverse inventories. Fluid Construction Grammar has been designed to satisfy these various requirements and the system is now fully operational and has already been used in a number of experiments. In this document the unification and merging algorithms used in FCG were formally defined as they form the core of the system. It was shown that FCG unification is a special type of multi-subset-unification, which is inherently of exponential complexity in the length of the expressions that are unified. FCG unification always returns a complete but not necessarily minimal set of unifiers. FCG merging was properly defined and it was shown that it always terminates. The unification of a source with an includes list $(==)$ was formally defined and the unification of a permutation list $(==_p)$ and of an includes-uniquely list $(==_1)$ were shown to be special cases hereof. These made it possible to define the matching of structures, needed for FCG template application in terms of the general unification function. Non-destructive versions of these operators were introduced to enable the definition of FCG structure merging in terms of the general merging function. FCG can be used without considering all the technicalities discussed in the present paper, but these details are nevertheless of great importance when constructing new implementations.

Acknowledgment

The research reported here has been conducted at the Artificial Intelligence Laboratory of the Vrije Universiteit Brussel (VUB) and at the Sony Computer Science Laboratory in Paris. Joachim De Beule was funded as a teaching assistant at the VUB. Additional funding for the Sony CSL activities has come from the EU FET-ECAgents project 1170. Many other researchers have been important in shaping FCG. We are particularly indebted to Nicolas Neubauer for early work on the unification and merge algorithms, Josefina Sierra for an early re-implementation in Prolog, and to Martin Loetzsch for recent contributions towards making FCG a more professional software engineered artifact. Other contributions have come from Benjamin Bergen, Joris Bleys, Remi Van Trijp, and Pieter Wellens.

References

1. Batali, J. (2002) The negotiation and acquisition of recursive grammars as a result of competition among exemplars. In Ted Briscoe, editor, Linguistic Evolution through Language Acquisition: Formal and Computational Models. Cambridge University Press.
2. Bergen, B.K. and Chang, N.C.: Embodied Construction Grammar in Simulation-Based Language Understanding. In: Ostman, J.O. and Fried, M. (eds): Construction Grammar(s): Cognitive and Cross-Language Dimensions. John Benjamins Publishing Company, Amsterdam (2003)
3. Briscoe, T. (ed.) (2002) Linguistic Evolution through Language Acquisition: Formal and Computational Models. Cambridge University Press, Cambridge, UK.
4. Cangelosi, A. and D. Parisi (eds.) (2001) Simulating the Evolution of Language. Springer-Verlag, Berlin.
5. Chomsky, N.: Logical Structure of Linguistic Theory. Plenum (1955)
6. Croft, William A. (2001). Radical Construction Grammar; Syntactic Theory in Typological Perspective. Oxford: Oxford University Press.
7. De Beule, J. and B. Bergen (2006) On the emergence of compositionality.Accepted for the Sixth Evolution of Language Conference, Rome, 2006
8. De Beule, J. and Steels, L. (2005) Hierarchy in Fluid Construction Grammar. In Furbach U., editor, Proceedings of KI-2005, pages 1–15. Berlin: Springer-Verlag.
9. Degyarev, A., Voronkov, A.: Equality Elimination for Semantic Tableaux. Tech. report **90**, Computer Science department, Uppsala University, Upsalla, Sweden (1994)
10. Dovier, A., Pontelli, E., Rossi, G.: Set Unification. arXiv:cs.LO/0110023v1 (2001)
11. Goldberg, A.E. (1995) Constructions: A construction grammar approach to argument structure. University of Chicago Press, Chicago.
12. Hashimoto, T. and Ikegami, T. (1996) Emergence of net-grammar in communicating agents. Biosystems, 38(1):1–14.
13. Hagoort, P.: On Broca, brain and binding: a new framework. Trends in Cognitive Science **9(9)** (2005) 416–423
14. Jackendoff, R.: Foundations of Language: Brain, Meaning, Grammar, Evolution. Oxford University Press (2002)
15. Kay, M.: Functional unification grammar: A formalism for machine translation. Proceedings of the International Conference of Computational Linguistics (1984)
16. Kapur, D. and Narendran, P.: NP-completeness of the set-unification and matching problems. In: Proceedings of the Eighth International Conference on Automated Deduction. Springer Verlag, Lecture Notes in Computer Science **230** (1986) 289–495
17. Langacker, R.W. (2000) Grammar and Conceptualization. Mouton de Gruyter, Den Haag.
18. Minett, J. W. and Wang, W. S-Y. (2005) Language Acquisition, Change and Emergence: Essays in Evolutionary Linguistics. City University of Hong Kong Press: Hong Kong.
19. Pollard, C. and Sag, I.: Head-driven phrase structure grammar. University of Chicago Press (1994)
20. Russell S.J., Norvig, P.: Artificial Intelligence: A Modern Approach, 2nd edition. Upper Saddle River, New Jersey 07458, Prentice Hall, Inc. (2003)
21. Sierra-Santibàñez, J.: Prolog Implementation of Fluid Construction Grammar. Presented at the First FCG workshop, Paris (2004)

22. Sterling, L. and Shapiro, E.: The art of PROLOG. MIT Press, Cambridge, Massachusetts (1986)
23. Steels, L.: Self-organizing vocabularies. In: Langton, C. (ed.): Proceedings of the Conference on Artificial Life V (Alife V) (Nara, Japan) (1996)
24. Steels, L., M. Loetzsch and B. Bergen (2005) Explaining Language Universals: A Case Study on Perspective Marking. [submitted]
25. Smith, K., Kirby, S., and Brighton, H. (2003) Iterated Learning: a framework for the emergence of language. Artificial Life, 9(4).371-380
26. Steels, L. (1998) The origins of syntax in visually grounded robotic agents. Artificial Intelligence, 103(1-2):133-156.
27. Steels, L. (2004) Constructivist Development of Grounded Construction Grammars Scott, D., Daelemans, W. and Walker M. (eds) (2004) Proceedings Annual Meeting Association for Computational Linguistic Conference. Barcelona. p. 9-19.
28. Steels, L. (2005) The emergence and evolution of linguistic structure: from lexical to grammatical communication systems. Connection Science, 17(3-4):213-230.
29. Steels, L., De Beule, J., Neubauer, N.: Linking in Fluid Construction Grammar. In: Transactions Royal Flemish Academy for Science and Art. Proceedings of BNAIC-05. (2005) p. 11-18.
30. Steele, Guy L. Jr.: Common Lisp, the language (2nd ed.) Digital Press (1990).

Utility for Communicability
by Profit and Cost of Agreement

Ryuichi Matoba, Makoto Nakamura, and Satoshi Tojo

School of Information Science,
Japan Advanced Institute of Science and Technology,
1-1, Asahidai, Nomi, Ishikawa, 923-1292, Japan
{r-matoba, mnakamur, tojo}@jaist.ac.jp

Abstract. The inflection of words based on agreement, such as number, gender and case, is considered to contribute to clarify the dependency between words in a sentence. Our purpose in this study is to investigate the efficiency of word inflections with HPSG (Head–driven Phrase Structure Grammar), which is able to deal with these features directly. Using a notion of utility, we measure the efficiency of a grammar in terms of the balance between the number of semantic structures of a sentence, and the cost of agreement according to the number of unification processes. In our experiments, we showed how these were balanced in two different corpora. One, WSJ (Wall Street Journal), includes long and complicated sentences, while the other corpus, ATIS (Air Travel Information System) does shorter colloquial sentences. In the both corpora, agreement is surely important to reduce ambiguity. However, the importance of agreement in the ATIS corpus became salient as personal pronouns were so often employed in it, compared with the WSJ corpus.

1 Introduction

Grammatical rules of human language enable us to generate an infinite range of expressions. Because a long sentence may contain ambiguities in its meaning, language is equipped with devices to indicate dependency. Among them, we consider the function of agreement.

Types of agreement such as number, gender, and case change word forms by inflection or agglutination of prefix/suffix. Inflection is a grammatical affix that attaches to a word to mark it as a particular part of speech [3], in English, for example, the use of *-ed* to make the word *show* into the past tense form *showed*, and the use of *-s* to make the word *actor* into the plural *actors*. Agglutination is to combine words with sets of stable affixes to produce complicated phrases like *judgemental* or *helplessness* in English. In technical terms, the case change of nouns or adjectives is called declension, and words are classified into declinable ones and other indeclinable ones, while verb inflection is called conjugation [1]. Among we said above, those words which are often used in daily expressions, such as, *I, my, me, mine*, or irregular verbs tend to totally change their forms. However, these irregular inflections are an obvious barrier for language learners such as toddlers and foreigners.

P. Vogt et al. (Eds.): EELC 2006, LNAI 4211, pp. 224–236, 2006.

These types of agreement are considered to assist to identify or reidentify referents [2]. The languages with rich inflectional systems often allow more freedom in word order, while those which only have few inflectional systems such as modern English requires strict word order instead [3,6]. This relationship between word order and agreement is one of the sign to represent characteristics of languages. Because these grammatical features are considered to be diachronically developed, studying languages through the aspect of agreement and word order may contribute to the field of language evolution.

Kirby's model [8], claimed that human beings had a skill to develop and create grammars spontaneously for compositionality and recursion. Considering these two functions, we presume that we can generate an infinite variety of expressions. However, his model seems rather to have neglected the aspect of understanding. Such a free proliferation of language may decrease the communicability, if we can generate long and complicated sentences, then they inevitably include ambiguities. Thus, we contend that a grammatical feature which decreases ambiguity such as agreement should also contribute to developing spontaneity. Our work is based also on Jäger [7], who has used the notion of *utility* to describe the efficiency of language generation. We will utilize this notion, and define our own utility function later. In our study, we bring HPSG (Head–driven Phrase Structure Grammar) which is indebted to a wide range of research traditions in syntax, like categorial grammar, generalized phrase structure grammar, lexical–functional grammar etc. Compared with other grammars dealing with phenomena of language evolution [4,12], HPSG is simple enough to handle our experiment. Because in HPSG every part of speech, category, and partial tree is represented by feature structures or DAG's (directed acyclic graphs), we can embed the restrictions on agreement in grammar formalisms.

In this study, we scramble the word order of sentences artificially, and measure how they become ambiguous. For this purpose, (i) we define a utility function, the value of which is higher if the meaning is less ambiguous with less effort. (ii) Next, we show the difference of utility values between inflectional and non-inflectional languages. We expect that inflectional language will have less ambiguity, though it will cost more in the parsing process. We show the value of the utility against the ratio of randomization of word order. (iii) Then, we compare two sample corpora. One is ATIS which consists of rather simple short sentences. The other is WSJ, which includes many complicated sentences. We hypothesize that in ATIS the non-inflectional language will suffice for communication and show high values in the utility, while in WSJ the inflectional one will show high values.

This paper is organized as follows: in Section 2 we explain the mechanism of HPSG and a programming language which we use to build our system. Section 3 presents the details of our experimental model, as well as the explanation of the utility function. We show our experimental results in Section 4, and Section 5 summarizes this study and outlines the further work.

2   HPSG and Parser

2.1   Briefing HPSG

Feature structure, Type, and Head. In HPSG, each word and phrase is not a single symbol but a set of feature–value pairs called a *feature structure*. A feature structure is a directed graph, in which all the nodes and edges have associated names. The name associated with a node is called *type* and the name associated with an edge is called *feature*. The types of edges or attributes that can be associated with a node are determined uniquely by the type. In case the feature takes multiple candidates as its value, it is represented by a list '⟨ ... ⟩'.

In Fig. 1, we illustrate a parsed tree of 'A man walks.' Note that each node of the tree is a feature structure; because the value of feature NUM is fixed as '3sg' (third person, singular), feature structures with different NUM values cannot be accepted to form a tree.

We metaphorically call the upper node a *mother* and the lower one a *daughter* in a tree structure. In a verb phrase or a noun phrase, we can find the prime daughter who mainly decided the features of her mother, that is, a verb and a noun, called *head*.[1] In Fig. 1, the head of the phrase 'A man' is a noun 'man.'

In HPSG, various categories are classified into types. Each category, that is a feature structure, owns a type and it is usually placed at the top of the whole structure, headed by '~' (tilde).[2] The upper type inherits the features of all the lower types, and thus, all the types form a *type-hierarchy*. We use '⊑' for the *subsumption* relation in types. The feature structure of type a of $a \sqsubseteq b$ is a subset of the structure of type b. The bottom type ($\perp$) is the most general type with no features.

Heads are often represented by a bar '—' over the type labels. Because the type of 'man' is N, that of 'a man' becomes $\overline{N}$. Similarly, the head of a verb phrase $\overline{V}$ is a verb V, and because the whole sentence can be considered to be formed by a verb phrase, the type of the sentence becomes $\overline{\overline{V}}$. The process in which a head is combined with other daughters into a mother is called a *subcategorization*, such that 'man' (N) takes an article 'A' to $\overline{N}$, or 'walks' ($\overline{V}$) takes 'A man' ($\overline{N}$). As in Fig. 1, a type requires other types specified in SUBCAT feature to be a mother structure.

ID-schemata and Principles. The grammar rules of HPSG consist of *ID-schemata* and principles. An ID-schema corresponds to a generation rule of Context–Free Grammar (CFG), viz., the left-hand side of '→' is a mother category and the right-hand side is daughter categories. The feature HEAD contains the structures of the head feature and DTRS (daughters) contains the structures

---

[1] Some linguists define that the head of a noun phrase is a determiner because without it a noun cannot be a phrase, but the discussion is out of the scope of this paper.

[2] In this paper, we may omit type labels unless they are necessary.

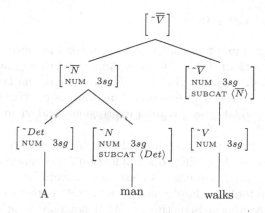

Fig. 1. A tree structure of a natural language sentence

of HEAD-DTR and COMP-DTR (complement daughter). Consecutive feature names delimited by '|' access the value of the last feature.[3]

A *pointer* indexed by '$\boxed{i}$' points to another structure headed by the same label, and denotes that the labeled structure is shared. The operation which merges multiple feature structures into one, without losing consistency, is called *unification*. This is utilized when looking up lexicons and grammar rule applications.

Principles are the constraints which all the feature structures must satisfy a priori. For example, *Head Feature Principle*, shown in Eqn (1), declares that both mother HEAD features and those of daughters must be common.

$$\begin{bmatrix} |\text{HEAD} & \boxed{1} \\ \text{DTRS}|\text{HEAD-DTR} & \left[|\text{HEAD} & \boxed{1} \right] \end{bmatrix} \tag{1}$$

Subcategorization Principle, shown in Eqn (2), limits the mother SUBCAT feature to the list of all the daughter SUBCAT features minus those which are already subcategorized.

$$\begin{bmatrix} |\text{SUBCAT} \langle \boxed{2} \rangle \\ \text{DTRS} \begin{bmatrix} \text{HEAD-DTR} & \left[|\text{SUBCAT} \langle \boxed{1}, \boxed{2} \rangle \right] \\ \text{COMP-DTRS} & \boxed{1} \end{bmatrix} \end{bmatrix} \tag{2}$$

The parsing process of HPSG is to acquire the mother feature structure, filling out its initially vacant HEAD-DTR and COMP-DTRS features, taking two other structures, with ID-schemata and principles. Although the order of this composition is not specified, the possible combinations are limited by the given initial set of structures.

---

[3] Hereafter, we abbreviate the description of consecutive feature names. '|' denotes that several feature names which are located the left side of two vertical bars are omitted.

2.2 LiLFeS and UP Parser

LiLFeS[4] is a programming language that processes linguistic formalisms, developed at University of Tokyo [9]. It is similar to Prolog in that its syntax includes disjunction, negation, and cut. The library of the language has been well developed, and we can utilize such functions as copying of feature structures, multi-dimensional arrays, regular expressions, and so on. Thus, LiLFeS is well suited to implement HPSG.

The UP parser which is written in LiLFeS is included in the MAYZ toolkit[5]. It analyzes a sentence according to a unification–based grammar, e.g., HPSG. Users can give the target sentence as a string or a word lattice to the parser.

Using these two tools, we implemented our HPSG parser which enables us to derive Predicate-Argument Structures (PASs) not only from ordinary English sentences but also from artificial ones with scrambled word order.

3 Utility Investigation Model

3.1 Word Order Variation

In this section, we introduce the methods to represent scrambling in HPSG [5]. In Japanese, for example, beside the standard subject–object–verb (SOV) order, the object–subject–verb (OSV) order is admissible as below, both of which give the same meaning as "Ken loves Naomi."

Ken–ga (NOM) Naomi–wo (ACC) aisiteiru (verb).
Naomi–wo (ACC) Ken–ga (NOM) aisiteiru (verb).

The syntactical structures of the above two sentences are composed using SLASH feature. Briefly, if a category contains the SLASH feature it dominates a gap (missing constituent). To help readers identify the location of the gaps, we mark them with an underlined space in the following example sentences.

What did you say they handed _ to the baby?
The presents that it annoys me that the children discover _ ...

The gap in the phrase "hand to the baby" from which an NP is absent is represented as [SLASH <NP>], as in Fig. 2 [11].

In this paper, because we basically deal with English grammar, we adopt this SLASH feature to represent word migration. Using the SLASH feature, a verb, "love," is represented in Fig. 3.

The languages of the Latin family such as Italian and Spanish apply the rule of the left-hand side of Fig. 3 when an object of a verb is a pronoun. The Germanic languages whose word order is called SOV-V2 such as German and Netherlandic

---

[4] http://www-tsujii.is.s.u-tokyo.ac.jp/lilfes/
[5] http://www-tsujii.is.s.u-tokyo.ac.jp/mayz/

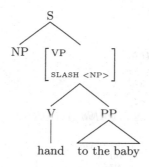

Fig. 2. Example of handing SLASH feature in HPSG

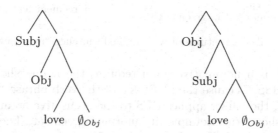

Fig. 3. Lexical item of "love" for the scrambled expression

apply this rule. The rule of the right-hand side of Fig. 3, long distance dependency, is applied to question forms and relative clauses of English. According to these migrating rules, a sentence "Subj *loves* Obj" may change to "Obj Subj *loves*" or "Subj Obj *loves*", but may not change to "*loves* Subj Obj" or "*loves* Obj Subj'.'

3.2 Parsing Process of Scrambled Sentences

We explain the characteristics of our parser, shown in Fig. 4, which is an example of a parsed tree after scrambling of "she loves me" in HPSG. In this figure, *nom, acc*, HSS, HCS, HFS are the abbreviations of nominative (Subject), accusative (Object), head–subject schema, head–complement schema, and head–filler schema, respectively. These schemata are explained as follows:

Head-complement schema. This schema is for a verb phrase to take a complement. Only those words, the category of which has been specified in SUB-CAT, can be unified to the verb phrase.

Head-subject schema. This schema is for a verb phrase to take a subject. The subject candidate can be applied to the schema only when the verb phrase has satisfied all the complements.

Head-filler schema. This schema is for a relative clause, and wh–question. Only a word which is categorized as SLASH can be unified as a complement.

With the rule of the right-hand side of Fig. 3, the sentence is parsed as in Fig. 4(a) by the SLASH feature. The verb "loves" in which the first argument

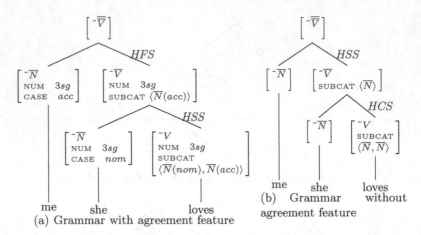

Fig. 4. Tree structures of a scrambled sentence "me she loves"

of the SUBCAT is a nominative noun requires the noun "she" whose case is nominative by HSS. Because the SUBCAT of the verb phrase "she loves" is an accusative noun, the parser applies HFS to the accusative noun "me".

In Fig. 4(b) shows the example of ignoring agreement. The information of the SUBCAT of the verb "loves" lacks the information on case. Therefore, the parser cannot figure out whether the noun "she" is the subject or the object of the verb. At this time, Using HCS, the verb phrase "she loves" is constructed. The SUBCAT of the verb phrase "she loves" is the noun, and the only remaining noun is "me"; this verb phrase does not have a subject yet, thus with HSS this verb phrase subcategorizes a noun "me".

The output of this parser is a Predicate–Argument Structure (PAS), that is one of the characteristics of HPSG. Figure 5 shows the outputs of parsing dependent upon the agreement features. "Pred (argument1, argument2)" means that "argument1 Pred argument2". For the parsing result with the agreement features in Fig. 4(a), we can figure out what this sentence means without any ambiguity, though the sentence is scrambled. However, the result of Fig. 4(b), in which the grammar does not consider agreement features such as CASE and NUM, shows that we cannot figure out the meaning either "me loves she" (meaning "I love her") or "she loves me."

3.3   Experimented Procedure

In this section, we explain the procedure of our experiment (see Fig. 6). Due to defects of the grammar set of our parser, not all the sentences in the corpora can be parsed. Therefore, first, we extract only those sentences which can be parsed. Next, we scramble the word order of the parsed sentences, and embed them into each original corpus at the rate of 0 % to 100 %. Then, we parse them with our HPSG parser which tolerates scrambled sentences. Also using a function of LiLFeS which can ignore arbitrary features, we parse the sentences disregarding agreement.

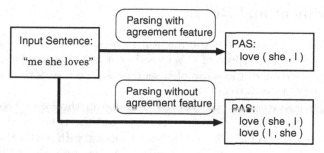

Fig. 5. Outputs of parsing depend on agreement

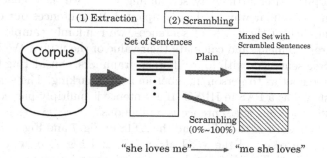

Fig. 6. Procedure of experiment

Finally, using these outputs, we calculate a value of the utility to evaluate grammars with regard to the balance between word order and the cost of unification.

3.4 Utility

In our model, based on the utility formula of Jäger's research [7], we propose a utility function for a sentence, U, such that:

$$U = \frac{N}{|PAS|} - w \cdot C(unif),\tag{3}$$

where $|PAS|$, N, $C(unif)$, and w are the number of predicate argument structures extracted from the sentence, the word length of the sentence, the number of unifications for the agreement feature, and the weight for $C(unif)$, respectively.

As the number of PASs represents ambiguity, the first term of (3) indicates profit. The less ambiguous the sentence is, the higher the value of the first term is. The second term of (3) indicates cost of unification. In Fig. 4(a), for example, the number of unification of agreement is four times, while the number of unification of agreement in Fig. 4(b) is zero. The low value of this second term means that the sentence is parsed more efficiently. The weight w is a positive coefficient by which the priority of the second term is assessed.

4   Experiment and Result

In this section, we show our experimental results, based on the model in the previous section. The purpose of this experiment is to observe the utility value against the proportion of the scrambled sentences. In our experiment, we set the weight in Eqn (3) to $w = 0$ and 0.1.

We apply our system to two corpora recorded in the Penn Tree Bank; one is the Wall Street Journal (WSJ, hereafter), and the other is the Air Ticket Information Service (ATIS). These corpora contrast with each other; while the WSJ includes many grammatically complicated sentences, the ATIS consists of comparatively short and simple sentences. We extracted 5,856 sentences out of the WSJ corpus. After artificially scrambling them, we have generated 4,390 sentences. In the similar way, we have employed 210 sentences out of the ATIS corpus. From each of these sets of sentences, we randomly sample 10,000 sentences with replacement, and calculate their value of the utility. We have parsed these word-free sentences with four different grammars, considering the requirements of agreement as to person/number and case marking. The semantics of a sentence is shown as a PAS in HPSG. If a sentence is multiply parsed, we obtain multiple PASs and thus the sentence is ambiguous.

We show the results of the WSJ and the ATIS in Fig. 7 and Fig. 8, respectively. Figure 7(a) is the result of the WSJ at $w = 0$, and Fig. 7(b) at $w = 0.1$. The same holds for Fig. 8. The horizontal axis denotes the mixture ratio of scrambled sentences, and the vertical axis is the average of utility. The solid line tagged by *PERNUM&CASE* shows the grammar in agreement both with person/number and case marking, the long dashed line by *CASE* denotes the one regarding only case, the short dashed line by *PERNUM* regarding only person/number, and the dotted line by *NONE* is the grammar disregarding agreement. The chain line tagged by *Difference* denotes the difference of the utility between *PERNUM&CASE* and *NONE*. All these lines include spline interpolation.

As we can see in Fig. 7and Fig. 8, the more the mixture ratio of scrambled sentences increases, the more the utility values decrease. According to Eqn (3), the profit term is inversely proportional to the number of PASs, which implies the degree of ambiguity for a sentence. Because, in most cases, scrambled sentences are more difficult to identify a nominative and an accusative of a verb than normal sentences with strict word order of English, the average number of PASs for the scrambled sentences is greater than that of the normal ones. As a result, the increase of scrambled sentences simply makes the average of utility low.

Here, we focus on Fig. 7(a). The weight in Eqn (3) is set to $w = 0$, which means that language users do not care the cost of agreement. The utility value of *PERNUM&CASE* is the highest over all the mixture ratio of scrambled sentences, while that of *NONE* is the lowest. Because the grammatical features such as agreement with person/number and case marking are considered to contribute to identify referents, the grammar using them reduces the number of PASs. The figure represents the effect of these grammatical features in the order of agreement with person/number and case marking (*PERNUM&CASE*), only person/number (*PERNUM*), and only case marking (*CASE*). Because the

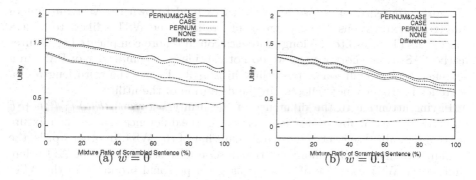

Fig. 7. Utility and the ratio of scrambled sentences: WSJ

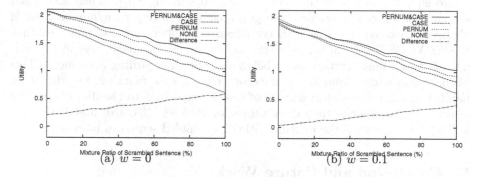

Fig. 8. Utility and the ratio of scrambled sentences: ATIS

frequency of unification processes for agreement with person/number was 14.7 times as much as that of case marking, the grammatical feature for agreement with person/number is considered to be more efficient than that of case marking. We can see that the more the mixture ratio increases, the greater the difference between *PERNUM&CASE* and *NONE* is. Thus, the use of these features for scrambled sentences is more effective in the reduction of ambiguity. It is consistent with the fact that the languages with rich inflectional systems often allow more freedom in word order.

Figure 7(b) shows the result of the WSJ at $w = 0.1$. In this situation, language users are annoyed by taking agreement. Therefore, the utility value of *PER-NUM&CASE* becomes close to that of *NONE*, and when $w = 0.2$, it eventually becomes worse than *NONE*. Second language learners may not be accustomed to dealing with agreement, i.e., in their case, the weight of cost becomes large. This means that the grammar disregarding agreement brings them a high value of the utility.

We show the result of the ATIS at $w = 0$ in Fig. 8(a). Although the order of the utility values for each grammatical feature is the same as the WSJ, it is entirely higher than that of the WSJ. Compared with the WSJ as written English sentences, the corpus of the ATIS as colloquial sentences contains many of shorter sentences. Because long sentences tend to own the vast amount of ambiguous expressions, the average utility value of the WSJ is likely to be less than the ATIS. Despite the long sentences contain more complicated structures in the PASs than shorter ones, we do not consider the complexity of PASs in a sentence in the definition of the utility in Eqn (3). Hence, the word length of a sentence is properly not reflected in the definition of the utility.

Paying attention to the difference of the utility between *PERNUM&CASE* and *NONE*, we can observe the increase rate of the difference against the mixture ratio of scrambled sentences is greater than that of the WSJ. In other words, the grammatical features are more effective in scrambled sentences in the ATIS than that in the WSJ. Because of a heavy usage of personal pronouns in the ATIS corpus, the case marking is more important than in the WSJ. In fact, 28.1 % of the sentences contained personal pronouns in the ATIS while 10.9 % in the WSJ.

We show the result of the ATIS at $w = 0.1$ in Fig. 8(b). When scrambled sentences are rarely contained, the grammar with only person/number,that is *PERNUM*, exceeds the one with both person/number and case marking, that is *PERNUM&CASE*, in terms of the utility values. Similarly, the utility values of the grammar with case is below the one disregarding agreement. This phenomenon comes from the unification cost for case marking. On the other hand, because grammatical feature of case is important to the disambiguation of scrambled sentences, the utility values for *PERNUM&CASE* and *CASE* are still kept high, even if the mixture ratio of scrambled sentences increases.

5   Conclusion and Future Work

In this study, we have investigated the utility of word inflections based on agreement, which can clarify dependency and can reduce the ambiguity. We have measured the ambiguity by (a) the number of probable PASs, i.e., possible semantic structures of a sentence, and (b) the cost of agreement by the number of unification processes. We defined our utility function by (a)−(b) and showed how these were balanced in two different corpora. One was the Wall Street Journal corpus which contains long and complicated sentences, in the other corpus, Air Travel Information Service corpus which contains shorter sentences.

In the experiment, we prepared four types of grammar which are (i) the grammar regarding person/number and case, (ii) only person/number, (iii) only case, and (iv) disregarding all of them.

As a result, the more the mixture ratio of scrambled sentences increases, the more the utility value decreases. Also, we have observed that the more the mixture ratio increases, the greater the difference between the grammar with agreement and the one without it. Because the word order is strict in English, the grammar without agreement has shown higher utility than those with any agreement. For those who are accustomed to dealing with agreement, Grammar (i) showed the highest utility. On the other hand, for those who are not, Grammar (iv) became efficient. The latter case may often happen in the second language acquisition.

Thus far, in many studies concerning language change and language evolution, grammar has only been regarded as an abstract notion, as a virtual parameter set of Universal Grammar. However, in this study, we actually wrote grammar rules to investigate how each rule affects the features of language. We owe the benefits of our experiment greatly to the adoption of HPSG, which is one of the advanced style of grammar formalism, in that we could calculate the profit by the number of PASs in the analysis of SLASH features, and the cost by the number of feature unification. However, in this grammar, there are many other features which we have not dealt with yet. Employing these features, we will be able to analyze practical phenomena more precisely, also modeling in the future.

In our system, understanding of a speaker's utterance in actual situations corresponds to deriving a unique PAS from the sentence. Our present rule–based parser, however, does not disambiguate multiple PASs semantically, i.e., we do not determine a unique PAS from the multiple candidates. For solving this problem, a stochastic parsing method is necessary. If the parser chose one from the candidates, we could calculate a precision of the PASs against the correct answer, which is recorded in the corpora as parsed tree structures. Also, in this study, we have not considered the complexity of PASs in a sentence in the definition of the utility, even if a long sentence contains complicated structures in the PASs than shorter ones. In the near future, we will develop a stochastic system based on Enju[6], which is a stochastic HPSG parser [10], and then redefine a new utility including a precision and a term for complexity of PASs.

References

1. J. Anward. Word Classes / Parts of Speech : Overview. In Keith Brown, editor, *The Encyclopedia of Language and Linguistics*, Vol. 13, pp. 628–629. Elsevier Science Publishers, Amsterdam, NL, second edition, 2006.
2. M. Barlow and C.A. Ferguson, editors. *Agreement in Natural Language: Approaches, Theories, Descriptions*. CSLI, Stanford, CA, 1988.
3. B.J. Blake. *Case.* Cambridge University Press, 1994.
4. T. Briscoe. Grammatical acquisition and linguistic selection. In *Linguistic Evolution through Language Acquisition.* Cambridge University Press, 2002.
5. T. Gunji. *Japanese Phrase Structure Grammar.* Reidel, Dordrecht, 1987.
6. R. Jackendoff. *Foundations of Language: Brain, Meaning, Grammar, Evolution.* Oxford University Press, 2002.
7. G. Jäger. Evolutionary Game Theory and Typology:a Case Study. In *Proceedings of the 14th Amsterdam Colloquium*, pp. 108–117, 2003.
8. S. Kirby. Learning, Bottlenecks and the Evolution of Recursive Syntax. In *Linguistic Evolution through Language Acquisition.* Cambridge University Press, 2002.
9. T. Makino, K. Torisawa, and J. Tsujii. Lilfes–Pactical Programming Language For Typed Feature Structures. In *Natural Language Pacific Rim Symposium '97*, 1997.

---

[6] http://www-tsujii.is.s.u-tokyo.ac.jp/enju/

236   R. Matoba, M. Nakamura, and S. Tojo

10. Y. Miyao and J. Tsujii. Probabilistic Disambiguation Models for Wide–Coverage HPSG parsing. In *ACL–2005*, 2005.
11. I. Sag, T. Wasow, and E. Bender. *Syntactic Theory -A Formal Introduction. Second Edition.* CSLI PUBLICATIONS, 2003.
12. L. Steels and J.D Beule. A (very) Brief Introduction to Fluid Construction Grammar. In *Proceedings of the 3rd International Workshop on Scalable Natural Language (ScaNaLu06)*, to appear.

Author Index

Lecture Notes in Artificial Intelligence (LNAI)

Vol. 4020: A. Bredenfeld, A. Jacoff, I. Noda, Y. Takahashi (Eds.), RoboCup 2005: Robot Soccer World Cup IX. XVII, 727 pages. 2006.

Vol. 4013: L. Lamontagne, M. Marchand (Eds.), Advances in Artificial Intelligence. XIII, 564 pages. 2006.

Vol. 4012: T. Washio, A. Sakurai, K. Nakajima, H. Takeda, S. Tojo, M. Yokoo (Eds.), New Frontiers in Artificial Intelligence. XIII, 484 pages. 2006.

Vol. 4008: J.C. Augusto, C.D. Nugent (Eds.), Designing Smart Homes. XI, 183 pages. 2006.

Vol. 4005: G. Lugosi, H.U. Simon (Eds.), Learning Theory. XI, 656 pages. 2006.

Vol. 3978: B. Hnich, M. Carlsson, F. Fages, F. Rossi (Eds.), Recent Advances in Constraints. VIII, 179 pages. 2006.

Vol. 3963: O. Dikenelli, M.-P. Gleizes, A. Ricci (Eds.), Engineering Societies in the Agents World VI. XII, 303 pages. 2006.

Vol. 3960: R. Vieira, P. Quaresma, M.d.G.V. Nunes, N.J. Mamede, C. Oliveira, M.C. Dias (Eds.), Computational Processing of the Portuguese Language. XII, 274 pages. 2006.

Vol. 3955: G. Antoniou, G. Potamias, C. Spyropoulos, D. Plexousakis (Eds.), Advances in Artificial Intelligence. XVII, 611 pages. 2006.

Vol. 3949: F. A. Savacı (Ed.), Artificial Intelligence and Neural Networks. IX, 227 pages. 2006.

Vol. 3946: T.R. Roth-Berghofer, S. Schulz, D.B. Leake (Eds.), Modeling and Retrieval of Context. XI, 149 pages. 2006.

Vol. 3944: J. Quiñonero-Candela, I. Dagan, B. Magnini, F. d'Alché-Buc (Eds.), Machine Learning Challenges. XIII, 462 pages. 2006.

Vol. 3930: D.S. Yeung, Z.-Q. Liu, X.-Z. Wang, H. Yan (Eds.), Advances in Machine Learning and Cybernetics. XXI, 1110 pages. 2006.

Vol. 3918: W.K. Ng, M. Kitsuregawa, J. Li, K. Chang (Eds.), Advances in Knowledge Discovery and Data Mining. XXIV, 879 pages. 2006.

Vol. 3913: O. Boissier, J. Padget, V. Dignum, G. Lindemann, E. Matson, S. Ossowski, J.S. Sichman, J. Vázquez-Salceda (Eds.), Coordination, Organizations, Institutions, and Norms in Multi-Agent Systems. XII, 259 pages. 2006.

Vol. 3910: S.A. Brueckner, G.D.M. Serugendo, D. Hales, F. Zambonelli (Eds.), Engineering Self-Organising Systems. XII, 245 pages. 2006.

Vol. 3904: M. Baldoni, U. Endriss, A. Omicini, P. Torroni (Eds.), Declarative Agent Languages and Technologies III. XII, 245 pages. 2006.

Vol. 3900: F. Toni, P. Torroni (Eds.), Computational Logic in Multi-Agent Systems. XVII, 427 pages. 2006.

Vol. 3899: S. Frintrop, VOCUS: A Visual Attention System for Object Detection and Goal-Directed Search. XIV, 216 pages. 2006.

Vol. 3898: K. Tuyls, P.J. 't Hoen, K. Verbeeck, S. Sen (Eds.), Learning and Adaption in Multi-Agent Systems. X, 217 pages. 2006.

Vol. 3891: J.S. Sichman, L. Antunes (Eds.), Multi-Agent-Based Simulation VI. X, 191 pages. 2006.

Vol. 3890: S.G. Thompson, R. Ghanea-Hercock (Eds.), Defence Applications of Multi-Agent Systems. XII, 141 pages. 2006.

Vol. 3885: V. Torra, Y. Narukawa, A. Valls, J. Domingo-Ferrer (Eds.), Modeling Decisions for Artificial Intelligence. XII, 374 pages. 2006.

Vol. 3881: S. Gibet, N. Courty, J.-F. Kamp (Eds.), Gesture in Human-Computer Interaction and Simulation. XIII, 344 pages. 2006.

Vol. 3874: R. Missaoui, J. Schmidt (Eds.), Formal Concept Analysis. X, 309 pages. 2006.

Vol. 3873: L. Maicher, J. Park (Eds.), Charting the Topic Maps Research and Applications Landscape. VIII, 281 pages. 2006.

Vol. 3864: Y. Cai, J. Abascal (Eds.), Ambient Intelligence in Everyday Life. XII, 323 pages. 2006.

Vol. 3863: M. Kohlhase (Ed.), Mathematical Knowledge Management. XI, 405 pages. 2006.

Vol. 3862: R.H. Bordini, M. Dastani, J. Dix, A.E.F. Seghrouchni (Eds.), Programming Multi-Agent Systems. XIV, 267 pages. 2006.

Vol. 3849: I. Bloch, A. Petrosino, A.G.B. Tettamanzi (Eds.), Fuzzy Logic and Applications. XIV, 438 pages. 2006.

Vol. 3848: J.-F. Boulicaut, L. De Raedt, H. Mannila (Eds.), Constraint-Based Mining and Inductive Databases. X, 401 pages. 2006.

Vol. 3847: K.P. Jantke, A. Lunzer, N. Spyratos, Y. Tanaka (Eds.), Federation over the Web. X, 215 pages. 2006.

Vol. 3835: G. Sutcliffe, A. Voronkov (Eds.), Logic for Programming, Artificial Intelligence, and Reasoning. XIV, 744 pages. 2005.

Vol. 3830: D. Weyns, H. V.D. Parunak, F. Michel (Eds.), Environments for Multi-Agent Systems II. VIII, 291 pages. 2006.

Vol. 3817: M. Faundez-Zanuy, L. Janer, A. Esposito, A. Satue-Villar, J. Roure, V. Espinosa-Duro (Eds.), Nonlinear Analyses and Algorithms for Speech Processing. XII, 380 pages. 2006.

Vol. 3814: M. Maybury, O. Stock, W. Wahlster (Eds.), Intelligent Technologies for Interactive Entertainment. XV, 342 pages. 2005.

Vol. 3809: S. Zhang, R. Jarvis (Eds.), AI 2005: Advances in Artificial Intelligence. XXVII, 1344 pages. 2005.

Vol. 3808: C. Bento, A. Cardoso, G. Dias (Eds.), Progress in Artificial Intelligence. XVIII, 704 pages. 2005.

Vol. 3802: Y. Hao, J. Liu, Y.-P. Wang, Y.-m. Cheung, H. Yin, L. Jiao, J. Ma, Y.-C. Jiao (Eds.), Computational Intelligence and Security, Part II. XLII, 1166 pages. 2005.

Vol. 3801: Y. Hao, J. Liu, Y.-P. Wang, Y.-m. Cheung, H. Yin, L. Jiao, J. Ma, Y.-C. Jiao (Eds.), Computational Intelligence and Security, Part I. XLI, 1122 pages. 2005.

Vol. 3789: A. Gelbukh, Á. de Albornoz, H. Terashima-Marín (Eds.), MICAI 2005: Advances in Artificial Intelligence. XXVI, 1198 pages. 2005.